D1611450

MEET ME at the ROCKET

MEET ME at the
ROCKET

A History of the South Carolina State Fair

RODGER E. STROUP

Foreword by **Walter Edgar**

THE UNIVERSITY OF
SOUTH CAROLINA PRESS

© 2019 University of South Carolina

Published by the University of South Carolina Press
Columbia, South Carolina 29208

www.sc.edu/uscpress

Manufactured in China

28 27 26 25 24 23 22 21 20 19 10 9 8 7 6 5 4 3 2 1

Library of Congress Cataloging-in-Publication Data can be found at http://catalog.loc.gov/.

CONTENTS

Foreword vii
Walter Edgar

Preface ix

1 Colonial and Antebellum Fairs, 1720–1865 1

2 The Fair on Elmwood Avenue, 1869–1903 10

3 The Greater State Fair, 1904–1920 26

4 The Colored State Fair, 1890–1969 40
"The greatest event for Negroes in the state"

5 The Depression and World War II, 1921–1945 49

6 "The Grooming Ground of Champions," 1890–1969 62

7 Integration and the Civic Center, 1946–1964 70

8 County and Regional Fairs 82

9 From Disaster to a New Vision, 1965–1983. 89
"We have a story of a disaster, we have lost the Steel Building"

10 Entertainment and the Midway 99
"All to win a stuffed animal I really didn't want"

11 The State Fair into the Twenty-first Century, 1984–2019 126
"Nothing Could Be Swiner"

12 Exhibits and Premiums. 136

13 Icons of the State Fair. 146
"_____, meet your mother at the rocket"

Conclusion. 162

Appendix 165
The State Agricultural and Mechanical Society of South Carolina

Notes 167

Index 175

FOREWORD

Fairs have been an integral part of South Carolina culture since the 1720s, when the Commons House of Assembly authorized them for the rural market crossroads of Dorchester, Ashley Ferry Town, and Childsbury. These annual, four-day events were the harbingers of later county fairs and, eventually, a state fair. Within a generation, the colonial South Carolina fairs evolved from simple bazaars or markets into something that would be familiar to fairgoers today. There were agricultural exhibits, horse races, food, and games—in short, fun for the entire family.

In this account of the South Carolina State Fair, Rodger Stroup has mined a myriad of sources to compile a fascinating account not just of the fair itself but also its various components. And, importantly, it answers a lot of questions.

For example, it is commonly believed today that the State Fair is a governmental agency. It is not; it is operated by a nonprofit organization, the State Agricultural and Mechanical Society of South Carolina, for the benefit and enjoyment of nearly a half-million South Carolinians every year. How and why this occurred makes for entertaining reading.

And, inquiring Carolinians might also want to know....

Where did one of the fair's signature icons—the Rocket—come from?

Did you know that world-class thoroughbreds, including the famous Seabiscuit, once spent the winter training at the fairgrounds? Or that the Palmetto Trials were a feature on the American horse racing circuit?

Big Thursday, for decades the annual gridiron clash between Clemson and Carolina, was the highlight of fair week. Why is it now just a memory?

Why, for more than seventy years, were there two State Fairs?

When and why did "girlie" and "freak" shows disappear from the midway?

How have outside events such as the Civil War, the Great Depression, and avian influenza affected the fair?

In answering these questions and many others, Stroup has written much more than an institutional history. He sets the South Carolina State Fair in the broader context of South Carolina history.

Scattered throughout the text are dozens of interesting—and rare—illustrations, including the National Corn Building that brought the country's National Corn Show to Columbia; a turn-of-the-twentieth-century poster for the Colored State Fair; foreign visitors at the Palmetto Trials; a view of the midway in the 1950s; Gene Autry, the "Singing Cowboy," performing at the grandstand; a "petrified man" from an old "freak" show; a list of premiums (prizes) awarded in 1859; and a 4-H Club exhibit from the 1930s.

Rodger Stroup and the State Agricultural and Mechanical Society of South Carolina are to be congratulated for producing *Meet Me at the Rocket*. It will be a welcome addition to my bookshelf.

Walter Edgar

PREFACE

In 2013 Walter Edgar contacted me and asked if I would be interested in writing a history of the South Carolina State Fair. For the 150th anniversary of their founding, the State Agricultural and Mechanical Society of South Carolina had decided to publish a history of the society and the State Fair to commemorate its sesquicentennial. Even though I knew very little about the State Fair, other than it was a fun place to go in the fall, I told Walter that I would like to take on the project. After a survey of the secondary sources I discovered that the story of the society and the fair were only mentioned in passing, and most of the research would need to come from primary sources. The society's institutional history, published in 1916, and its board minutes from 1918 to the present provided a general outline but contained little detailed information.

I quickly realized that the best source of primary material was the newspapers. I did not relish the idea of reading through 150 years of newspapers on microfilm. Fortunately, a wealth of South Carolina newspapers are available online through NewsBank and Chronicling America, all searchable by words or phrases. Without the online newspapers, the research would have taken much longer, and many articles buried on the back pages would probably have been missed.

A major challenge was locating the illustrations to accompany the story. Except for the 1872 bird's eye view of the map of Columbia, I was unable to find an image of the Elmwood Avenue fairgrounds. Most disheartening is the lack of an image of Columbia's Main Street during the fair, where many of the midway activities happened between the 1870s and 1914. But I was able to find a wealth of fascinating images thanks to the staff members of the South Caroliniana Library, the State Archives of North Carolina, the Richland Library, the South Carolina Department of Archives and History, the South Carolina State Library, the Thomas Cooper Library Government Information & Maps Department, the Strates Shows, the South Carolina Chapter of the American Institute of Architects, the Library of Congress, the South Carolina Department of Parks, Recreation and Tourism, the University of South Carolina Archives, and the Greater Columbia Chamber of Commerce. Several individuals also shared their images, including Bill and Trish Eccles, Jack A. Meyer, Ralph N. Riley, Rice Music House, Mike Safran, and David C. Sennema.

In addition to the images, the illustrations depict many fair-related artifacts. Institutions and individuals who allowed me to share photos of their treasures include Tom and Beth Evers, Barry Gibbes, Burl R. Kennedy, Jo Mewbourn, the South Carolina State Museum, and Four Oaks Farm. Since starting this endeavor in 2013, I have perused online and live auctions and roamed through local antique malls acquiring several artifacts used in the book. A special thanks to Hunter Clarkson, who not only took many of the photographs but whose attention to detail in preparing all of the illustrations for publication ensured each image was of the highest quality possible.

Working with Gary Goodman, retired general manager of the society, and Nancy Smith, the current general manager, was a pleasure. They were both very supportive and always ready to provide whatever resources I needed. Thanks to the society's board of directors for entrusting me with this opportunity and for allowing me to go where the research led. I hope I discovered things about the State Fair that they did not know.

Finally, a very special thank you to Susanne R. Kennedy, a longtime member of the society board, and her son Burl R. Kennedy. Susanne has a wealth of knowledge about the fair, and I frequently called on her to help me verify facts and clarify issues where I was in doubt. In addition to his mother's service on the society's board, Burl's grandfather was the general manager of the fair during the 1960s. Burl grew up with the fair in his blood, and he generously shared not only his knowledge of the fair but also his extensive collection of fair memorabilia.

Last and certainly not least, my wife, Martha, deserves a special commendation for her support and patience. For the past couple of years, our study, then porch, and now dining room have been cluttered with "State Fair stuff." Martha provided encouragement as I have worked through challenges, and her careful reading of the manuscript has alerted me to items that need to be clarified.

Since 1969 fairgoers have frequently heard the phrase "meet your mother at the Rocket" blast from the public address system escalating the rocket to icon status. While the Rocket would be unknown to fairgoers of an earlier time, each era of the fair had icons that would be unfamiliar to current fairgoers. From the State Ball in the 1870s through the 1910s or Big Thursday from the 1890s to the 1950s, each of these icons was closely aligned with the fair until their demise.

Colonial and Antebellum Fairs

In the early years of colonial South Carolina, farmers and planters came together to exchange information about crops and livestock. Primarily social occasions, these events also featured competitive activities and prizes. In the 1780s a state-wide agricultural society sponsored annual gatherings but focused on activities and orations encouraging agriculturalists to adopt scientific farming practices. By the 1820s several county and regional agricultural societies existed across the state, and many of them sponsored fairs. The success of these societies led to the founding of South Carolina Agricultural Society in 1839 and South Carolina's first state fair in 1840. The statewide fairs from 1840 to 1845 and again from 1856 to 1861 brought together the political and economic leadership of the state and focused on improving agricultural practices. But the fairs also provided an opportunity for social interaction and competitive events.

Rural fairs had been established by 1723 at Dorchester, Ashley Ferry Town, and Childsbury, market towns located on the rivers approximately twenty miles

Constructed in 1828, the Pendleton Farmers' Society Hall housed one of the state's earliest regional farmers' organizations. **The society is still active today.** Courtesy of the Library of Congress

from Charleston. Held in the spring and fall, these four-day events provided an opportunity for residents to buy and sell enslaved persons, cattle, horses, provisions, and other merchandise. The fairs also provided diversions including horse racing, shooting matches, raffles, and dance exhibitions, with prizes frequently awarded to the winners. In 1751 the *South Carolina Gazette* reported that "a Role of Tobacco and 3 Gross of Pipes *to be grinn'd for by old Women*." While these fairs allowed local citizens a break from their rigorous work schedules, they were not intended to be educational or to promote scientific farming methods.[1]

In 1785 lowcountry planters organized the South Carolina Society for Promoting and Improving Agriculture and Other Rural Concerns. After ten years the organization became the Agricultural Society of South Carolina, and it continued to exist into the middle of the twentieth century. Following a movement that began in Great Britain and other states, the society encouraged farmers to adopt scientific farming methods and lessen the state's dependence on rice and indigo, urging planters to set aside a small portion of their land for experimentation with various crops and promoting the practice of crop rotation. The society also wanted planters to test new ways of weeding, hoeing, and watering. To support these new practices the society offered premiums (prizes) for raising peanuts, rhubarb, castor beans, hops, madder (a red dyestuff), figs, and merino sheep.[2]

By 1823 there were at least eleven local agricultural societies spread across the state. During the 1820s and 1830s

The grounds and chamber of the House of Representatives of the first statehouse was the site of the State Fair from 1840 to 1845. Courtesy of the South Carolina Department of Archives & History

there were other attempts to establish a statewide organization devoted to improving agricultural practices. In 1818 the South Carolina Society was organized with William R. Davie as president, but it was defunct by 1823. In 1826 several local societies organized the United Agricultural Society of South Carolina, with Whitemarsh B. Seabrook as president. This organization held periodic meetings featuring speakers on agricultural topics. The last meeting was held in 1831. These failed attempts at a statewide organization laid the groundwork for the establishment of the first agricultural organization to successfully organize and stage a State Fair in Columbia.[3]

In late 1839, at a meeting in the chamber of the House of Representatives, the State Agricultural Society of South

Carolina was created, and its first annual fair and stock show was held in November 1840. The annual meeting and fair were planned to coincide with the meeting of the General Assembly each year in Columbia. At the 1839 meeting, the society proposed several things, including establishing an agricultural professorship at the South Carolina College, creating an agricultural school, establishing a state board of agriculture, introducing in the free schools some elementary work on agriculture, and appropriating funds in the Legislature to defray the costs of a geological and agricultural survey of the state. The last one was the only one of these recommendations that was carried out.[4]

From 1840 through 1845 the society held an annual meeting and fair in Columbia. The meetings were held in the

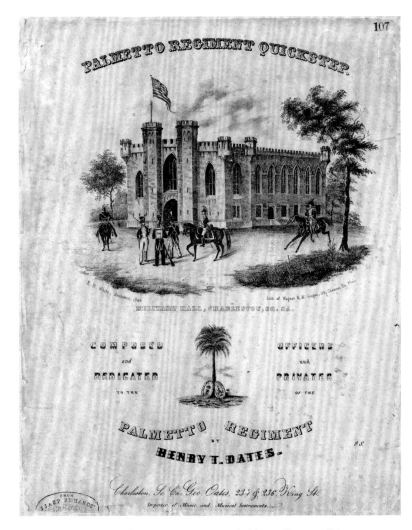

The State Agricultural Society of South-Carolina
PREMIUM LIST FOR 1841.

For the best Stallion for Agricultural purposes, $30
For the best Mare for Agricul-
    tural purposes,   A Silver Cup, $20
For the second best Mare,   "   15
For the best Colt,   "   10
For the best Filly,   "   10
For the best Bull,   "   20
For the second best Bull,   "   15
For the best two year old Bull,   "   12
For the best yearling Bull,   "   10
For the best Cow,   "   15
For the second best Cow,   "   12
For the best Heifer under 3 years old, "   15
For the 2nd best Heifer   "   "   "   10
For the best yearling Heifer,   "   10
For the best Bull Calf,   "   10
For the best Heifer Calf,   "   10
For the best Boar,   "   10
For the best Sow,   "   10
For the second best Boar,   "   8
For the second best Sow,   "   8
For the best pair of Pigs under 1 year, "   5
For the best pair of Pigs under 6 mos. "   5
For the best Ram,   "   15
For the second best Ram,   "   10
For the best Ewe,   "   10

The premium list for the 1841 State Fair was published in the *Charleston Courier.* At the bottom, note the premium for the best ewe is a silver cup. See chapter 12 for a photo of the 1842 silver cup for the best ewe. *Courtesy of the Charleston Courier*

In 1850 the South Carolina Institute Fair was held in Military Hall in Charleston. This image of Military Hall is from a musical score composed to commemorate the Palmetto Regiment, which served during the Mexican War, 1846–48. *Courtesy of Dr. Jack A. Meyer*

chamber of the House of Representatives, and the fair was on the statehouse grounds. The activities included a business meeting, exhibitions of livestock and domestic goods, and an annual oration focused on agricultural topics. At the 1840 meeting and fair, the society awarded premiums for cattle, sheep, hogs, and mules. By 1845 premiums were also awarded for corn, cotton, wheat, oats, rye, sweet potatoes, and domestic products made with cotton mixed with wool, silk, or other materials. To attract members from outside the Columbia area, a fair was held in Newberry in 1841 and Greenville in 1844. Despite the best efforts of the society's leadership, the

last fair was held in Columbia in 1845.[5] A primary reason the creation of a statewide agricultural organization failed at this time was the difficulty of transportation. When the meeting and fair was held in Columbia, it was attended almost exclusively by farmers and planters from the center of the state. The 1844 Greenville event was heavily weighted to attendees from Greenville, Spartanburg, and Pendleton. In 1845 the railroads only provided service on routes from Charleston to North Augusta and Columbia. Moving livestock and equipment over dirt roads any distance was expensive and time consuming.[6] However, by 1855 railroad service was greatly expanded,

No.	Articles.	Residence.
51	Crotchet Work,	Miss J. B. Whitney, Charleston, S. C.
52	Worsted Work,	"
53	Oil Painting, "Interior of City Hall, and Calhoun's body lying in state,	A. Caraduc, Charleston, S. C.
54	Oil Painting, An Indian Female,	"
55	Parkhurst's Cotton Seed and Batting Machine,	H. Redfield, New-York.
56	Pine Burr Baskets, and Palmetto Mats.	Miss Given, Beaufort, S. C.
57	Fruit and Preserves, Oranges, Olives, Lemons, &c.	Robert Chisolm, Beaufort, S. C.
58	Picket Fence,	J. M. Gamewell, Camden, S. C.
59	Walking Sticks, Gold and silver headed, native wood.	J. Peckham, Columbia, S. C.
60	Mineral Paints, Red, Yellow, Fire Proof Paints, Purple and Yellow. Fine Georgia Tripoli,	W. Haines, Augusta, Geo.,
61	Patent Leather Boots,	Vogel & Lassalle, Columbia, S. C.
62	Pump Sole Boots,	S. G. Barkly, Winnsboro, S. C.
63	Embroidery in Gold,	Miss A. L. Solamon, Charleston, S. C.
64	Chenille Work,	"
65	Portrait in Oil, John C. Calhoun,	Master Robert Boggs, Augusta, Geo.
66	Portrait in Oil, "Rembrandt."	"
67	Portrait in Oil, Washington.	"
68	Crotchet Work,	Miss L. C. Smith, Charleston, S. C.
69	Negro Shoes, Manufactured in Thomas Co. Ga.	E. W. Bancroft. Charleston, S. C.
70	Plough, For Nut Grass.	Mr. Philips, Augusta, Geo.
71	Card Clothing,	J. & J. Murdoch, Leicester.
72	Crotchet Work,	Miss M. E. Smith.
73	Pen Knife,	C. U. Parks, Knoxville, Tenn.
74	Jeans, 125 Samples—Manufactured in Alabama.	Sent by L. Bowie,

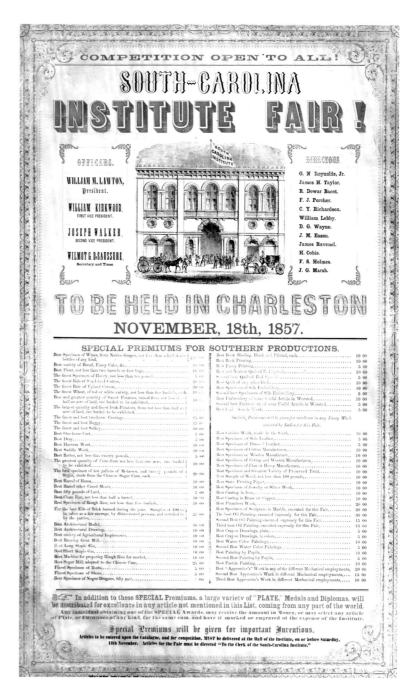

In 1850 the South Carolina Institute Fair published a catalog of all 257 exhibits at the fair. This page shows the wide variety of entries. Courtesy of the South Carolina State Library

A poster advertising the 1857 South Carolina Institute Fair features special premiums for southern productions. Courtesy of the South Caroliniana Library, University of South Carolina, Columbia, S.C.

with daily service from Columbia to Charleston, Greenville, Sumter, and Florence and to Charlotte, North Carolina. The fate of the next revival of the agricultural society would be sealed by a much more significant event—the Civil War.

Between 1846 and 1855 no major effort was made to revive the society. The establishment in 1848 of the South Carolina Institute for the Promotion of Art, Mechanical Ingenuity, and Industry in Charleston was probably a factor in the slow resurrection of the State Agricultural Society's fair. The primary goal of the South Carolina Institute Fair was to exhibit and promote South Carolina–made goods including art. As political tension increased between the North and South, the initial promoters of the institute's fair stated in the *Charleston Courier* on October 22, 1856, "The South is backward and slow in the construction and manufacture of such smaller articles of domestic use, as we are now dependent on the North.... Our Institute has done much to encourage and promote these desirable proofs of independence, and we flatter ourselves that the approaching Exhibitions will evidence improving taste and excellence in the Mechanic Department especially."

Beginning in 1849 the South Carolina Institute held fairs in Charleston. Following the revival of the State Agricultural Society's fair in 1856, the institute's fair was usually after the State Fair, and many of the same domestic goods were entered in both fairs. Likewise, mechanical and manufactured goods were featured at both, but the institute's fair had limited exhibits of livestock and crops.

While the State Fair struggled to gain traction between 1846 and 1855, the county and regional fairs continued to thrive. At the Newberry Agricultural Society's fair in June 1855, an invitation was issued by the society to agricultural societies across the state to meet in Newberry on September 19, 1855, to form a state agricultural society. This action by the Newberry Agricultural Society was one of many calls for action. As the editor of the *South Carolina Agriculturist* reported: "During the year 1855 a new spirit sprang into life among our rural population which resulted in a call of an agricultural convention in Columbia on the 8th of August, and the organization of the State Agricultural Society of South Carolina, on a new, and we trust, successful plan." At the August convention the State Agricultural Society of South Carolina was revived with a new plan that included a salary for the officers and the creation of an executive committee to oversee the whole organization. The convention was confident that the new plan would succeed because of "the central position of Columbia, with railroads radiating in all directions, its proverbial health, and the hospitality of its citizens, its beautiful gardens, its magnificent streets, its abundance of water—all combining to make it one of the most attractive points of assembly in the

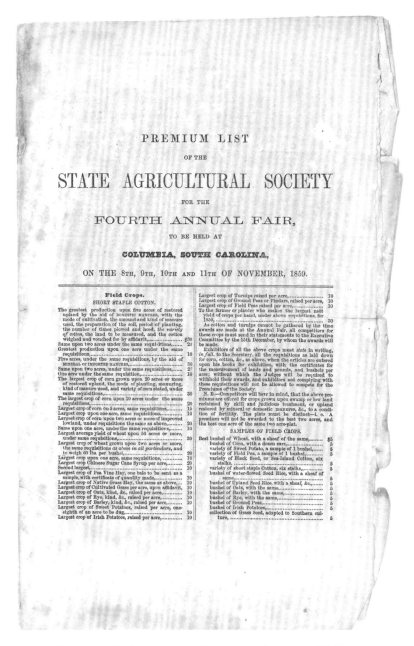

By 1859 the State Agricultural Society of South Carolina was publishing a separate eight-page premium list for the State Fair. Courtesy of the South Caroliniana Library, University of South Carolina, Columbia, S.C.

country."[7] In addition, the Legislature appropriated $5,000 to assist in the payment of premiums for agricultural products, and the City of Columbia provided land just north of Elmwood Avenue for the construction of a fairground. The state appropriation enabled the society to offer premiums substantially higher than those at the county fairs seeking to attract exhibitors from outside the Midlands. For example, at

YOUNG'S MILL PAINTING

At the 1856 State Fair a painting by Columbia artist Eugene Dovilliers was "greatly admired" by fairgoers. The large painting depicted Young's Mill located on the Congaree River near present-day Elmwood Avenue. On November 17, 1856, a correspondent for the *Charleston Courier* wrote that "Several connosieurs [*sic*] have pronounced it to surpass any oil painting on exhibition." In 2006 the South Carolina State Museum acquired two painting by Dovilliers from a local donor, one a view of the Columbia skyline from the west side of the Congaree River and the other of an unidentified mill. Attempts by the museum staff to identify the location of the mill were unsuccessful until research for the current work discovered an article in the *Charleston Courier* on November 17, 1856, containing a detailed description of the painting on exhibit at the State Fair.

Painting of Young's Mill by Eugene Dovilliers exhibited at the 1856 State Fair.
Courtesy of the South Carolina State Museum

the State Fair the best stallion received a cash prize of fifteen dollars while the Newberry County Fair presented a silver cup valued at five dollars.

The revived society's first State Fair was held in November 1856 at the new fairgrounds. The earlier fairs held on the statehouse grounds depended on temporary facilities, but according to the *Winnsboro Register,* the new "grounds and buildings are said to be the best in the United States."[8] Also important to the success of the new fair were the recently completed railroad connections in Columbia. The railroads were eager to assist in moving livestock and exhibits, and the Charlotte Railroad Company provided round-trip tickets at one fare.[9] For the 1857 fair, the Charlotte and South Carolina Railroad provided free passage for all exhibition articles and one-half fare for fair visitors.[10]

The 1856 State Fair was a resounding success. On November 11, 1856, a correspondent for the *Charleston Courier* reported, "Never, in the memory of the 'oldest inhabitant,' have so many visitors been congregated in this city. At an early hour this morning thousands were seen hurrying to the Fair grounds to see the 'sights,' and the universal opinion is, that the exhibition is an honor to the State. All doubt of its success is vanished, and the Annual Fair of this State may now be looked on as an institution." Among the prized livestock on exhibit was an eighteen-month-old Devon bull named "Press Brooks" owned by Leroy Springs of Charlotte. The bull was obviously named after South Carolina congressman Preston Brooks, who, in May 1856, had strode into the U.S. Senate and caned Massachusetts senator Charles Sumner following Sumner's verbal attack on slaveholders aimed at Brooks's second cousin, Sen. Andrew Butler. Sumner's injuries were so extensive that he was unable to return to the Senate for three years. The incident was one of many that polarized the nation in the years leading to the Civil War.

The State Fair's southern domestics department featured blankets, coverlets, counterpanes, rugs, and silk hose. Also featured was a "Lady's Reclining Chair, made by a Negro man

The Alexander Foundry of Columbia exhibited sugar cane mills at the State Fair in the late 1850s. This Alexander syrup kettle is one of a series of decreasing-size kettles used during the clarifying and evaporating process of making sugar from sugar cane. Courtesy of the South Carolina State Museum

who never served a day in a cabinet maker's shop…and is a job which would do credit to any cabinet maker." Among the curiosities were the "Maine Giantess" and the bearded woman with her wooly child. In the industrial display visitors' attention was riveted on the portable steam engine exhibited by William Lebby of Charleston.[11]

The 1856 and 1857 fairs were both very successful and received high marks from visitors. The 1858 fair opened with all of the exhibit areas overflowing and visitors facing "no vacancy" signs throughout Columbia. By the close of the fair the lack of rooms was a major concern, and on November 12, 1858, a correspondent for the *Charleston Courier* suggested the State Fair should be moved to Charleston, where there were adequate accommodations for the crowds. On August 26, 1859, as the opening of the fair approached, the *Charleston Mercury* reprinted an article from the *Columbia Guardian,* recalling, "Last year many were prevented from attending the Fair from the common report that there were no accommodations to be had in Columbia, and hundreds on their way hither on hearing these reports returned to their homes." Fearing that the lack of adequate accommodations might impede the fair, the citizens of Columbia held a public meeting in September 1859. According to the *Charleston Mercury* on September 9, 1859, committees were appointed to work with the hotel owners, to consult with the citizens in each ward, and to welcome visitors to the city. On November 14, 1859, the *Charleston Mercury* reported that the city's actions alleviated the housing problem during the fair. "Another cause for general congratulation was the provision made for visitors. We have not heard of any complaint. Ample accommodations were provided by the Committee of Reception, to whom the thanks of the whole city—it would not be too much to say the entire State—are due."

The 1859 event was the most successful State Fair held prior to the outbreak of the Civil War. In November 1860 and 1861 the society sponsored the fair in Columbia, but the impending crisis in 1860 and the ongoing war in 1861 took their toll on the activities at the fair. Even before the 1861 fair, Confederate authorities were using the fairgrounds as a mobilization camp. After several months a more permanent camp was established at Killian, about nine miles north of Columbia. Shortly after the war began the ladies of Columbia established a hospital at the fairgrounds to care for the sick and wounded from the Confederate encampment at Killian. However, in 1862 the hospital was moved to the campus of South Carolina College and used buildings that were empty because of decreased enrollment due to the war. In 1863

Joseph LeConte, a professor of chemistry and geology at the South Carolina College, was appointed to head a large-scale Confederate operation for manufacturing medicines using the facilities at the fairgrounds. This laboratory was one of the few domestic suppliers of alcohol, nitrate of silver, chloroform, and other chemicals available to the Confederates. A fire that engulfed much of Columbia on the evening of February 17, 1865, spared the fairgrounds, even though the origin of the fire was bales of cotton burning on Elmwood Avenue only a few blocks away. Fortunately for the Fair Grounds, the winds that evening blew the fire away from the fairgrounds and toward Main Street. However, on February 19 the building at the fairgrounds, along with many other buildings in Columbia, were designated as legitimate military targets and deliberately burned by the occupying Union Army.[12]

From 1840 to 1845 and from 1856 to 1861 the State Agricultural Society of South Carolina sponsored successful State Fairs that advanced the agricultural interests. In addition to recognizing outstanding livestock and crops, the fairs highlighted the need to employ scientific farming practices. The exhibits at the fairs also introduced farmers to the latest machinery for increasing productivity. The domestic and cultural exhibits expanded the scope of the fairs to individuals not directly associated with farming. Finally, the entertainment offerings, including musical performances and curiosities, became very popular attractions for all fairgoers.

2

The Fair on Elmwood Avenue

The end of the Civil War brought major changes in the economic, political, and social atmosphere of all South Carolinians. In addition to the physical devastation left by Sherman's Army and five years of war along the coast, the population also suffered substantially. Between eighteen thousand and twenty-one thousand men, or one in fourteen white South Carolinians, were either killed, mortally wounded, or died from disease. Over four hundred thousand former slaves were now freedmen struggling to find their place in the new order. Large landholders sought a labor system that would enable them to produce crops equivalent to their prewar yields. The prewar political leadership of the state was out of power and forced to stand on the sidelines while carpetbaggers, scalawags, and many of the new freedmen who had no experience in politics ran state and local governments. In 1867 the U.S. Congress passed the Reconstruction Acts that required all the Southern states to ratify the Fourteenth Amendment and adopt a constitution that would allow all males to vote regardless of color.

Subsequent elections in 1868 saw Republicans in control of the major statewide offices as well as a majority (134 to 22) in the General Assembly. The Republican administrations, while addressing many of the state's problems, especially in the areas of education and economic development, were viewed by most of the state's white citizens as an occupation government made possible only by the presence of federal troops.

While the revival of the State Fair was promoted as a method to improve agricultural practices and encourage industrial development, there was an underlying agenda as well. Democratic leaders wanted to keep the poor white farmers from allying with the poor black farmers. With the support of the poor white farmers, they hoped to have the votes to take back control of the state government at the next election. While a statewide executive committee was initiating the revival of the State Fair in Columbia, the *Charleston Courier* reported on October 7, 1869, that the business community in Charleston was encouraged to "aid the committee in raising the limited amount of funds necessary to accomplish a creditable exhibition. Let us knit and bind the up- and lowcountry together more closely by harmonious and mutual sympathy of action, in a common effort to advance our natural welfare and all will yet come right." Having lost control of state and local governments, the Democrats created several resistance organizations. The founding of the State Agricultural and Mechanical Society coincided with the rise of other organizations determined to resist Radical Reconstruction. The Confederate Survivors' Association, headed by Gen. Wade Hampton, and the Young Men's Christian Association, directed by future Democratic Party chair Alexander Haskell, were organized. Two other resistance organizations had their initial meetings at the 1869 State Fair. The South Carolina Club, led by future Democratic paramilitary leader Martin W. Gary, and the South Carolina Monument Association, a women's organization established to erect a monument honoring South Carolina's Civil War soldiers, held their organizational meetings in November 1869 during the State Fair.[1]

RADICAL MEMBERS OF THE So. Ca. LEGISLATURE.

One objective of the new State Fair was to help rid the state of the Radical Legislature. Courtesy of the South Carolina Department of Archives & History

On April 29, 1869, several of the leading citizens of the state, including James Lide Coker of Hartsville, Johnson Hagood of Barnwell, David Wyatt Aiken of Abbeville, and Thomas Green Clemson of Pendleton, called for a convention to meet in Columbia to reorganize the State Agricultural Society. Gen. Johnson Hagood was elected president and the group quickly adopted a resolution "that this Convention resolve itself into a permanent agricultural, mechanical and industrial society." Unlike its prewar predecessors, which focused primarily on agricultural interests, the new organization realized it was important for the state to diversify its economy. The constitution adopted by the convention stated that its aim "shall be to develop and promote the entire material interests of the State." President Hagood appointed standing committees in

THE CARPET-BAGGER

While the accounts of the State Fair touted the progress made in agriculture and manufacturing since the end of the Civil War, the political turmoil was ever present. On November 11, 1869, a reporter for the *Charleston Courier* lamented the presence of carpetbaggers in the state capital: "In this dusty, windy city, the *genus homo* carpet-bagger finds a congeniality which must be very pleasing to him. Radicals do most congregate here, and you may not pass through a street without meeting a number of them. They may be known by a peculiarity which I heard described by a *Northern Man* as follows: Said he, 'You may know him (meaning the carpet-bagger) because he has the appearance of one who has been half starved all of his life until within the past six months, since which time he has been over-fed.' Albeit, the influx has not yet fully set in. When the Legislature meets there will be a grand gathering of them, and Columbia will have become metamorphosed into one vast carpet bag, in which the carpet-bagger will live and move and have his being, in close affection with him 'man and brother'." This same sentiment was echoed on November 11, 1870, when a Columbia newspaper, *The Daily Phoenix,* reported that "a large sum of money has been spent in improving the Fair Grounds, and Columbia seems determined to show all South Carolina that the capital, oppressed as it is by the presence of radical rascality, has life and energy enough to gather the people together in good cause of industrial progress."

616   HARPER'S WEEKLY.   [JULY 25, 1874.

MOSES JUNIOR VIEWING THE PROMISED LAND FROM MOUNT RUIN.

Scalawag governor Franklin J. Moses Jr. is depicted in this cartoon attempting to cover up the scandals that characterized his term in office. Courtesy of the Richland Library Historical Collections, Richland Library

the areas of agriculture, manufactures, mechanics, labor, and immigration—all areas that were subsequently addressed by the convention. The activities at the convention focused on industrialization, labor, and the need to publish a magazine promoting scientific agricultural practices.

Col. John B. Palmer spoke about the need to bring manufacturing to the state. He argued that the state was an ideal location for textile mills because of the abundance of water-power, a mild climate, low wages, a skilled work force, and lower freight rates. T. S. Boinest, from Newberry and the chairman of the committee on immigration, encouraged the convention to follow the lead of the Immigration Society of Newberry and seek immigrants from abroad to supplement the present inadequate labor force.

The convention adopted a resolution supporting the publication of a monthly magazine devoted to the agricultural, mechanical and industrial interests of the state. The first volume was published in 1869 with D. H. Jacques as editor.

NOW IS THE TIME

TO SUBSCRIBE FOR 1872

TO THE

RURAL CAROLINIAN,

THE GREAT

SOUTHERN

AGRICULTURAL MAGAZINE.

NOW IS THE TIME

TO PURCHASE YOUR

ACCOUNT BOOK FOR 1872.

SEND FOR

"THE RURAL ACCOUNTANT."

JUST THE THING FOR THE FARMER.

Price—*Small Size, by Mail, $1 40; Large Size, by Mail, $2 30.*

PUBLISHED BY

WALKER, EVANS & COGSWELL,

STATIONERS, PRINTERS AND BINDERS,

Nos. 3 BROAD AND 109 EAST BAY STREETS,

CHARLESTON, S. C.

The Rural Carolinian was published by the society from 1869 to 1876 and promoted the agricultural, mechanical, and industrial interests of the state. Courtesy of the South Caroliniana Library, University of South Carolina, Columbia, S.C.

During the first twenty years of the society's existence there was confusion about the name. The 1869 constitution of the society lists the name as "Agricultural and Mechanical Society of South Carolina." By the late 1870s some of the premium lists show the name as "State Agricultural and Mechanical Society." The 1890 constitution has the name as the State Agricultural and Mechanical Society of South Carolina. During the twentieth century, "The," with a capital "T" was added to the formal name of the society.*

Even though the formal name of the organization is the State Agricultural and Mechanical Society of South Carolina, since the 1890s this abbreviated name was used on medals awarded as premiums. Courtesy of the State Agricultural and Mechanical Society of South Carolina

Society History, 37–38.

Walker, Evans & Cogswell of Charleston published *The Rural Carolinian* from 1869 to 1876. From 1870 to 1876 David Wyatt Aiken, the secretary of the society, was co-owner and correspondent. For several years after the magazine ceased publication, the work was carried on by the agricultural department of the *News and Courier* with Aiken as the editor. While the society's resolution might have inspired creation of the magazine, it was not a publication of the organization.

Following speeches and reports from the committees, the convention passed a resolution calling for the first fair to open on the second Wednesday of November 1869. While the new organization included promoting the industrial interests of the state along with its traditional agricultural focus, there were still ties to the prewar agricultural society's fairs. The leadership of the new organization was composed of former planters and merchants, but only one was active in the leadership of the prewar society. Robert J. Gage from Union County served as the secretary of the society in 1855 and as the treasurer of the postwar organization in 1869. As the 1869 fair approached, newspapers across the state heralded it as the sixth annual State Fair, thereby linking the two organizations. The first premium list printed in the *Charleston Courier* for the 1869 fair was headlined as "Premium list of the State Agricultural and Mechanical Society for the Sixth Annual Fair...." However, by 1878 the society was using the 1869 fair as its founding date, confirming that the postwar organization considered itself separate from the prewar agricultural society.

Another resolution authorized the executive committee "to proceed to raise the necessary funds, by subscription or otherwise, for the purpose of erecting on the Fair Grounds in this city, the buildings necessary for the annual fairs of the Society." The members of the convention realized that they would not be able to get any support from the state because the interests of the farmers and industrialists were "inadequately represented in the present State Government."[2]

The *Charleston Courier* reported on July 28, 1869, that, at a meeting of the taxpayers of Columbia, the following resolution was adopted: "That in the opinion of this meeting, the interest of Columbia imperatively require that such an appropriation be made, the amount to be left to the discretion of the city." In addition to the appropriation from the city, the

meeting established a committee of two members from each ward of the city to solicit subscriptions from citizens to construct the buildings for the State Fair. In addition to the solicitation of members from Columbia on July 31, 1869, the executive committee placed a circular in the *Charleston Courier* asking citizens to detach a promissory note for twenty dollars payable on October 1. Individuals would be able to redeem the note by obtaining either ten annual members at two dollars each or two life members at ten dollars each. Other funds were received from outside the Columbia area. On October 20, 1869, the *Charleston Courier* reported that the board of trade in Charleston donated $200 and other Charleston merchants contributed an additional $800. The Charleston Chamber of Commerce donated a one-hundred-dollar silver cup for the best ten bales of cotton.

The most enthusiastic supporter of the revived fair was the sitting Democratic Columbia City Council. Shortly after the organization of the society the city council leased the fairgrounds to three members of the society's executive committee, John B. Palmer, John P. Thomas, and William Wallace, because the society was not yet incorporated. Since the property was not actually being used by the city, Richland County sent the society a tax bill for 1869. Fortunately, Columbia mayor John McKenzie provided the county with a letter certifying that the property was being used for a public purpose—the State Fair. The county subsequently removed the fairgrounds from the tax roll.[3] The council also appropriated $8,000 for the construction of the necessary buildings at the fairgrounds. Following the city elections in 1870 the now Republican-controlled council challenged the legality of the land transfer and filed a lawsuit. After three years of litigation the Columbia City Council dropped the suit, and the fair continued every year until 1904, when it moved to the Rosewood Avenue location.[4]

As the opening of the 1869 State Fair on November 10 approached, the final preparations were hindered by heavy rains turning the fairgrounds into a quagmire of mud. As he made his way to the fairgrounds on November 11, 1869,

This 1872 view of Columbia is the earliest known image of the fairgrounds on Upper Street showing the main building, outside exhibit area, and the racetrack. Courtesy of Library of Congress

a correspondent for the *Charleston Courier* commented, "the good people of this community, together with the thousands of visitors to the State Fair, are pushing, wading, paddling through the slush of yellow clay-mud that encumbers the streets." The roads leading to the fairgrounds were jammed with wagons, buggies, ox carts, pedestrians, steam engines, horse plows, and other portable machines. The large crowds that poured into Columbia once again taxed the available restaurants and hotel accommodations. In the days preceding the grand opening, the railroads transported goods intended for the exhibitions to Columbia at no charge and offered special passenger rates.

From November 11th through the 15th, the *Charleston Courier* carried extensive coverage of activities at the State Fair. The 1869 State Fair contained many of the activities found in the prewar fairs sponsored by the State Agricultural Society of South Carolina. The exhibits contained manufactured products from across the state including the gold-medal-winning Tozer portable steam engine from Columbia, a patented saw sharpener by Shields & Glaze from Columbia, submerged pumps by Jennings & Tomlinson from Charleston, Brinly's plows exhibited by C. Graveley of Charleston, and Hinckley's knitting machine exhibited by J. W. Thomas from Abbeville. Among the products exhibited were flour from

THE TOZER ENGINE.

BEST!

The undersigned, being exclusively engaged in the manufacture of THE TOZER ENGINE, beg to call the attention of all who contemplate purchasing engines to the advantage you secure in making your purchases from manufacturers at home. You get the best that is made, (all Yankee manufacturers acknowledge this fact,) adapted to the class of work for which they are needed. They will do more work with the same amount of fuel than any other engine. They are made outright at your own beautiful capital. They are more simple and less liable to get out of repair than any other, and if anything gets broken we are within a few hours of you to replace what is wrong. We guarantee satisfaction to all. Engines made from SIX TO FIFTY HORSE POWER. Saw Mills any size. Repairing done at short notice. Fitting, Belting, Hose, Hancock Inspirators, etc., for sale.

Also, Agents for Wheeler, Malick, and Cardwell and other Separators.

TOZER & DIAL,
COLUMBIA, S. C.

A frequent premium winner, Tozer engines were manufactured in Columbia during the late nineteenth century. This advertisement is from the 1883 premium catalog. Courtesy of the State Agricultural and Mechanical Society of South Carolina

BUILDINGS AND GROUNDS

When the Union troops under the command of Gen. William T. Sherman occupied Columbia in February 1865, the buildings at the fairgrounds were intentionally destroyed because they were used as a laboratory by the Confederacy. Prior to the war the city had deeded the land to the agricultural society, but when the city burned, the records were destroyed. With the establishment of the society and the reopening of a State Fair, the city once again deeded the property north of Upper (now Elmwood) Street with the stipulation that an annual fair would be held there. Columbia also provided the funds for a substantial two-story structure forty feet by eighty feet with wings on each end measuring thirty feet by sixty feet. By 1884 the State Fair had outgrown the facilities, and a new building, more than twice the size of the original building, was constructed at a cost of $8,000. The new building was used for the field crop, needle and fancy work, and fine art and literary exhibits. The ground floor of the original building held the mechanical exhibits while the upper floor became a restaurant. In addition to the new building, the stalls for the livestock were expanded more than fourfold. The 1869 fair featured a one-half-mile horse racing track. Encouraged by Robert C. Shiver and the State Auxiliary and Joint Stock Company, a three-quarter-mile track was constructed after 1873 to expand equestrian events.[*]

*Society History, 26–37.

Campsen Mills in Charleston, breads and biscuits from Claussen' Steam Bakery in Columbia, sugar and molasses from Passmore & Wilhelm of Greenville, and brooms manufactured by convicts at the state penitentiary. The highlights of the stock exhibitions were the horses and cattle. Over five thousand spectators watched as hundreds of horses were led around the show-ring by their grooms. The cattle exhibition included some very valuable Brahman bulls and an excellent group of Devon bulls and heifers. The domestic department overflowed with fancy work from the ladies of South Carolina, including quilts, needlework, and knitting. Finally, the fertilizer manufacturers had a large exhibit touting the attributes of their products.

In addition to the exhibitions, fairgoers were treated to a

According to the *Charleston Daily News* on November 12, 1869, one of the highlights of the 1869 exhibits was the Jackson Vase. Made by the Philadelphia silversmiths Fletcher and Gardiner, the vase was presented to Gen. Andrew Jackson by the ladies of South Carolina after his victory at the Battle of New Orleans in 1815. On Jackson's death in 1845, his will directed his son that, should the United States become involved in a war with any foreign country, the vase should be given at the close of the war to the South Carolinian "who shall be adjudged by his countrymen or the ladies the most valiant in defense of his country and our country's rights." Following the Mexican War of 1848, Jackson's son sent the vase to Gov. F. W. Alston, instructing him to give it to the Palmetto Regiment Association to be handed down to the last survivor. The association voted to give the vase to the state, and it was in the custody of the South Carolina Department of Archives and History until it was transferred to the South Carolina State Museum in 1986, where it is on exhibit in the military spirit exhibit.

The vase given to Andrew Jackson by the ladies of South Carolina following his victory at the Battle of New Orleans in 1815 was a featured exhibit at the 1869 State Fair. Courtesy of the South Carolina State Museum

variety of entertainment. Horse racing was a major attraction at the fair, but according to a reporter the competition was disappointing and overshadowed by the death of William Guignard of Columbia after he was thrown from his horse during one of the races. The plow demonstrations attracted large crowds interested in comparing the latest innovations.

Another important result of the 1869 fair was the creation of the South Carolina Club. As noted above, one reason for re-establishing the State Fair was to oppose Reconstruction that allowed the freedmen, carpetbaggers, and scalawags to run state and local governments. The *Orangeburg News* reported on November 27, 1869, that during the State Fair there was a meeting of young men "with a view to the organization of a so-ciety for the purpose of promoting social intercourse amongst the gentlemen of South Carolina." The South Carolina Club elected as its president William T. Gary of Edgefield; vice presidents included Wade Hampton of Richland, J. S. Heyward of Colleton, Paul Haskell of Abbeville, William D. Aiken of Fairfield, and David Hampton of Chester. An executive committee was charged with drafting a constitution and with arranging an anniversary ball that would be held in conjunction with the 1870 fair. The account of the meeting concluded: "Gentlemen desiring to become members will forward applications to Mr. Wade Manning, at Columbia." Based on the leadership, "gentlemen" clearly referred to those families who provided the prewar leadership in South Carolina.

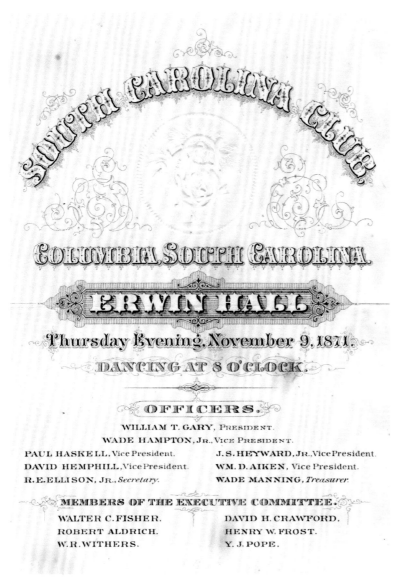

Invitation to the second annual state ball in 1871 sponsored by the South Carolina Club. Courtesy of Rodger E. Stroup

Following the successful 1869 fair during the remaining years of Reconstruction, the State Fair continued to provide an opportunity for the citizens of the state to gather in Columbia to see the latest agricultural and mechanical equipment, exhibit their products, and compete for prizes and premiums. In 1876 the turmoil surrounding the national and state elections resulted in an unusual State Fair. With the white citizens focused on electing former Confederate general Wade Hampton to the governor's office, little attention was paid as fair week approached. Recalling that the city's land donation stipulated that a State Fair must be held each year,

Col. J. Washington Watts of Laurens County shipped by rail a variety of stock from his farm, and they were exhibited each day at the fairgrounds with an audience composed primarily of Hampton supporters who came to Columbia to ensure a fair election.[5]

From 1869 until 1878 the society depended on gate receipts and membership to cover expenses. Bad weather during fair week often made it difficult to meet expenses. Nevertheless, the society was always able to provide recognition to the winners in each category. Cash awards were limited to the field crops and livestock. The manufacturing, mechanical, and fine arts departments presented diplomas, while the domestic, needle, and fancy works departments awarded pieces of silver. In 1878 the State Legislature began an annual appropriation of $2,500 to the society.[6]

The society and the annual fair provided the state's farmers an opportunity to review the latest in agricultural sciences and mechanized equipment. However, in addition to sponsoring the State Fair, the society was a strong advocate for the needs of the agricultural community. In the early 1870s the state's farmers began to join the Patrons of Husbandry, also known as the Grange, a national organization that championed agricultural interests such as railroad rate regulation and rural free postal delivery. David Wyatt Aiken from Abbeville was an officer in the National Grange and from 1869 to 1875 and was the secretary-treasurer of the State Agricultural and Mechanical Society of South Carolina. By 1875 South Carolina membership in the Grange began to decline because it was apolitical and had not accomplished much. The Grange started holding joint summer meetings with the State Agricultural and Mechanical Society. These meetings featured exhibitions of farm machinery, crops, and livestock along with essays on scientific farming practices.

As the state Grange disappeared, new, stronger farmers' organizations emerged during the late 1880s. In 1886 Benjamin F. Tillman united many local farmers' groups and founded the Farmers' Association. Under Tillman's leadership the organization advocated agricultural, educational, and governmental reform while challenging the conservative wing of the Democratic Party that was primarily composed of the pre–Civil War planters who were the founders and active leadership of the State Agricultural and Mechanical Society. Ironically, "Pitchfork Ben" began his rise in politics in 1885 in Bennettsville with a powerful speech at the ninth annual joint meeting of the state Grange and the State Agricultural and Mechanical Society. In addition to the Farmers' Association, the Southern Farmers' Alliance also began to attract members during the late 1880s. It originated in Texas in the mid-1870s, but the first chapter in South Carolina was not started until 1887 in Marion County. By 1890 the alliance had more than sixty thousand members statewide.

From 1877 until the State Fair moved to the Assembly Street location in 1904, the annual event grew larger each year, offering more premiums, exhibits, and entertainment. At the same time, Columbia became more involved in making the city an integral part of fair week. In the 1880s the Columbia Fair Association was organized to sponsor and coordinate events along Main Street. This organization of primarily Columbians was autonomous from the society and each year solicited funds to help defray the cost of staging activities downtown. For the 1889 fair, the group raised the funds to erect six arches across Main Street between the statehouse and the post office, each containing fifty-two gas jets with different colored globes.[7] In 1890 the association collected and expended $858.[8] In addition to sponsoring events downtown, the association also coordinated housing for out-of-town visitors. The lack of adequate hotel rooms was a constant problem during fair week. Beginning in the 1890s the association's housing bureau provided information on rooms available in private homes as well as hotels. In 1900 the association reported an excess of two hundred available rooms.[9] While the association assisted the society, it struggled each year to raise the necessary funds. However, on November 27, 1898, the *State* reported that the association had a surplus and they refunded to their subscribers 64 percent of each subscription amount. In 1902 the Elks joined forces with the association

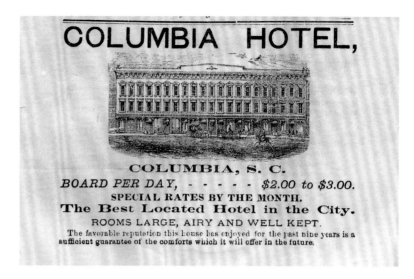

Even though rooms were at a premium during fair week, local hotels promoted their accommodations in ads like this one from the 1878 premium list.
Courtesy of the State Agricultural and Mechanical Society of South Carolina

and sponsored the Cincinnati Carnival Company, which provided the sideshows, parades, and open-air attractions along Main Street. Finally, in 1903 the association disbanded. At a meeting of the executive committee of the association, they determined "that the necessity for the continuance of this organization has ceased to exist in view of the fact that Columbia now has a permanent and well-established organization to the same end—the advertisement of the city and the entertainment of its visitors."[10] The Columbia Chamber of Commerce coordinated the downtown events until 1915, when all activities were moved to the new fairgrounds on Rosewood Avenue. While the midway attractions were not at the fairgrounds until 1915, there were still several spaces under the racetrack grandstand that were rented each year by the society, primarily for food service during the day. Each year the society auctioned these "privileges" to the highest bidder. In 1891 the fifteen booths available sold for between $15 and $17 ($406 to $460 in 2016). However, the big prize was the beer "privilege," which sold for $320 ($8,670 in 2016).[11]

For the 1888 fair, the city completed the installation of electric lights along Main Street.[12] In preparation for the fair on November 5, 1891, a writer for the *State* reported that "the city is taking on carnival attire, and the buntings are floating

The Governor's Guard of Columbia poses with Main Street in the background at the 1877 State Fair.
The military was frequently a part of the State Fair. Courtesy of the South Caroliniana Library, University of South Carolina, Columbia, S.C.

to the breeze." He went on to report: "Yesterday the work of erecting handsome arches of colored globes across Main street was continued, and now they span nearly every crossing to be decorated thus, ready to be lighted." Additionally, many buildings on Main Street were handsomely decorated. Each year the opening parade grew larger, always striving to entice fairgoers to visit all of the attractions at the fairgrounds.

During the 1890s the cost of attending the State Fair could be an impediment to many citizens. Writing to her father from Winthrop Normal and Training School, Annie Perry Jester estimated it would cost her $1.60 ($46.79 in 2016), including $1.00 round-trip train fare, $.25 admission, $.10 trolley fare, and $.25 for dinner served by the ladies of several churches.[13]

Always cognizant of the need for exposure in the media, the 1898 fair featured the first press room, which was warmly received by reporters. Writing in the *State* on November 17, 1898, one reporter commented, "One of the best features of

An 1898 poster advertising the State Fair highlights the entertainment activities over the "instructive exhibits." Courtesy of the South Caroliniana Library, University of South Carolina, Columbia, S.C.

this fair in the opinion of the newspaper men, is the press room which has been fitted up especially for their exclusive use. Tables and chairs have been provided and there, safe from the noise and bustle outside, the reporters can write their allotted 'grind' of what is going on at the fair. This is the first step taken for the comfort of the newspaper men by the fair authorities."

Every year the State Fair sought to offer special events and exhibits to attract larger crowds. In the early 1880s both Union and Confederate Civil War veterans began to attend reunions at the fair, recounting the heroic battles of the war. In 1883 French artist Paul Philippoteaux completed a monumental painting of the Battle of Gettysburg that was displayed in Chicago. By 1885 numerous illicit copies were touring the country. On November 10, 1885, *The Abbeville Messenger* reported that the State Fair exhibited a painting of the battle that was 18 feet high by 300 feet long, smaller than the original painting, which was 42 feet high by 359 feet long, but it still proved a major attraction. The State Fair obviously had one of the copies of the painting rather than the original. In 1895 a petrified man found on the banks of the Saluda River created a sensation and a controversy. On October 30, 1903, the *State* reported that the fair featured an exhibit of Catawba pottery made by the Indian women and offered a premium for the best specimen. According to the article, the fair would offer a regular premium next year for the best piece of Catawba pottery.

During the late nineteenth century, a major feature at the State Fair was the state ball sponsored by the South Carolina Club, a social organization composed of gentlemen from most of the counties of the state. The state ball began in 1870 as a part of the State Fair. From the outset the state ball was a major social event in the state. *The Daily Phoenix* commented on November 17, 1870, that "The grand ball of the South Carolina Club was a model of refined taste, courteous care and skillful management." The *State* newspaper reported on November 18, 1898, that the state ball was one of the most elaborate. Held in the chambers of the State House of Representatives, the ball required removing the legislators' desks and putting down a dance floor. The fifteen-piece Columbia Orchestra provided the music for waltzes, quadrilles, lancers, and two-steps. Prepared by H. H. Shiver, the dinner included turkey with cranberry sauce, smoked tongue, fried oysters, chicken salad, rolls, cakes, fruit, champagne, sherry, and coffee. On October 30, 1903, page one of the *State* included the headline "The State Ball a Great Success." The paper's correspondent touted the event as "one of the proud events in the south that

Since its inception in 1870 the state ball was held in several different venues in Columbia, including Parker's Hall, Craven Hall, the Shandon Pavilion, the Jefferson Hotel, and the House Chamber in the statehouse. The last state ball was held during fair week in 1917. Several factors contributed to the demise of the state ball. For several years the House of Representatives had attempted to prohibit the use of its chamber for private events. In February 1911 the House passed a resolution by a vote of 56 to 40 that the House Chambers could not be used during the recess except for the Democratic State Convention. The reasons given for this policy change included the need to protect the new furnishings recently installed in the chamber and concern about allowing a private group the exclusive use of state property. For the next several years the state ball was held at other venues. In 1918 the ball was scheduled at the Jefferson Hotel but when the State Fair was canceled because of the influenza epidemic, the South Carolina Club also canceled the state ball. In both 1919 and 1920 there was some sentiment for resuming the state ball, but it did not occur. In 1921 an article in the society section of the *State* reported that the South Carolina Club was exploring having the ball in October, but some dissenters pointed out that "since they have been held outside the capitol, losing as they did a prestige such as only this setting can give and being deprived of the stateliness and dignity of the legislative hall." Other club members commented "with a sigh, that never can the balls be the brilliant events of former years so long as the pop, sparkle and inspiration of champagne are lacking" since, with the beginning of Prohibition in January 1920, serving alcoholic beverages was illegal.* The final factor that spelled doom for the state ball was the establishment of local social clubs including the Assembly, which was sponsoring a ball as early as 1918, and the Tarantella, which sponsored a ball during fair week beginning in 1922.† In 1935 a final attempt was made to resurrect the state ball, but that ball was poorly attended and the *State* reported that the "Tarantella has filled in the gap, with a gay party that is perhaps better suited to Fair week than the State Ball."‡

* "A State Ball This Year?" *State* (Columbia), July 7, 1921.

† "News of Columbia Society, Women's Clubs, Philanthropies," *State* (Columbia), January 17, 1918; and "Tarantella Dance Club Is Formed," *State* (Columbia), October 7, 1922.

‡ "Gaiety Reigns as Informality Marks Occasion," *State* (Columbia), October 13, 1935.

is intimately connected with the proud days of the old south. Down the years it has come and people of other States now regard it as one of the greatest social events of the year in the country."

A major feature of the state ball was the presentation of "many fair debutantes, graceful, vivacious, modest and lovely…such women as South Carolina is noted for." Among the young ladies who debuted in 1898 was Blondelle Malone, the daughter of Mr. and Mrs. Miles Alexander Malone of Columbia. The *State* newspaper's account of the affair included detailed descriptions of the ladies' attire. Miss Malone wore a "lovely white lace dress, over white silk, trimmed with ruching of the same; low waist outlined with lace and lace girdle; flowers, lilies of the valley."[14]

While the fairgrounds were used each November for the annual State Fair, they were also used for other activities during the year. Horse racing, carnivals, baseball games, and other activities used the fairgrounds. In 1891 Trinity College (now Duke University) beat Furman College 96–0 in one of the state's earliest football games.[15] In 1891 the first celebration of Labor Day was held at the fairgrounds, but following that event the executive committee of the society passed a resolution prohibiting the use of the grounds and buildings "for any purpose except for holding fairs and similar exhibitions."

Over the years one of the expectations of State Fair goers has been to see unique objects. Sometimes these were bearded ladies or freaks of nature, and other times they were outright fakes. In 1895 a petrified man was exhibited at the State Fair. A farmer who noticed toes sticking out of the water discovered the man in the Saluda River five miles north of Columbia. Weighing over four hundred pounds and standing six feet tall, the figure appeared to be a white man based on the moustache and hair. According to an advertising poster for the exhibition of the petrified man, sixty-four doctors and scientists had "examined the body and guarantee it to be a genuine specimen of petrification of the human body."[*] Following the State Fair, the petrified man toured areas in the eastern United States over the next two years. In March 1896 a suit was brought against the owner alleging that the object was removed from his family's burial ground.[†] In 1896 the petrified man was again an attraction at the State Fair. The mystery surrounding the petrified man saw one author write a fictional account published in the *New York Herald* portraying the figure as a Federal soldier killed during the Civil War.[‡] Until 1899 the petrified man continued to travel until two small pieces were sent to scientists in Berlin, Germany. After a careful examination, they determined that the figure was actually Portland cement that might have been cast from an Indian mummy.[§]

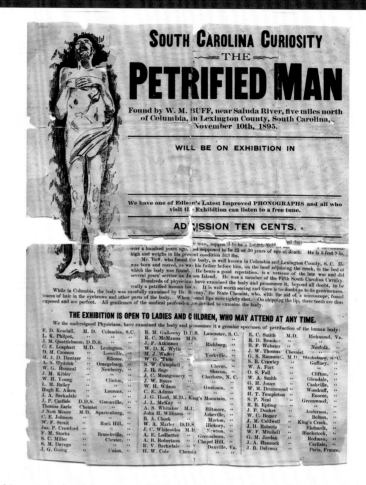

This poster advertising the petrified man lists the South Carolina doctors who verified that it was "a genuine specimen of petrification of the human body." Courtesy of the South Caroliniana Library, University of South Carolina, Columbia, S.C.

[*] "A Petrified Man," *State* (Columbia), November 12, 1895.
[†] "A Novel Suit Action to be Instituted to Recover the Petrified Man," *State* (Columbia), March 11, 1896.
[‡] Cited in "Readable Fiction: A Story about Lexington's 'Petrified Man,'" *State* (Columbia), October 12, 1897.
[§] "Our Petrified Indian in Berlin," *State* (Columbia), January 8, 1899.

In 1892 the society declined the use of the fairgrounds for the Labor Day celebration. However, in 1893 the society reversed its earlier prohibition and permitted the Labor Day celebration to use the facilities with the condition that "all the property of the society be left in first-class order."[16] Extant records do not reveal any details, but apparently the 1891 Labor Day celebration had left the fairgrounds in disrepair.

Except during this short-lived prohibition, the fairgrounds frequently hosted events like the celebration of Columbia's centennial gala, a May Day carnival, and a football game in 1897 between the local Pigskin Pushers and a pick-up team.[17] In 1898, at the outbreak of the Spanish American War, the fairgrounds were the site of Camp Prospect, one of four small training camps in the Columbia area. Among the units at Camp Prospect were the 2nd South Carolina and the Charleston Heavy Battery.[18]

At the opening of the twentieth century the thirty-acre Elmwood Avenue fairgrounds was running short of space for the State Fair's ever-growing activities. Since the 1880s the carnival activities and midway had been held on Main Street in the evenings so they would not conflict with other fair events and would not take up space on the fairgrounds. The space limitation was especially evident after the 1903 fair, when the Barnum & Bailey Circus was a feature on the fair schedule for Friday and Saturday. The circus, arriving with

THE COLUMBIA CARNIVAL, 1893

In May 1893 the society allowed the Columbia Carnival to use the fairgrounds. Always looking for a way to promote the city, local businessmen organized the carnival, intending for it to become an annual event in the spring. The success of the State Fair each fall brought substantial business to the city, and the Columbia Carnival committee sought a similar event for the spring. On May 18 and 19, 1893, visitors from across the state came to Columbia to attend the events highlighted by the increasingly popular sport of bicycle racing. Unfortunately, attendance was not what the organizers anticipated. One reporter noted "that in the spring, the season of work, there cannot be the number of visitors possible in the fall, the season of recreation." However, the reporter also pointed out that Gov. Ben Tillman had encouraged his followers to boycott the carnival. A few weeks before the carnival, the governor had supported the lynching of a Negro for allegedly raping a fourteen-year-old white girl. Led by N. G. Gonzales, editor of the *State* newspaper, Columbians were indignant at the governor's action, and Tillman used his bully pulpit to keep his followers at home, contributing to the carnival's lackluster results.* The 1893 carnival was the only year the city held the spring carnival.

* Francis Butler Simkins, *Pitchfork Ben Tillman: South Carolinian* (Baton Rouge: Louisiana State University Press, 1944), 224–25; and "Thoughts on the Carnival," *State* (Columbia), May 19, 1893.

over one thousand employees on eighty-eight railcars, was housed in tents covering twelve acres.[19] Further reducing the fairgrounds, part of the land where the racetrack was located, owned by Charles Logan, was divided and sold as home lots after Logan's death.

At the annual meeting of the society on October 29, 1903, members received a report from the Joint Greater State Fair Committee appointed by the Columbia City Council, the Chamber of Commerce, and the society. The joint committee recommended moving the annual State Fair to a location that had at least seventy-five acres of land. After a lengthy discussion, the proposal was referred to the society's executive committee, which held the power to act. During meetings on November 30, 1903, and February 3, 1904, the executive committee examined four potential sites and settled on a one-hundred-acre site that was previously the demonstration field of the Agricultural Department of the University of South Carolina. The site provided more than adequate space with electricity from the Olympia Power House and water provided by wells on site. The streetcar line was being extended through the Olympia Mill village, and the site had an excellent view of the city skyline, dominated by the new dome on the statehouse. The purchase price was $15,000. Working with the city, the society issued $30,000 in bonds to purchase the property and construct the necessary buildings. The city agreed that the proceeds from the sale of the old fairgrounds could be used to retire this debt. Subsequently the old fairgrounds were sold for $30,000 and the society was able to retire the mortgage.

The new fairgrounds were located about two miles south of the city between the Southern Railway and Bluff Road. On April 20, 1904, the society engaged architects Shand & LaFaye to design the main building and the women's building.[20]

From 1869 to 1903 the fairgrounds on Elmwood Avenue saw the State Fair develop into an event featuring not only agricultural and industrial activities but also expanded

BLONDELLE MALONE

Born in Bostwick, Georgia, in 1877, Blondelle Malone was to become a respected American artist who one critic dubbed "The Garden Artist of America." She grew up in Columbia and later frequently visited her parents in Columbia. While a student at Converse College in 1896, Malone won the first premium for the best landscape made from a copy. That same year she also entered hand-painted china and crayon portraits. In 1915 her mother died, and Blondelle returned from an extended stay in Europe to be with her father. In 1917 she entered five paintings in the State Fair and won the first premium with a painting of crepe myrtle trees in Columbia.*

domestic exhibits, entertainment opportunities, and state-wide social events including the state ball and the annual Carolina–Clemson football game. With limited space on the fairgrounds, the society partnered with the City of Columbia and used the city's main streets as venues for the midway activities. The move to a much larger fairgrounds in 1904 paved the way for the development of an even greater State Fair.

Debutante Blondelle Malone with the dress she wore to the state ball in 1898. Courtesy of the South Caroliniana Library, University of South Carolina, Columbia, S.C.

*Louise Jones DuBose, *Enigma: The Career of Blondelle Malone in Art and Society 1879–1951, as Told in Her Letters and Diaries* (Columbia: University of South Carolina Press).

The Greater State Fair

The decision to move the State Fair to a larger venue was necessitated by a lack of space and adequate facilities to house the growing crowds. The success of the fair required the use of Columbia's streets for the midway activities. By 1900 fairgoers were more sophisticated and were seeking larger and better facilities, along with professional entertainers. In 1902, for the first time, the society engaged the Cincinnati Carnival Company to provide the midway activities and shows. Over the next several years, professional carnival companies coupled with better facilities made possible a greater state fair.

When the 1903 fair closed, the location for the 1904 fair was uncertain. Working quickly the society's executive committee completed the necessary plans to move the 1904 fair to the new site on Rosewood Drive. On May 11, 1904, the *State* paper reported that all of the stock stalls were completed, and work on the racetrack would begin within a few days. The old buildings on the Elmwood Avenue site were being demolished, and much of the lumber was being used on the new site. Work on the new building was well along under the supervision of the architects Shand & LaFaye and the Greater State Fair building committee.

The main entrance to the new fairgrounds was on present-day Rosewood Drive. The main building was 138 feet by 68 feet and housed the major industrial exhibits. To the right of the main building was the women's building, 112 feet by 68 feet, where all the domestic and art exhibits were displayed. To the left was the agricultural building. Behind the agricultural building was the poultry building, measuring 150 feet by 50 feet. Behind the agricultural building were stalls for three hundred blooded stock and quarters for three hundred cattle. Adjacent to the stock buildings were thirty sleeping rooms for exhibitors. There was a one-mile racetrack and a smaller one-half-mile track inside the mile track. A polo ground was inside the small track. A new 2,000-seat grandstand and a paddock completed the racing facilities. The two large restaurants each had seating for 150 patrons. Finally, the athletic field was located at the corner of Rosewood and Bluff Roads and featured the grandstand moved from the old fairgrounds.

The facilities at the new fairgrounds contained amenities focused on accommodating larger crowds. For example, the main building at the old fairgrounds was a two-story structure, and there were frequent delays while using the stairs.[1] All the buildings at the new fairgrounds were on one level.

After the fair was under way, the *State* proclaimed on October 27, 1904: "From Farm and Factory, Field and Fireside, the Fashionings of Man's Hands Are Gathered for Exhibition at the Greater State Fair." When the gates opened, not all the facilities were finished, but they were all far enough along that they were used. Despite bad weather on opening day, thousands of visitors flocked to the fairgrounds and packed the exhibits in the new buildings. One of the highlights of the stock exhibits were the Berkshire hogs presented by farmers from across the state. On October 29, 1904, the *State* reviewed the stock exhibits, reporting that the Berkshires were favored by the state's farmers because "they are sound, adapted perfectly to the climate, are handsome animals, hardy, fatten

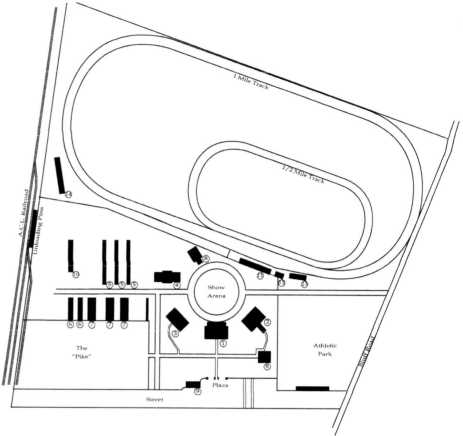

Map showing the location of the facilities at the new fairgrounds in 1904.
Courtesy of the State Agricultural and Mechanical Society of South Carolina

1. Commercial Building	8. Restaurants
2. Women's Building	9. Administration Building
3. Agriculture Building	10. Sleeping Rooms
4. Poultry Building	11. Grand Stand
5. Horse Stalls	12. Pool Room
6. Hog & Sheep Pens	13. Paddock
7. Cattle Sheds	14. Racing Stalls

GREATER STATE FAIR

As the 1904 fair approached, all the publicity touted the "Greater State Fair." The origin of this term is unknown because the society's board minutes from this period are not extant. The first use of the term appears during the October 1903 annual meeting when the society appointed the Joint Greater State Fair Committee. Following this committee's report, the use of the term "Greater State Fair" begins to appear in the press and becomes the primary marketing focus for the 1904 fair.

COLUMBIA, S. C.   State Fair Grounds.

This early-twentieth-century postcard features the grandstand and racetrack. Courtesy of Dave Sennema

with a nice distribution of lean and fat and produce meat of the keenest flavor." The horse shows in the arena and the cattle sale, while the prices were low, attracted large crowds. On October 27, 1904, the *State* reported that the women's building had only been completed on the evening prior to opening day, with beautiful roses and chrysanthemums highlighting the flower exhibits. A wide variety of fancy work, handcrafted pillows, quilts, counterpanes, and handkerchiefs were featured in exhibit cases. In another area were entries of jellies, preserves, dried fruit, and other domestic goods such as soap and lye. Also in the women's building was an exhibit by the Laurens Manufacturing Company of quarter-sawn oak furniture whose "design, workmanship and finish...are not surpassed by any of the older manufacturers. The company is three years old and is doing a fine business, increasing trade monthly over a wide territory."

In the commerce building the exhibits featured and promoted South Carolina agricultural and industrial products. Horry County had the best county exhibit featuring a five-pound sweet potato while Rock Hill had the best city exhibit highlighted by a carriage manufactured by the Rock Hill Buggy Company. The Southern Railway exhibit touted the wide variety of agricultural products grown in the state including

lumber, cotton, pecans, peaches, pears, apples, grapes, corn, and vegetables. Adjacent to the Southern Railway exhibit was the Coca-Cola exhibit featuring free samples for all fairgoers. The Southern Scale and Fixture Company exhibited its products and featured a sixteen-horsepower Rambler automobile.

Even with the additional facilities at the new fairgrounds, there was not room for all the midway shows. Since the 1880s the Columbia Fair Association and the Columbia Chamber of Commerce sponsored the carnival and midway activities on Main Street. Anticipating larger crowds at the 1904 fair, the chamber continued to provide additional activities along Main Street. The activities included a balloon ascension each afternoon; a merry-go-round at Laurel Street; an electric theater and crystal maze at Taylor Street; a volcano at Plain (now Hampton) Street; a fat girl, big snake show, and old plantation at Washington Street; and Luna in Dreamland and the Marionettes at Lady Street. Other attractions included a trapeze artist, fancy shooting, high-wire act, and the Mardi Gras Company's band. On Tuesday evening all the Main Street activities were preceded by a grand parade. Each afternoon the Main Street carnival opened at 3:00 P.M., and when the State Fair closed at 5:00 P.M., fairgoers flocked to Main Street where the action continued well into the evening.

SOUTHERN RAILWAY COMPANY

PREMIER CARRIER OF THE SOUTH

CONVENIENT SHEDULES

HIGH CLASS EQUIPMENT

TO

ALL POINTS IN ALL DIRECTIONS

The Railway of the South

For the South

Penetrating All the South

COURTESY   EFFICIENCY

W. E. McGEE

Asst. General Passenger Agent

Columbia, South Carolina

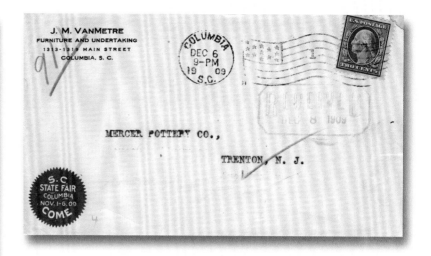

ACCOMMODATION BLANK

Cut out and mail to Columbia Chamber of Commerce.

I have......rooms and can take........people during the Harvest Jubilee and State Fair, October 23-27, 1916, for

Boarding ... ...)

) Per day.

Lodging.. ... ...)

Phone... ... ...   Name...... ....

                          Address ....

(left) In addition to offering special rates during fair season, the railroads also exhibited items during the fair and purchased advertisements in the annual premium list. This ad is from the 1915 premium list. Courtesy of the State Agricultural and Mechanical Society of South Carolina

(top) Fair week was an important time for retailers in Columbia, who helped market the fair by applying stickers to letters. Courtesy of Rodger E. Stroup

(bottom) 1916 accommodations blank. To accommodate the flood of visitors to Columbia during fair week, the city's housing bureau encouraged citizens to rent rooms to fair visitors. Courtesy of the State Agricultural and Mechanical Society of South Carolina

Attendance on Thursday surpassed twenty thousand, a single-day record. The society considered extending the fair through Saturday, but a much smaller crowd on Friday and the presence of the Adam Forepaugh & Sells Bros. circus on Friday persuaded them not to extend the fair. After the fair closed, the *State* printed a review of the State Fair as seen through the eyes of the state's newspapers. While the press unanimously declared the 1904 fair by far the best ever, they pointed out several areas that needed improvement. Foremost among complaints was the distance from Main Street (two miles) and Union Station (one mile) and the lack of adequate trolley cars to carry the crowds. Many arriving by train were forced to walk the mile from the station to the fairgrounds. As the *Sumter Item* noted, "The State fair has grown to be such a big thing that Columbia is unable to take care of the crowds. Columbia will have to grow some to catch up with the Greater State Fair." While the hotels, boarding houses, and private residences were able to handle the crowds, many complained that the prices were raised just because it was fair week. The *Manning Farmer* noted "that there were too many side shows and catch-penny devices allowed on the grounds." Despite these shortcomings, all agreed that the "Greater State Fair" was a resounding success. The *Abbeville Medium* reported that "The exhibits were of the highest excellence and the fair was a crowning success in every particular.... Greater successes await the Fair association in its new quarters for it is one of the most worthy of the established institutions of the State."[2]

Even with the success of the first fair at the Assembly Street fairgrounds, the society and the city were quick to address the concerns expressed by visitors. As the opening of the 1905 fair approached, the *State* newspaper reported on October 21 and 22, 1905, that the city had opened a bureau of information office in the YMCA building at the corner of Main and Lady that would be staffed throughout the fair, and it contained a telephone line (phone number 273). This office could provide information on lodging in private homes as well as the city's hotels. To help handle the expected overflow, the Columbia Hotel leased the vacant Columbia College building on Plain Street, which could accommodate several hundred visitors. The Columbia Street Railway added a double track between Sumter Street and Union Station and from the station to the fairgrounds that could handle five thousand riders per hour. Various locations in town also offered a combination trolley and fair ticket.

The 1905 fair saw the first reference to a new challenge, an issue that continues to this day—where to put the automobiles that fairgoers were beginning to use. Fairgoers with automobiles were directed to enter off of Bluff Road and park in the ballpark near the corner of Bluff Road and Rosewood Avenue. Even with all the advanced planning, the trolleys were still overwhelmed on "Big Thursday." But there were few complaints, as most visitors enjoyed the carnival atmosphere.[3]

In 1907 the state participated in celebration of the tricen-

COLUMBIA STREET RAILWAY

As the 1905 fair approached, the Columbia Street Railway experienced a problem with its electric generating plant. An ongoing dry spell caused a lower than normal flow of water in the river. General Manager Elliott of the power plant called his counterpart in Union, South Carolina, Col. T. C. Duncan, and requested that he allow a greater amount of water to come down the Broad River. Colonel Duncan consented to let about four feet of water more than usual come down the river each day.* Without adequate power, the trolley cars would not have been available to transport people between downtown and the fairgrounds.

* "Capital City Chat," *State* (Columbia), October 24, 1905.

tennial of the settling of Jamestown, Virginia. The Legislature appropriated funds to create an exhibit highlighting the various industries of South Carolina. At the conclusion of the exposition, the unexpended balance of $4,519.91 was given to the society for the erection of an agricultural building on the fairgrounds. The society matched the funds in 1908 and erected a structure that housed the exhibits from the Jamestown Exposition, an exhibit from Clemson College and other agricultural exhibits.[4]

Every year the core attractions at the fair remained the agricultural and industrial exhibits, horse racing, sporting events, and the midway activities. To ensure returning visitors and entice new ones each year, the society sought unique attractions and amenities. In 1909 President William Howard Taft visited the fair, and the anticipated crowds were so large that in addition to the streetcars, the Atlantic Coast Line ran trains from Union Station (now California Dreaming restaurant) to the fairgrounds.[5] On November 1, 1910, the *State* described one featured attraction: "Among the free attractions that have been booked for the State fair is California Frank's diving horse that will leap from a tower 70 feet high into a tank of water 12 feet deep with a lady rider on his back." Frequently events were held in Columbia during fair week that were not part of the fair. In 1911, for example, for the fourth year in a row the state board of health held a clinic at the State Hospital for physicians across the state. The 1911 clinic addressed the ongoing problem of pellagra.[6]

In addition to the attractions, the 1910 fair was a pivotal one during this era. After moving to the Rosewood Fairgrounds, the society wanted to eliminate the use of the city streets for the midway activities and move them to the fairgrounds. Since the 1870s the midway activities were on Main Street and controlled by the city. In February 1905 the annual meeting of the society adopted a resolution: "That it is the sense of this society that sideshows and other attractions on the streets be prohibited during fair week and that the city give its aid to the attractions at the fair." The society appointed it secretary, A. W. Love of Chester, a committee of one, "to see the city and county authorities to ask that these attractions be prevented during fair week and to arrange for suitable transportation facilities."[7] Despite the resolution and Love's efforts, the midway activities continued to be held on Main Street for several more years. In 1909 they were jointly overseen by the Chamber of Commerce and the society. After the 1909 fair the society decided to open the fairgrounds in the evening and discontinue activities on Main Street. Some Columbians were unhappy with this decision because it took fair visitors away from the downtown restaurants and shops. In his address at the annual meeting of the society, outgoing president John G. Mobley accused some Columbians of attempting to undermine the evening events at the fair for their own selfish interests. He went on to say that Columbia "does not show sufficient appreciation of the great good that the society is doing to the development of our State, and to the commercial interests of Columbia."[8] A. McP. Hamby, secretary of the Chamber of Commerce, said he thought the Chamber of Commerce "had acted unselfishly in this matter, and I believe that it has injured Columbia for Main street to have had no street shows. They enliven and inspirit the crowd."[9] Three days later Columbia mayor Thomas H. Gibbes sent a letter to the new president of the society, J. Arthur Banks: "We suppose that it is a matter of almost as much regret to you as it is to the city council of Columbia that expressions were used by your predecessor…which might possibly have been construed into an implication of hostility between the city of Columbia and the society." Mayor Gibbes pointed out that the city had abstained from hosting events on Main Street since the fair was going to open at night and that the city believed hosting those events would show that opening at night would not be successful.[10] Mayor Gibbes was correct because the cash receipts at night had been only $343, well below the amount needed to cover expenses. This disagreement quickly dissipated, and by June 1911 the society and the city jointly agreed to purchase a new building for the fairgrounds to replace the main building that had burned during the 1910 fair.

On the final night of the 1910 fair, a fire destroyed the commercial building, which housed exhibits featuring furniture, pianos, automobiles, and concessions. The November 3, 1910, edition of the *State* disclosed the details of the fire: "The blaze was one of the most spectacular ever seen in Columbia. The rich pine wood burned freely and quickly and within an hour the building was in ashes." Thanks to the quick response of many at the fairgrounds, some of the contents were salvaged, but the loss of the building and contents was valued at $20,000. One of the exhibits that escaped damage was "the colonial exhibit, consisting of several thousand dollars' worth of old furniture displayed by Dr. J. W. Babcock, Jno A. Willis and a number of others." An extensive investigation failed to determine the cause of the blaze that had started under the front steps.

In retrospect, the fire that destroyed the commercial building proved to be a blessing in disguise. In early 1911 the Columbia Chamber of Commerce invited the National Corn Show to meet in Columbia in December 1912. The chamber approached the society regarding the use of the fairgrounds but realized that the current facilities were inadequate to accommodate the more than forty thousand anticipated exhibits. Minneapolis, Minnesota, also issued an invitation

Originally acquired to house the National Corn Show in 1912, this building became known locally as the "old steel building" and was the primary exhibit facility until it burned in 1966. This postcard was produced for the National Corn Show.

Courtesy of David Sennema

to host the National Corn Show and provided assurances of adequate facilities. In March 1911 the site selection committee for the National Corn Show visited Columbia and were assured that the society and the city would ensure the construction of a building capable of housing the exhibits. Despite the lack of adequate existing facilities at the fairgrounds, the selection committee awarded the 1912 show to Columbia. An important factor in their decision was a desire to see increased corn production in the South, a goal that was also promoted by agricultural interests in the South that wanted to further diversify southern farming practices. The decision for Columbia to host the National Corn Show was important opportunity for the city to promote the state's agricultural possibilities. In October 1911 the Columbia Ad Club announced they were having moving pictures made of Columbia that would be seen by over 7 million people in the months leading up to the National Corn Show. The Columbia Ad Club's purpose was to show an "agricultural wave was swishing over the State, and it is the determination of those who realize its advantages and possibilities to let the outside world know what South Carolina has."[11] One of the stipulations the city accepted in hosting the National

Corn Show was to guarantee at least $45,000 in ticket sales. The city launched a campaign to solicit commitments from local businesses to underwrite the shortfall if necessary. As the final hour approached the city had only received $7,000 in pledges, whereupon Ambrose E. Gonzales, publisher of the *State* newspaper, said, "Put me and the *State* newspaper down for the balance."[12]

By June 1911 the city and the society located a building in Greensboro, North Carolina, that contained sixty thousand square feet of space. Originally constructed at the Jamestown Exposition in 1907 as a twenty-five-thousand-seat auditorium, the building was later moved to Greensboro. The building was purchased for $5,750 and the estimated cost to take down, move, and reconstruct it at the fairground was $7,500. The society announced that the new structure would be ready for the 1911 fair. The building was dismantled and moved to Columbia during the summer. Reconstruction began in September but was blown down when half erected due to faulty construction. At the last minute a large tent was secured to house part of the exhibits intended for the steel building, but because of the lack of space, the state department of agriculture's cotton exposition would be held at a later date.[13]

Interior of the old steel building during the National Corn Show in 1912. Courtesy of David Sennema

The building remained unfinished for several months until the society and the city sold $33,000 in bonds to pay for its completion in time for the National Corn Show's opening in December 1912.

Despite the failure to complete the new building in time for the 1911 fair, large posters encouraged visitors to attend the fair. John G. Mobley, the former president of the society, commented in the *State* newspaper on October 17, 1911, that the 1911 fair would be a "great success.... The fair is recognized throughout the State, not only as a great educational factor, but as a social gathering which is exceedingly beneficial to the interests of the people." In addition to horse racing and automobile races, the Carolina–Clemson game "is a feature and with the teams evenly matched, as they now appear to be, interest is already lively and the game will no doubt be witnessed by the largest crowd in the history of the fair association."

For the 1911 fair, the carnival and midway activities were back on Main Street. On October 31, 1911, the *State* newspaper heralded "Midway Shows in Full Blast." The Johnny J. Jones Exposition Shows & Trained Wild Animal Exhibition had seventeen attractions:

A tent on Assembly street, at the intersection of Washington, is said to be the "big" number. This is the animal show, where angry beasts of all kinds stay, and where one thinks he is in the wilds of Africa.... But the animal show is not the only thing to be seen. There is "Happy" Jack, the fat man; the diving girls; the flea circus; the Jesse James outfit; the educated horse; the ferris wheel; the merry-go-round; the

Exhibits in the old steel building in 1913, the first year it was used by the State Fair. Courtesy of Burl Kennedy

joy-mill; the Dixie minstrels; Jumbo, the big snake; Prince Irma; Joyland, and California; Frank's Wild West and other wonders. Dolleta and her baby is one of the stellar attractions. This is a midget, whose child, 6 years old, is larger than she is.

In addition "Two free acts will be given daily. Behind the post office a balloon ascension will be made each afternoon at 4 o'clock, Prof. Collins doing three parachute drops. This will occur promptly on time. A high dive by DeRalia, a one-armed man, will be made immediately after the balloon ascension, on corner Hampton and Assembly Streets."

However, by 1915 the Columbia Chamber of Commerce and the Columbia City Council decided to end their sponsorship of activities downtown. On March 24, 1915, the *State* reported that, at a meeting of city council on March 23, D. F. Efird, secretary of the society, told the Columbia City Council that, despite a splendid agricultural exhibition last year, the fair experienced a deficit of several thousand dollars primarily caused by the lack of revenue from concessions. Efird stated that, without competition from street shows, the fair could guarantee good shows on the midway. In return for abolishing the street shows, the State Fair announced that the gates of the fairgrounds "will be open free to all after 5:30 o'clock each afternoon and that at least three free acts will be shown." Following the vote by city council terminating the street shows, John W. Lillard, chairman of the board of director of the Chamber of Commerce, said "that the board was opposed

Color postcard of the Trades Parade from either 1915 or 1916. Courtesy of David Sennema

to street shows on the grounds that they made Columbia a 'small country town,' that they created filth and 'rowdyism,' and that they took away much money from Columbia without an adequate return." Lillard said that the Chamber of Commerce and the fair had several ideas for other types of entertainment for visitors while they were in Columbia during fair week.

On July 4, 1915, the *State* published the Columbia Chamber of Commerce's plans for fair week, which included the creation of the South Carolina Harvest Jubilee and a great trades parade on Thursday. The Harvest Jubilee featured a parade each day and street dances and concerts in the evening. Each daily parade had a different theme. On Monday the parade recognized state and local political leaders. The military parade

on Tuesday included the state militia and military colleges. On Wednesday, South Carolina day, floats touted the natural advantages of the state's counties. Friday was "Ladies Day," featuring automobiles and floats decorated in a floral theme. The winner of a silver mesh bag for the best-decorated car was Mrs. Thomas I. Weston. The car "was covered with a layer of white glittering cotton, with here and there a touch of red. As the car passed down the street the girls distributed loose balls of cotton for snowballs."

In 1915 and 1916 the Harvest Jubilee sponsored a trades parade featuring participants representing Columbia's products, resources, and businesses. The parade on Thursday, a highlight of the week, intended to help the downtown merchants overcome the loss of evening visitors. On October 29,

1916, the *State* featured a lengthy article describing the parade. The parade had sixty-eight units including three bands. The route of the parade began on Elmwood Avenue proceeding "down Main Street to Lady Street, Lady to Sumter, Sumter to Laurel, Laurel to Main where the head of the parade will close in closely behind the rear of the parade." The parade began at 4:30 P.M. so that, at its conclusion, parade goers would stay downtown and dine in the city's restaurants. The parade was held on Big Thursday—between the Carolina–Clemson football game and the state ball—and was listed on the State Fair's official schedule of events. The Harvest Jubilee, sponsored by the city to compensate for the loss of activity downtown during fair week, only lasted for two years. During 1917

the only remnant of the Harvest Jubilee was a mention in the *State* on June 24 of a concert by the Harvest Jubilee Band that afternoon.

During the remainder of the 1910s the fair continued to add additional attractions and events. As the 1914 fair approached, South Carolinians were faced with a crisis. The outbreak of World War I in June saw the price of cotton plummet to $.14 a pound as the export market fell, cotton markets closed for three months, and a bumper crop was whitening in the fields. On October 25, 1914, the *State* newspaper encouraged everyone to visit the fair even in these uncertain times because "the first object of the State fair is to educate the famers—to teach them more than they already know about their calling."

From 1915 to 1919 the premium list contained a notice that members of the society could purchase from Sylvan Jewelers a society lapel pin in either silver or gold. Courtesy of Jo Mewbourn

1916 MIDWAY ACTIVITIES

Even though all of the midway was inside the fairgrounds in 1916, fairgoers were still treated to a wide range of activities. Leon W. Washburn's Mighty Midway Shows featured Washburn's Big Trained Wild Animal Arena. Vincent Revere, "The Lion King," performed in the big steel cage with a mixed group of South African lions and Asiatic lioness. Mille Jewel, the leopard queen, entertained with her mixed group of East India leopards and Brazilian jaguars. "Master William Garner, considered to be the only boy trainer in showdom, handles in a capable manner a group of black performing bears." Other attractions on the crowded midway included "The Show of Living Freaks"; "Dion's Freak Animal Show"; "Beautiful Orient," scenes of the Far East; Captain Dunlap's "Shark Show"; "Murray's Sensational Diving Girls"; the latest of curiosities, "How Can She Live"; "Loveland," a show for spooners; "The Temple of Wonders," considered to be the best illustration show; "Ye Old Time Plantation"; "The Monkey Speedway"; "Elizabeth," the living doll, who was the smallest perfectly formed woman on earth; and the novel "Days of 49." The rides included the merry-go-round, the Ferris wheel, the Trip to Mars, and "the very latest, sensational, newest, and most fascinating of all riding devices, The "Whip."*

* "Midway Clear and Very Attractive," *Columbia Record*, October 26, 1916.

In response to the financial situation, the Carolina–Clemson Committee reduced the price for football tickets. Box seats fell from $2.50 to $2.00, with other seating options reduced accordingly. Following the 1914 fair, the society was asked by State Warehouse Commissioner John L. McLaurin if the steel building could be used to help store cotton. Before the matter could be brought before the society's executive committee, it became apparent that the insurance rates to store such a large quantity of cotton in one location would be prohibitive.[14]

As the war progressed, the plight of the cotton farmer improved as the price of cotton rose; after the United States entered the war in April 1917, cotton skyrocketed to $.40 a pound. The war did not have an immediate impact on the

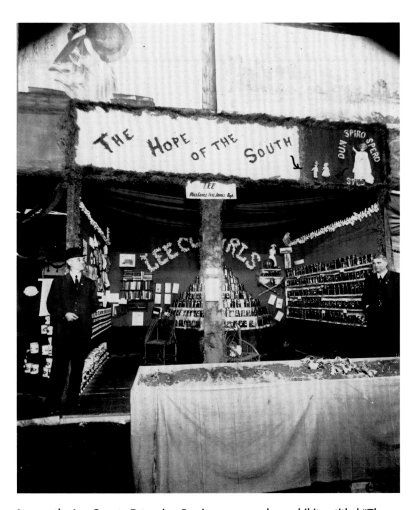

In 1914 the Lee County Extension Service sponsored an exhibit entitled "The Hope of the South," featuring the products of Lee County Canning Club. Look closely at the right side of the title and note the arrows pointing at two children who are the hope of the South. Courtesy of the South Caroliniana Library, University of South Carolina, Columbia, S.C.

1917 fair except the railroads were unable to run special trains or offer reduced rates to transport exhibits because of war mobilization efforts.[15]

Prior to 1917 the society membership was limited to men. At the annual meeting of the society in February 1917, it was pointed out that nothing in the organization's constitution prohibited women members. The names of four women were submitted and would be voted on at a future meeting.[16] However it was 1922 before the society again addressed women members. At the annual meeting in October 1922, the board decided that "the women of the State be asked to join the Society and co-operate with the men in making the State Fair what we would like to have it."[17]

In March 1918 the society executive committee discussed canceling the 1918 fair because of the ongoing war, but no decision was made. As fair week approached, however, a major influenza pandemic was sweeping across the nation, and on October 9 the State Board of Health ordered the indefinite postponement of the opening of the fair: "In consideration of the extent and the present rapid spread of the disease, I am of the opinion that the opening of the fair should be indefinitely postponed, as it is impossible to estimate the possible state of affairs on the date selected for the opening."[18] The hope was that the pandemic would ease and the fair would be able to proceed with its planned semicentennial celebration. By early November the pandemic was still raging, and the society decided to cancel the fair. "It is with many regrets that the management of the State fair announces that no fair can be held this fall. Health conditions throughout South Carolina caused the State board of health to postpone indefinitely the fair from the original dates, October 28–November 1, and it is deemed inadvisable to attempt to hold the fair at this late date. Also the present congested condition of transportation companies is such as to make the delivery of exhibits very uncertain. Further, the general unrest of the people on account of the war conditions and labor shortage makes attendance upon the fair decidedly problematical."[19] The 1918 fair is the only year since

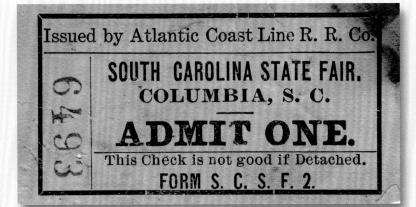

SOUTH CAROLINA STATE FAIR
COLUMBIA, S.C. OCT. 27-31, 1919
50TH YEAR

Issued by Atlantic Coast Line R. R. Co.

SOUTH CAROLINA STATE FAIR.
COLUMBIA, S. C.

6493

ADMIT ONE.
This Check is not good if Detached.
FORM S. C. S. F. 2.

SOUTH CAROLINA
STATE FAIR
Columbia, S. C.
October 27th to 31st, 1919

For the above occasion ROUND TRIP TICKETS WILL BE SOLD from all stations in South Carolina on the

ATLANTIC COAST LINE

For all trains on October 26, 27, 28, 29, 30 and for all trains scheduled to arrive Columbia by noon of October 31, limited, returning, to reach original starting point not later than midnight of November 3, 1919, at the following

Reduced Fares, Not Including War Tax

From	Fare	From	Fare
Alcolu	$2.54	Latta	$4.77
Charleston	5.81	Lanes	3.72
Darlington	3.65	Marion	4.68
Dillon	5.04	Mullins	5.04
Florence	3.65	Sumter	1.91
Kingstree	4.19	Timmonsville	3.14
Lake City	4.86	Walterboro	8.38

Corresponding fares from all stations in South Carolina

Children's Fares Will Be One-half the Above Adult Fares

For schedules and further particulars apply to Ticket Agents, or address the undersigned

THOS. E. MYERS, Dist. Pass. Agent
Union Station, Charleston, S. C.

E. CLIFF COHEN, Dist. Pass. Agent
813 Loan and Exc. Bank, Columbia, S. C.

W. J. CRAIG, Asst. Traf. Mgr., Passenger.; T. C. WHITE,
General Passenger Agent, Wilmington, N. C.

See the Nation's Strength
IN WAR AND PEACE
AT THE STATE FAIR

The Government Exhibitin of trophies from the battlefield of France is worth the cost of the trip.

Captured articles include everything from a Trench Mortar to a Canteen.

The display will also emphasize America's Military and Naval Equipment.

Soldiers from Camp Jackson will bring a Western Front Battle "Close-up" scene to the Fair. Nine big tanks and several batteries of field pieces will be used in the attack Thursday night by opposing forces from the camp.

While hunger stalked in enemy countries and empty stomachs overruled minds logic could not convince, a veritable flood of food poured from the rich agricultural acres of this country.

Uncle Sam is sending two carloads of exhibits to show how he is working to keep this production at flood tide. No problem of the farmer is being overlooked. The floor space required for these exhibits in the big steel building is 8,000 square feet. If you see only the Government Exhibits you will have seen a wonderful show.

(top) A 1919 felt banner commemorates the 50th State Fair. Courtesy of the State Agricultural and Mechanical Society of South Carolina

(bottom) A 1919 ad for the Atlantic Coast Line Railroad provides schedule and fare information and reminds fairgoers that the war tax is still in effect. Courtesy of Rodger E. Stroup

(top) The railroads often offered tickets that included admission to the State Fair. Courtesy of Rodger E. Stroup

(bottom) A newspaper advertisement for the 1919 State Fair highlights the nation's military prowess following World War I. Courtesy of the State Agricultural and Mechanical Society of South Carolina

its founding in 1869 that the society was unable to hold a State Fair.

South Carolinians anxiously awaited the opening of the 1919 State Fair. The high price of cotton during the war provided many of the state's citizens with additional income. One measure of the state's prosperity was a large increase in the number of motorcars at the 1919 fair. The *State* reported: "The distinguishing feature of this state fair was the aggregation of motor cars—not of the specimen cars exhibited in the buildings but the acres and acres of cars parked inside and outside of the fairgrounds and the unceasing streams of them that flowed through the streets." But the reporter's real motive was probably to decry the poor condition of the state's roads. "Five thousand automobiles that have come to Columbia from distances of 40, 50, 100 and even 150 miles this week are incontrovertible testimony that NOTHING SHORT OF A STATE HIGHWAY SYSTEM will make travel by motor car or hauling by motor truck economical."[20]

Visitors to the State Fair in 1919 were treated to exhibits featuring America's military and naval equipment and trophies from the battlefield of France, including heavy machine guns, light machine guns, and antitank guns. Soldiers from Camp Jackson staged a "Western Front Battle 'Close-up'" scene featuring nine tanks and several batteries of artillery. In addition to visitors arriving by car, the railroads offered reduced fares, although the rates still included the war tax, which would remain in place until February 1920.[21]

Moving the fairgrounds to the Assembly Street location in 1904 enabled the society to expand activities and amenities. Each year new attractions and larger exhibits proved the key to attracting larger crowds. With the help of the city and state, a new, large exhibition building enhanced both the exhibitors and fairgoers experience. Despite canceling the 1918 fair because of the influenza epidemic, the end of World War I brought a renewed optimistic outlook for the society.

4

The Colored State Fair

"The greatest event for Negroes in the state"

Today most South Carolinians don't know that from the 1890s to 1969 there were two separate state fairs. During most of these years the Colored State Fair, as it was known throughout most of its existence, was held the week following the White State Fair, more commonly just the State Fair. In most years both fairs were held on the fairgrounds, first on Elmwood Avenue and after 1904 on Rosewood Drive. Following the Civil Rights Act of 1964, the State Fair began to integrate all its activities. By 1970 the leadership of the Colored State Fair, then known as the Palmetto State Fair, was aging and that fair was unable to compete with the State Fair, so the separate colored fair disappeared following the 1969 fair.

Even before the Civil War African Americans attended and participated in the activities at the State Fair. In 1859 the premium awarded to a "white farmer" for winning the plowing contest was ten dollars, but the "black farmer" who won only received five dollars.[1] In 1878 the "white farmer" who won the plowing contest received twenty dollars while the "black farmer" received ten dollars.[2] By the early 1890s whites regained control of state governments in the South and were passing Jim Crow laws that established segregation. The southern states also passed restrictive voting laws that successfully disenfranchised most African Americans, relegating them to an inferior status.

During the years the two fairs existed, neither was totally segregated. Prior to 1909 Richard Carroll, the leader of the Colored State Fair, "protested against the indecent exhibitions by white women, in tent shows, open to both races."[3] In 1926 the society's board discussed the question of colored attendance at the State Fair, sending the matter to the executive committee, which was given the authority to take any necessary action.[4] No action is noted in subsequent society minutes but the minutes do indicate this as an issue that needed addressing. In 1932 a Negro man was arrested at the White State Fair. He was believed to be wanted in Youngstown, Ohio, for killing two police officers.[5] In the early 1960s, when the possibility of creating a civic center on the fairgrounds was under way, the society was concerned that it might be necessary to integrate the white fair if the property was owned by the city.

In 1889 African Americans disenchanted with their reception at the State Fair, and perhaps spurred on by one railroad's decision to experiment with segregated rail cars on excursion trains, organized the Colored Agricultural and Mechanical Exposition. After receiving permission to use the state fairgrounds on Elmwood Avenue, they held the Colored State Fair the first week of January in 1890.[6] Despite the poor weather conditions and the short planning time, the organizers were pleased with their first effort even though they only had six hundred exhibits compared to six thousand at the State Fair. In addition to using the state fairgrounds, the format of the fair emulated that of the regular fair, with exhibits, racing, orations, and premiums.[7] Like the White State Fair, they also auctioned off the sale of booths and privileges shortly before the fair opened. In fact, during the Colored State Fair in 1892, there was even a colored state ball held in agricultural hall.[8]

FOURTH ANNUAL STATE FAIR
—OF THE—
Colored State Fair Association.
DEC. 12TH TO 17TH, 1892.

This is a special appeal of the President, Rev. J. H. Williams, to the good people of the state. We earnestly request every colored person in the state to attend our Fair and prepare exhibits therefor. The people of Columbia have promised not to support the Hampton Fair—but will on Dec. 12th to 17th stand with open arms to receive all visitors. The First and Second Regiments, National Guards, of Charleston, S. C., will attend and will participate in the first sham battle ever fought by negro soldiers. This is one reason why you should attend. There will also be a grand trades display, calithumpian parade and fireworks. There will be cheap rates on all railroads. Special advantages will be granted all who present this card and it will pay all ministers to sign across the back of the card. There will be mass meetings in this city on Wednesday and Thursday of the white Fair week and at other stated times until Dec. 12th.

Trusting this to meet your approval I am, sincerely yours,

REV. J. H. WILLIAMS,
PRESIDENT.

In 1892 the Rev. J. H. Williams, president of the Colored State Fair, printed this card requesting "every colored person in the state to attend our fair and prepare exhibits therefor. The people of Columbia have promised not to support the Hampton Fair." Courtesy of the South Caroliniana Library, University of South Carolina, Columbia, S.C.

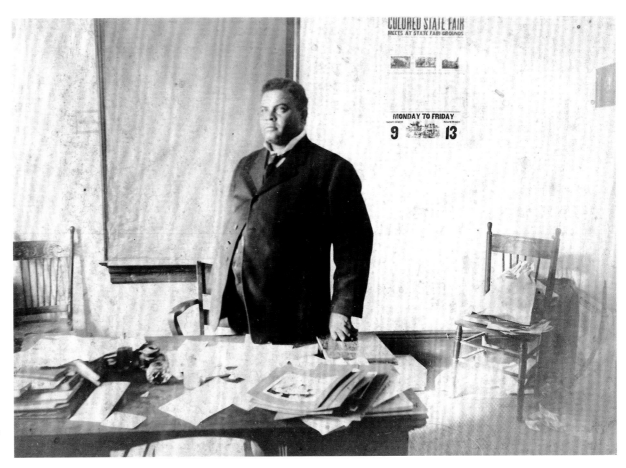

COLORED STATE FAIR
MEETS AT STATE FAIR GROUNDS

MONDAY TO FRIDAY
9 13

Colored Fair president Richard Carroll poses in his office beside a poster advertising the 1908 Colored State Fair. Courtesy of the South Caroliniana Library, University of South Carolina, Columbia, S.C.

Another successful Colored State Fair was held in the fall of 1890. One report noted that the fair was a great success and there was "quite a large attendance of whites last night."[9] The 1891 Colored State Fair provided many of the same attractions as the White State Fair. Activities included a colored band performing at various locations along Main Street on Wednesday evening. On Thursday a regiment of the South Carolina National Guard encamped at the fairgrounds. A trades parade featuring floats representing African American businesses entertained fairgoers on Thursday evening, followed by a fireworks display.[10] Despite the optimistic plans, the reporter for the *State* declared it was "Not a Howling Success," saying, "The crowd was very small, and, as on the previous days, there seemed to be a lack of interest."[11]

Following the 1891 fair, two factions emerged, both claiming to represent the Colored State Fair Association. One faction was led by A. E. Hampton, the founding president of the association. The other faction was led by J. H. Williams,

who accused Hampton of misappropriating funds, resulting in the inability to pay the promised premiums in 1891. Over the summer both factions applied to the society for the use of the fairgrounds. By September the Hampton faction was planning a fair from November 28 to December 3 and the Williams faction from December 12 to December 17. Both factions used the fairgrounds on Elmwood Avenue.[12] On December 1, 1891, the *State* reported that the Hampton Colored State Fair was "a dead failure." The small crowd saw no sideshows, only a few food booths, and "some two or three horses and a cow constitute all of the stock entries."[13] On the other hand, the Williams faction's fair "seems to be a success in every way.... There is about 100 head of live stock, including many horses and mules, some of which are quite blue blooded stock." At the conclusion of the Williams faction's fair, all of the premiums were paid and the organization was debt free.[14] Even though the Hampton faction received some state funds, the media reported that the Williams faction's fairs were "reasonably successful" and "represent the best and most intelligent class of colored people."[15]

Despite sponsoring two successful fairs, the Williams faction called off the 1894 fair because of "the unusually low price of cotton.... The scarcity of work and small wages so impoverishing the laboring classes and the widespread financial embarrassments so general throughout the State clearly indicate that it would be unwise to attempt to give a fair this year."[16] Over the next several years the Hampton faction continued to hold fairs, but they were characterized by the media as "fake fairs." In 1896 the *State* commented, "Nobody but A. E. Hampton, colored, ever attempted to construct a State fair out of one bottle of blackberry wine, three chickens, two crazy quilts, one pumpkin, and seven spectators."[17] In 1897 and again in 1904 there were abortive attempts to establish another organization to sponsor a colored fair, but they failed to get off the ground. Meanwhile the Hampton faction continued to hold "fake fairs" from time to time. While the Colored State Fair in Columbia continued to struggle, several successful colored county fairs were held each year.[18]

In 1907 Richard Carroll, a leading member of the African American community, proposed to the society that they explore ways to incorporate a colored fair into the regular fair schedule. He suggested "that a portion of the fair grounds be given to the negroes with a separate gate or entrance and also that the management put up a large building to contain the exhibits of negroes."[19] The society did not accept Carroll's proposal, but by the summer of 1908 the South Carolina Colored State Fair Association was organized with Carroll as president. However, the society did agree to rent the fairgrounds for the colored fair following the State Fair in 1908.[20] The Colored State Fair was held on the white fairgrounds from November 9 to 13 and was pronounced a success despite a lack of support from the Columbia business community. Local merchants and the railroads did not offer the same enticements for the colored fair as they did for the white fair.[21] Another major problem was the lack of hotel rooms that catered to Negroes. Because of the expense

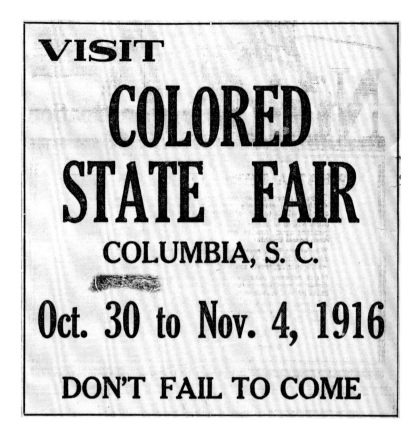

(top) A 1916 ad from the *Columbia Record.* Courtesy of the Colored State Fair Association

(bottom) "Like the Whites" 1927 advertisement in the *State* newspaper. Courtesy of the Colored State Fair Association

involved in renting the fairgrounds and the indifference from the business community, the 1909 Colored State Fair was held in Batesburg.[22] The Batesburg Colored State Fair far exceeded the expectations of the organizers, and the white citizens "highly commend[ed] Carroll and present[ed] him with a horse."[23] However, in 1910, following a pointed editorial in the *State,* the railroads and merchants realized the economic impact of the colored fair and it returned to the fairgrounds in Columbia.[24] After getting the Colored State Fair on a firm financial footing, Richard Carroll resigned as president in 1911 and was succeeded by E. J. Sawyer of Bennettsville. Sawyer was "a man of wide experience and a good farmer and a good business man."[25] By 1916 John H. Goodwin, president of the Colored State Fair, would comment, "Our own splendid financial condition with the hearty and generous cooperation of the merchants of the capital city—they who daily exude the 'greater Columbia spirit'—enable us to have it so."[26]

Like its white counterpart, there was no colored fair in 1918 because of the influenza epidemic. Despite the low price of cotton during the 1920s and 1930s, creating hardships for the state's farmers, the Colored State Fair continued to grow and attract large crowds. In 1922 a full-page ad in the *State* newspaper touted a large, high-class carnival, free circus acts, big farm demonstration day, and fireworks on three nights.[27] All of this in addition to the usual activities that by the early 1920s included a Big Thursday football game featuring Allen College, the State Agricultural and Mechanical College (South Carolina State), Benedict College, or Claflin College.

In 1927 there was an attempt to move the Colored State Fair to a separate venue. According to *The Palmetto Leader,* a leading newspaper in the African American community, two colored gentlemen expressed a willingness to finance a new location because the cost of renting the fairgrounds was too expensive. As the 1927 colored fair approached, the sentiment to move was evident. During that year's fair there were verbal altercations between the white fairground managers and some colored exhibitors who were denied timely entrance into the exhibit halls. These actions resulted in the

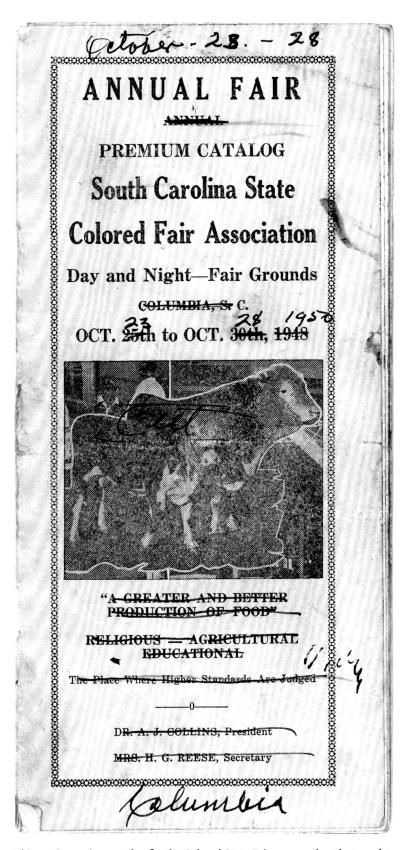

This 1948 premium catalog for the Colored State Fair was used as the template for the 1950 premium catalog—note the handwritten notations. Courtesy of the South Caroliniana Library, University of South Carolina, Columbia, S.C.

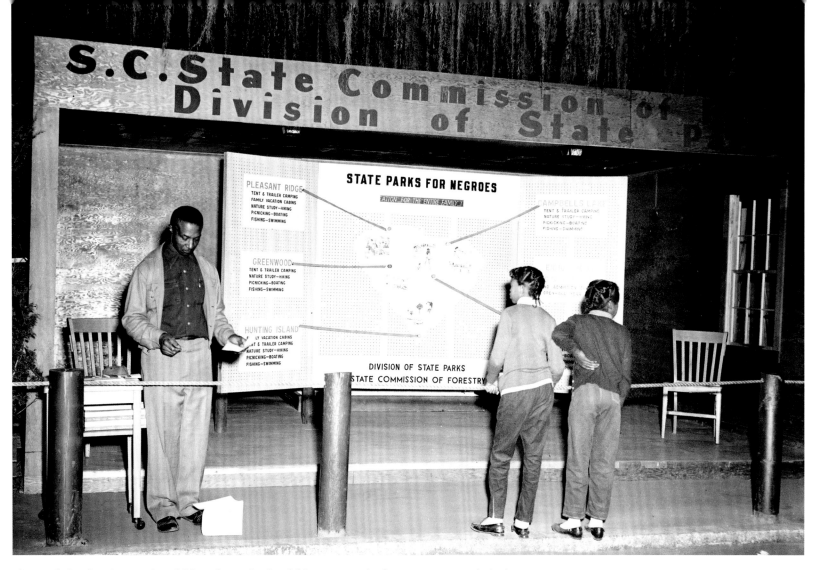

The South Carolina State Parks exhibit at the 1958 colored fair promotes the five Negro state parks in the state.

Courtesy of the South Carolina Department of Parks, Recreation & Tourism

Colored State Fair voting to purchase its own fairgrounds. *The Palmetto Leader* reported that "it looks certain that 1928 Fair will be held 'under its own vine and fig tree.'"[28] Apparently, however, the two sides settled their differences because the 1928 and subsequent colored fairs were held on the white fairgrounds.

During the 1930s cooperation increased between the white and colored fairs. Many of the displays from the white fair were held over for the colored fair. In a 1933 ad, the Seaboard Airline Railroad promoted their low fares for both fairs in the same newspaper ad.[29] A 1936 ad in the *State* newspaper encouraged subscribers to "Offer Your Servants an Opportunity to Attend the Colored State Fair, Dine. This week at Bihari's Restaurant."[30] The 1939 fair week once again featured a colored state ball at township auditorium featuring Joe Williams,

"the bronze Jimmy Dorsey," and his Manhattan Serenaders. Admission was $1.20 for colored spectators but only $.65 for white spectators.[31]

During World War II the colored fair continued to operate each year, providing a welcomed diversion from the routine of the war. Despite the shortages caused by the war, the usual activities were held at the fairgrounds, and even the football games were played. The 1943 fair featured twenty more concessions than in 1942, and the expanded exhibit offerings emphasized the fair theme "Food for Victory."[32] In 1945 the colored fair was the last week in October and was billed as a "Victory Celebration." A special feature that year was a western rodeo and the addition of a high school football game between Booker T. Washington High School and Mather Academy.[33]

The midway at the 1955 Colored State Fair. Courtesy of the State Newspaper Photograph Archive Richland Library

Following World War II, the colored fair continued to expand and add new attractions. In 1952 Friday School Day saw over fifty thousand school students from across the state admitted free.[34] In 1953 the Miss Colored State Fair beauty contest was won by Allen University freshman Bessie Eugenia Reed from Clarendon County. She received a fifty-dollar prize and was crowned at halftime during the Benedict versus Claflin football game. Another big attraction in 1953 was the auto daredevils, including Dan O'Neill jumping over three cars. O'Neill had been injured two weeks

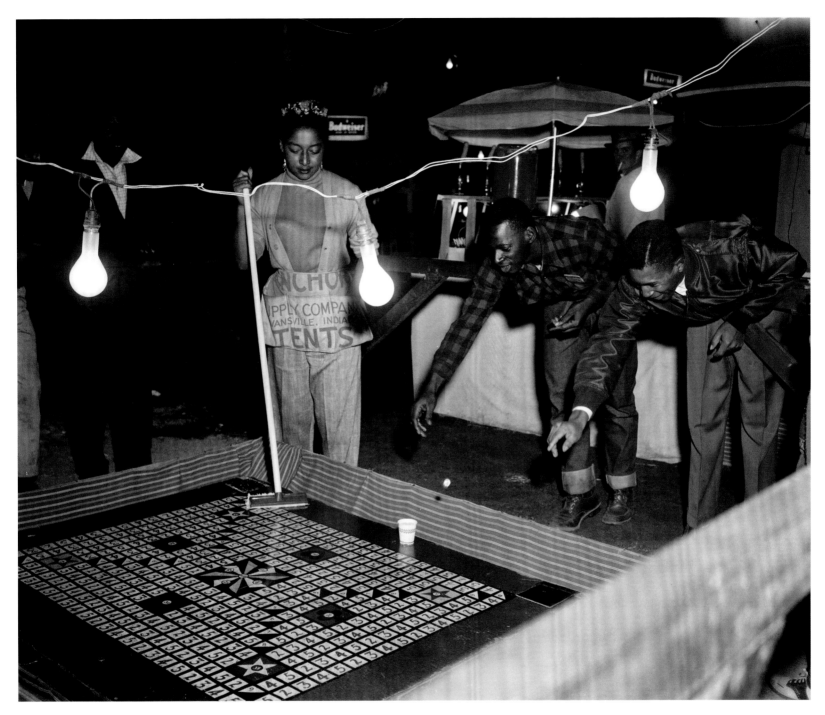

Two fairgoers play one of the games on the midway while the game's agent stands by.

Courtesy of the State Newspaper Photograph Archive, Richland Library

earlier performing the same stunt and, despite having "one arm in a cast, seven fractures ribs, a fractured collar bone, shoulder blade and a wrist" he would once again perform this "blood-curdling act."[35] The 1955 colored fair featured a colored high school band competition. In 1960, during the Cold War, a special atomic energy exhibit was held over from the white fair along with an exhibit on air raid shelters.[36] The 1963 colored fair featured Noell's Ark Gorilla Show, where prize money was offered to anyone who could stay in the cage with one of the gorillas. Only one fairgoer was game, reportedly only staying in the cage three-fifths of a second.[37]

The growth of the civil rights movement was reflected in the name of the colored fair. In 1897 the organization was chartered as the "Colored State Fair and Education Association of South Carolina." The group's purpose was "to develop and promote the agricultural, mechanical and educational interest of the negro race of South Carolina."[38] In 1941 the colored fair received a new charter as "The South Carolina Colored Fair Association," whose purpose was "to stress agricultural, educational and civic activities, and to promote social and religious interests."[39] Following advances during the civil rights movement, in 1955 the colored fair was referred to in a newspaper article as the Palmetto State Fair (Negro).[40] In 1965 the White State Fair was integrated, and the Colored State Fair formally adopted the Palmetto State Fair as its name.[41]

With the integration of the White State Fair, it only took a few years for the former Colored State Fair to fail. In 1970 a series of events led to the cancellation of the Palmetto State Fair. The secretary of the fair died during the year, and the superintendent of exhibits was hospitalized. The fair's president, Dr. A. J. Collins, announced they also could not get the carnival they wanted, so they were calling off this year's fair because, "after 65 years, we didn't want to have a low-grade fair." In 1971 Dr. Collins announced his retirement after forty-three years because many believed that the economy could not support two fairs in two weeks. Dr. Collins stated, "I wanted my people to have the best and that was available at the South Carolina State Fair."[42] On December 8, 1971, the *State* newspaper carried a notice announcing the dissolution of the Palmetto State Fair Association.

For over seventy-five years the Colored State Fair operated the week following the White State Fair on the same fairgrounds. While there was limited integration at the two fairs, the co-existence of the separate events paralleled the segregated society that developed in the state following Reconstruction and continued to plague the state even into the twenty-first century.

5

The Depression and World War II

During the years between the two world wars, the State Fair saw the construction of new facilities, the expansion of its membership base, and an ongoing effort to provide additional amenities and activities to attract more fairgoers. While the Depression years forced the society to carefully monitor activities and expenses, the annual fair operated every year at a profit except for 1931 and 1932. Following the outbreak of World War II in 1941, the State Fair was one of only a few fairs that operated every year during the war.

Following World War I, the price of cotton plummeted and the state began to slip into a depression during the 1920s. In 1921 the society passed a resolution encouraging farmers to cut their cotton acreage by 50 percent because of the glut of cotton on the market. The dependence on cotton by farmers throughout the state provided the impetus for the society to study the composition of the annual fair.[1] In April 1922 society president R. M. Cooper presented a report to the executive committee with thirty-four recommendations addressing

In 1920 a full-page ad in the *Columbia Record* highlights the activities at the coming State Fair. Courtesy of the State Agricultural and Mechanical Society of South Carolina

critical issues. Of primary concern was the nature of the fair itself. Cooper stressed the need to return the fair to its agricultural and industrial roots rather than the commercial fair it had become. Another major concern was the poor condition of the buildings and grounds. The report recommended developing closer ties to Clemson and the demonstration agents as well as coordinating with the county fairs and local chambers of commerce. Finally, Cooper noted that additional funds were necessary to accomplish his recommendations, and expanded advertising and promotion would help increase attendance, providing more funds to the society. Following

Cooper's report were detailed recommendations from each department.[2]

The society board endorsed President Cooper's report and authorized the sale of $100,000 of stock to raise the necessary funds.[3] By June the stock sale was deferred in favor of a statewide membership drive. The current society life membership was 1,400, and the goal for the campaign was 4,000 new life members at $25 each. The campaign goal for Columbia was 1,000 new members and $25,000. The campaign received enthusiastic support from groups across the state including the Chamber of Commerce, Bankers Association, Builders Exchange, Masonic Temple, and Clemson Extension Service as well as service clubs and women's clubs.[4] During the summer teams from various organizations canvassed Columbia soliciting memberships and donations.[5] For example, the Rotary Club of Columbia endorsed the plan and appointed a committee to solicit 1,000 new members from the Columbia area.[6] By August, despite the efforts of the Columbia's leaders, the city's campaign was lagging. An August 4 article in the *State* questioned Columbia's commitment to the fair, and within a few days both Rock Hill and Sumter indicated an interest in having the State Fair move to their communities. On August 8 Columbia's leaders called a meeting at the Columbia Theater; before the meeting was over, more than $25,000 was raised to meet the goal. Among those leading the successful campaign in Columbia were Charles H. Barron, Claud N. Sapp, W. D. Melton, and Christie Benet.[7] The statewide campaign did not reach its goal, so the society in March 1923 sold $75,000 in bonds to retire a $33,000 debt and pay for new construction at the fairgrounds.

In addition to holding a membership drive, the board also approved converting part of the fairgrounds into an amusement park that would be open during the spring and summer as well as during fair week. The amusement park would be developed with outside capital and management, but a portion of the proceeds would go to the society.[8] Two main construction projects were also approved. The first called for the construction of a new athletic field with seating for 12,200 that would be located at the south end of the racetrack. A new 5,000-seat grandstand for the racetrack was also approved. However, because of time and funding constraints, the only project completed for the 1922 fair was the racetrack grandstand.[9] The amusement park concept was dropped, and it would be ten years before a new athletic field was constructed on the site of the current Williams–Brice Stadium.

Despite the lack of progress on the amusement park and the new stadium, as the 1922 fair approached, workmen were busy constructing new buildings and converting existing structures for new uses. The most visible addition to the fairgrounds was the new grandstand at the racetrack. Seating five thousand people, the grandstand provided unhindered views of the new half-mile racetrack, and it included a performing stage inside the track directly in front of the stands. The former women's building was converted to house the poultry show, and along with the agricultural building received a new coat of white paint. The building that formerly housed the poultry was converted for judging cattle. In addition to work on the structures, the grounds also featured improvements. New palmetto trees bordered the walks, which were all smooth and covered with gravel. Around the buildings, plants and flowers enhanced the appearance of the grounds.[10] The landscape work was completed by George Baldwin, a local landscape artist who donated his services.[11] The interior of the steel building was divided into sections separated by aisles, providing better exhibition spaces. The *State* reported that so many changes were made "that the visitor almost feels that he is seeing a new fair." Since the former women's building had been converted to the poultry exhibit, a new one was planned and the cornerstone was laid during the fair's opening ceremony, which featured Mrs. George Vanderbilt.[12]

In keeping with President Cooper's recommendations, the 1922 fair featured new amenities. An enlarged parking lot on the corner of Rosewood and Assembly offered free parking. A nursery equipped with toys and beds provided a place where a qualified nurse watched over youngsters. There was also a

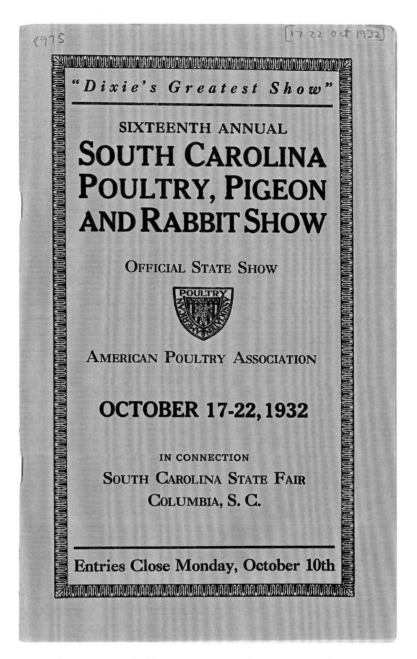

1932 poultry, pigeon, and rabbit show program. The conversion of the women's building to house the poultry exhibit resulted in the annual state poultry show happening at the State Fair. Courtesy of the South Caroliniana Library, University of South Carolina, Columbia, S.C.

restroom for men, featuring a barber shop "and other conveniences which are particularly needed by the male sex."[13] Finally, the Ringling Brothers Circus was the main attraction at the fair on Friday night with two performances.[14]

The construction of new buildings and the renovation of existing structures paid off for the society in 1925 when

A 1930 photograph shows the separate aisles layout in the old steel building providing more and better organized exhibit space.
Courtesy of the State Agricultural and Mechanical Society of South Carolina

two national poultry shows chose Columbia for their annual shows. The United Ancona Club's annual show was held in conjunction with the State Fair in October. In November the National Red show was held at the fairgrounds. This was the first time either of these shows had been held in the South.[15]

President Cooper's 1922 recommendations included attracting more children. In 1925 the society offered schoolchildren free admission on Saturday if they were accompanied by an adult. During the following years a variety of enticements were promoted to attract students.

By the mid-1920s more and more fairgoers were arriving by automobile, creating frequent traffic jams. In 1926, to alleviate traffic, the county approved construction of a road from the four-mile post on Garner's Ferry Road to Assembly Street, the present-day Rosewood Drive. The road provided direct access to the fairgrounds from the east and avoided all railroad crossings. Part of the road was built by contractors while the county chain gang completed other sections.[16]

In early 1924, following the completion of most of Cooper's recommendations of 1922, the society board appraised the value of its property and structures at $222,450. The one hundred acres was valued at $100,000, with the old steel building listed at $40,000. Other major structures and their values included the grandstand at $15,000; the new cattle barn #2 at $7,000; the main entrance at $6,000; and the racetrack at $5,000.[17] The renovation project that had started in 1922

Future Farmers of America (FFA) gather for a program in the grandstand circa 1940. Courtesy of the State Agricultural and Mechanical Society of South Carolina

resulted in a facility with updated structures and increased amenities for visitors.

In June 1926 the new grandstand at the racetrack burned. When the city fire department arrived to fight the fire, they were forced to run hoses two blocks into the Olympia neighborhood. Unfortunately, some of the hundreds of motorists attracted by the fire parked their cars on the hoses, causing them to burst and preventing the firefighters from getting an adequate water supply. Earlier that year the society had approved the use of the field for the Columbia Comers, the city's South Atlantic League baseball team, and for a Negro semipro team. L. L. Propst, president of the Columbia club, stated that he was not able to rebuild the grandstand and might have to move the franchise. Propst announced that the next scheduled home games would be played in Charlotte and Greenville.[18] Only five days after the fire, the society announced it would rebuild the grandstand at a cost of $19,000, including a grant of $2,500 from the City of Columbia. Only ten days after the fire, construction began on the new grandstand, which was completed by July 4. One positive result of the fire saw the city construct a six-inch waterline to the fairgrounds that for the first time provided an adequate water supply.[19]

The 1929 State Fair had concluded when the stock market crashed in late October. Following the 1930 fair, society secretary Paul V. Moore reported that, despite the current economic downturn, the fair was a "decided success," attested to by several individuals who attended other state fairs and "termed that of South Carolina the best they had seen."[20] Moore also told the society board that holding down expenses during the year helped the bottom line. He urged the board's members to err on the side of optimism as they approached the next year.[21] A notable event at the 1930 fair was the first radio broadcast from the fair featuring Victor's Band and radio announcements highlighting the week's activities. While the article in the *State* does not identify the radio station, the only one on the air in Columbia at the time was WIS (Wonderful Iodine State).[22]

Normally the election of the president of the society was uncontested. However, at the annual meeting in 1931, a small faction of the membership wanted a change in leadership.

Caughman Feed and Seed exhibit at the 1930 fair. Courtesy of the State Agricultural and Mechanical Society of South Carolina

Led by John J. McMahan of Columbia, they wanted to restore horse racing and questioned the availability of the society's financial statements. McMahan opened the controversy, noting "the time has come for a new move. I would like to see horses restored at the Fair grounds." In 1926 after several years of declining participation and loss of revenue at the horse races, the society had dropped horse racing. McMahan nominated A. B. Langley of Columbia for president. In addition, several members remarked that they had not seen financial statements in several years, and R. Beverly Herbert, a Columbia attorney, commented, "It looks to me like the society is run secretly." Others jumped to the defense of President D. D. Witcover, pointing out the many improvements at the fair under his leadership. David G. Ellison of Winnsboro remarked that the financial statements had been presented at the February meeting after the books were closed and were available to any member who requested a copy. When the vote was called, Witcover won by a margin of 39 to 15.[23] Despite this challenge to his reelection, President Witcover served as the society president from 1925 to 1952, the society's longest-serving president.

With the full impact of the Depression felt in South Carolina, the 1931 and 1932 fairs operated at a loss. In 1931 the $1,900 loss was attributed to a $4,000 shortfall at the gate. With the high unemployment rate in the state, many people could not afford to come to the fair. In 1932 several factors contributed to the deficit, including the loss of the $3,000 state appropriation, the inability of the Clemson demonstration program to participate because of a prior commitment to the federal cotton reduction program, and the necessity to refinance an outstanding loan of $75,000. In response to the deficits as the 1933 fair approached, the society decided to limit premiums to South Carolina citizens only due to a shortage of funds. All "open-to-the-world classes" were eliminated.[24]

As early as 1922 the society planned to replace the wooden stadium used for the Carolina-Clemson football games. However, financial restraints prohibited any action until 1933, when the City of Columbia applied and received a loan of $82,000 from the Reconstruction Finance Corporation. The new municipal stadium would be owned and operated by the city. It would not be located on the current fairgrounds but on

The South Carolina State Fair is one of the few state fairs in the United States that still operates under the auspices of a private organization. Some other state fairs began as private entities but at some point became affiliated with a state agency under whose sponsorship they now operate. The only record of public funds for the antebellum fairs occurred in 1856 when the Legislature appropriated $5,000 to help pay the premiums.* From 1869 to 1877 the society depended on gate receipts and memberships. Following Reconstruction, the Legislature was once again controlled by the prewar leaders of the state and the fair received an appropriation of $2,500 from 1877 to 1890.† When Ben Tillman and his allies took control of the state in 1890, they discontinued the state appropriation for the fair. However, by 1896 Senator Tillman was representing the state in Washington, and the society, still controlled by the families of the prewar leadership, once again began receiving a state appropriation in the amount of $2,500. Between 1896 and 1975 the society received state appropriations most years ranging up to $10,000, although some years it did not receive any. Each year the society lobbied the Legislature for funds, and its success frequently depended on friendly legislators inserting an appropriation in the budget.

Since the inception of the State Fair, the city understood the importance of the fair each year and provided not only appropriations but also property. In 1869, in addition to deeding the land to the society, the city also appropriated $8,000 to build the main building. Beginning in the 1870s the city assisted the fair each year by coordinating and hosting the carnival and midway activities on Main Street because there was not adequate space at the fairgrounds. In the mid-1890s, when the state funds were lost, the city provided funds to ensure the fair would continue. Beginning in 1918 until 1975, in all but a few years, the city provided a small appropriation ranging from $750 to $2,000.‡

Despite the small amount of public funds available, the society has a remarkable record of staging a financially successful State Fair each year. Prior to 1918 the financial records of the society are not extant, so it is not possible to assess the success or failure of the first fifty years. However, since 1918 the fair has only run a deficit in six years, and those all occurred between 1918 and 1932, due primarily to the early onset of the Depression in the agricultural economy of the state. Since 1932, despite innumerable challenges including bad weather and the burning of the main building on the eve of the fair, the society has operated with a surplus each year.

* *Society History,* 19.
† *Society History,* 34.
‡ Review of financial audits 1918–1980 by the author, documents in Society Archives safe.

property that was adjacent to the fair property and owned by the Taylor family.[25] The stadium would be used by the University of South Carolina, Columbia High School, Benedict College, Allen College, and other institutions of the city.[26] To address the society's concern that the loss of the Carolina–Clemson game from the fairgrounds would be a severe blow to the fair, the city agreed that all admissions to the game would be through the fairgrounds, thereby preventing the loss of revenue for the society. As the stadium neared completion, Clemson pointed out that the old stadium was constructed with the assistance

of the athletic associations of the two schools, and the State Fair society and these organizations needed to be involved in how the stadium was used during fair week. The Columbia City Council agreed that, during fair week, the stadium would be under the control of the athletic associations of Carolina and Clemson and of the State Fair society.[27]

Work began on the stadium in early 1934, and it was completed for the October 6 game between South Carolina and the Virginia Military Institute.[28] Constructed of steel and concrete, the new stadium had 18,000 seats and was designed so

The 1909 "Big Thursday" football game. The old wooden stadium inside the fairgrounds hosted the Carolina–Clemson game from the early 1900s until the completion of the new stadium in 1934.

Courtesy of the University of South Carolina Archives

it could easily be expanded to 30,000. The stadium featured cypress seats, modern restrooms, locker rooms with showers, and a roomy press box. The first Carolina–Clemson game in the new municipal stadium was won by Clemson 19–0 in front of a record crowd of 17,500.[29]

However, the ownership of the stadium by the city did not last long. In January 1935 the city was behind in making loan payments and began discussions with the University of South Carolina regarding the ownership of the stadium. After the university agreed to take over the payment of the loans and provide for the maintenance and upkeep of the stadium, the city transferred ownership to the university.[30] On October 24, 1935, the Carolina–Clemson game was played in the newly named Carolina Stadium. Since its construction in 1934, the stadium has undergone many renovations and expansions and, as of 2015, seats 80,250 fans with all of the amenities necessary for the Gamecock faithful.

PASSING OF WOODEN BOWL

In November 1933 the last game was played in the "wooden bowl" on the fairgrounds between South Carolina and Furman. An article in the *State* lamented the end of an era: "Starting from a single covered grandstand, built when the fairgrounds were moved from Elmwood Avenue to the present site, the pine stadium was a gradual growth which finally saw the whole field enclosed with seats and the original capacity of around 800 into one seating about 14,000—the biggest by far in this state. The wooden stands have required constant attention and great repair expense in order to maintain them and while everyone admitted that the arrangement gave an exceptionally good view of the play, at the same time that the seats were far from comfortable."*

* "Saturday's Game Marks Passing of Wooden Bowl," *State* (Columbia), November 16, 1933.

The new football stadium adjacent to the fairgrounds opened for the 1934 Big Thursday game. Courtesy of the University of South Carolina Archives

A 1938 aerial photograph shows the racetrack, the old steel building, and the recently completed football stadium. Courtesy of the Thomas Cooper Government Information & Maps Department

Fairgoers stream into the fairgrounds in October 1940. In the left foreground is a poster advertising the auto races on Saturday. Courtesy of the State Agricultural and Mechanical Society of South Carolina

Despite the Depression, the society not only sponsored a comprehensive fair each year but also managed to make continued improvements to the fairgrounds. In his 1938 report to the society, President D. D. Witcover pointed out many of the accomplishments in his thirteen years as president. The bonded debt that was due during the Depression was instead refinanced at 5 percent, a reduction of 2 percent, saving $1,500 in interest annually—and the society was now retiring three $500 bonds each year. The arrangement with Winter Stables Incorporated resulted in new stables and improvement to the racetrack.

The winter facilities at the fairgrounds were "now one of the foremost training quarters for thoroughbred horses and is the source of much favorable advertising for the fair and the city of Columbia." One of the most important accomplishments was negotiating a working contract with the University of South Carolina for controlling fair-week football games. President Witcover also reviewed improvements to the facilities. A permanent fence was erected around the entire fairgrounds, providing increased security. The unsightly lunch row was replaced by new permanent structures. The antiquated electric system was modernized. The grandstand, which had been damaged during two separate storms, was rebuilt and reinforced to withstand stronger winds. All of the buildings were repaired and repainted. President Witcover concluded, "We now owe nothing but the bonded debt, which has been reduced to $69,000. I am happy to state that we are now operating on a cash basis."[31]

The 1940 annual meeting once again saw a challenge to Witcover's leadership. Ben Adams nominated J. P. Kilgo, a

World of Mirth advertising poster. World of Mirth was the carnival operator for the
State Fair from 1936 to 1961. Courtesy of Burl R. Kennedy

prominent Darlington businessman, for president. Adams expressed concern that the current administration had dropped horse racing from the program in favor of automobile races. Joseph L. Nettles supported Kilgo, saying that he thought that there should be a rotation in the leadership of the society (President Witcover had been first elected to lead the society in 1925). When the vote was called, a "decided majority" voted to reelect President Witcover.[32]

The German invasion of Poland and the start of World War II in September 1939 had very little impact on the 1939 and 1940 State Fairs. It wasn't until early 1941, following the German occupation of continental Europe and with the United States drifting toward war, that the society began to consider the war's impact on the fair. At a meeting of the society's executive committee in January 1941, the officers felt that continuing an annual fair "plays a very definite part in building up morale and state production of agriculture and livestock. The Committee went on record as being in favor of substantially adding to our premiums."[33] Also at this meeting the executive committee initiated the process of getting the society recognized as a charitable organization. Working with the General Assembly, the necessary legislation was passed in October 1941.[34]

After the American entry into the war, at a meeting in April 1942, the executive committee "manifested a very strong spirit of cooperating with the Federal Government in its efforts to Win the War" by encouraging agricultural production focusing on oil-producing products and foodstuffs.

In 1945 a Victory Fair pennant was available as a souvenir at the fair. But the question is which fair—the White State Fair or the Colored State Fair? In early October 1945 the Colored State Fair began encouraging people to come to the Victory Fair. After the fair closed the "fair executives explained that the Victory Fair had surpassed all expectations in every way."* But the phrase "will help win the war" rings hollow. How could a fair help win the war? Or was this a souvenir from the White State Fair? During the fall of 1945 the U.S. government continued to sell war bonds in the Victory War Bond campaign. By purchasing a war bond, you could "help win the war."

* "Negro Fair Attendance Hits Record," *State* (Columbia), November 3, 1945.

By working with the Clemson Extension Service, the society would promote exhibits dealing with peanuts, soybeans, lespedeza, crotalaria, wheat, sugarcane, and sorghum.[35]

In the summer of 1942 the possibility arose that the fair might be canceled. In June Joseph B. Eastman, the director of the Office of Defense Transportation, requested that "all state and county fairs as well as non-essential conventions" be deferred for the duration of the war. Director Eastman pointed out that travel for such events would not only require the consumption of gasoline but even more crucial would be the loss of rubber products needed for the war effort.[36] With the planning well under way and contracts already executed, the society decided to proceed with the fair. The 1942 fair featured "no shortages on good entertainment" provided by the World of Mirth Shows. The midway was crowded with the newly erected

Victory fair pennant.
Courtesy of Burl R. Kennedy

idway that, despite a manpower shortage of 150 workers due
 the war, were all set up on schedule. The fairgrounds were
vishly decorated with patriotic colors "as a constant reminder
at the nation is at war."[37]

The society decided to again hold the fair in 1943. The ex-
:utive committee "was decidedly of the opinion that the Fair
uld make a greater contribution than ever before this year
 the agricultural drive around which so much of America's
opes for victory are built."[38] The fair featured a huge exhibit
onsored by the armed forces as well as spaces provided
r other war exhibits such as bond sales.[39] Even the midway
atured more than fifty modern, streamlined amusement de-
ces provided by the World of Mirth Shows, the world's largest
aveling amusement company. Even during the midst of the
ar, "the show itself [had] taken on a world's fair appearance
ith gigantic light towers and searchlights supplemented by
ousands of electric light lamps and miles of colorful neon
bing providing illumination....The show's own train of
-72-foot flatcars [was] used in transporting the 130 circus
agons loaded to the hilt with amusement devices."[40] Since
iving private automobiles would use precious rationed
asoline, the society assured visitors that the city bus service
ould be adequate to transport people from downtown to the
irgrounds. This was especially important because the city
anned the use of taxicabs for pleasure.[41] School day at the
ir was a big success even though school buses could not
e used to transport students, but they managed to get there
omehow, according to President Witcover.[42]

In July 1945 the headlines in the *State* declared "Richland
air Planned as SC Fair Canceled." The society agreed to can-
el the fair after a mandatory order from the Office of Defense
ransportation because of wartime travel difficulties. Society
ecretary Paul Moore stated that with "mandatory orders hav-
1g been received from Col. Monroe Johnson, director of the
ffice of Defense Transportation that no state or regional fairs
ould be allowed to operate in 1945, the state fair has notified
1r. Johnson that we will comply with the order." Instead, a

localized fair was planned for fair week at the fairgrounds and
the Carolina–Clemson game would be played on Big Thursday,
as usual.[43] However, following the Japanese surrender in early
August, the Office of Defense Transportation lifted the ban
on state and regional fairs on August 14 and, according to
Secretary Moore, "this office went in high gear. Result—a
successful Fair from all angles with the largest net operating
profits in the Society's history." The $32,266 net profit was the
society's largest until the 1963 fair's $34,340 profit.[44]

Between the world wars, the State Fair constructed new facilities, increased attendance, and began partnerships for
the wintering of horses that saw the equine facilities used
for several additional months each year. The agreement with
the University of South Carolina to locate its football stadium
adjacent to the fairgrounds ensured that Big Thursday would
continue to be an important part of fair week. The South
Carolina State Fair was one of only a few state fairs that managed to operate each year during the war.

6

"The Grooming Ground of Champions"

Both Camden and Aiken, South Carolina, are nationally recognized as winter equestrian centers and each year attract a strong contingent of trainers who take advantage of the mild winters to train their horses. However, from the 1890s until the late 1960s, a winter training facility at the fairgrounds in Columbia was also a destination for many northern stables. Nationally known trainers like Max Hirsch and Woody Stephens discovered the Columbia stables in 1926, and until the demise of the Palmetto Trials following the 1968 race, the fairground facilities hosted many prominent stables including the Buxton Brothers, Cain Hoy Stable, King Ranch, Brookmeade, Maine Chance Farms, Guggenheim, and Brookfield Stables. Among the thoroughbreds who wintered at the fairground stables were five Kentucky Derby winners (Assault, Bold Venture, Middleground, Cavalcade, and Jet Pilot), and one triple-crown winner (Assault). Other well-known horses trained in Columbia included Seabiscuit, Sun Beau, Stymie, High Gun, and Columbiana (named after the city).[1] Since the winter

Mrs. Robert L. Sumwalt, P. Brady, W. J. Beatie, and jockey T. Grogan at the Palmetto Trials horse race at the State Fairgrounds. Beatie's horse, Mill Isle, ridden by Grogan, won the first race of the day at the 1962 Palmetto Trials. Courtesy of the State Newspaper Photograph Archive, Richland Library

training facilities operated from November until late spring, they were not part of the annual State Fair. However, the story of the fairground stables and racetrack is an integral part of the history of the State Agricultural and Mechanical Society of South Carolina and the development of the State Fair property.

Breeding and racing horses became an important part of the South Carolina's recreational activities even in colonial days. As soon as the early white colonists began to prosper and acquire significant land and resources, they sought to emulate the lifestyles of wealthy landowners in England and the Caribbean. As early as 1723, horse racing was an integral part of the regional fairs held throughout the lowcountry. These early races were loosely organized contests, and there is no mention of prizes, but the winner was able to claim bragging rights. In 1734 the first jockey club in the state was formed in

Charleston. In 1735 "The York Course" was established, and by the middle of the eighteenth century the rules of racing were formalized and prizes of gold or silver were awarded.

During the antebellum era the interest in horse racing spread across the state. Columbia, St. Matthews, Pendleton, Greenville, Barnwell, Newberry, Laurensville, Deadfall, Beaufort, Georgetown, Camden, Orangeburg, and Pinewood all held regular races, and some even had jockey clubs.[2] The State Agricultural Society of South Carolina sponsored its first State Fair in 1840, but there is no mention of horse racing at that fair probably because the fair was held on the statehouse grounds and there was no racetrack nearby.

The first horse races at the State Fair occurred in 1856 after the fair developed its own facility just north of Elmwood Avenue. Horse racing would be a major draw each year until its popularity began to wane in the early twentieth century. In

A 1959 aerial photograph features the racetrack in the center with the stables located in the upper right above the racetrack. **For football games and special events, the infield of the racetrack was used for parking.** Courtesy of the State Agricultural and Mechanical Society of South Carolina

1859 the *Charleston Mercury* reported, "A grand pacing match came off between N. Drayton's three-year old stallion, *Seneca Chief,* from New York, and Messrs. Lanham and Glover's six year old pacing bay horse*, Swamp Robin,* from Edgefield, S.C. The former came in one length ahead of the latter. On the second round the latter paced the course in 2:15."[3]

The end of the Civil War saw most of the prewar aristocracy unable to maintain their stables, and the racetracks were abandoned. In 1869, following the Civil War, the rebuilt fairgrounds on Elmwood Avenue featured a one-half-mile racetrack that was expanded to three-fourths of a mile in 1873.

When the State Fair moved to its new location on Assembly Street in 1904, a one-mile track was constructed with a half-mile track built inside the larger track. Even though horse racing was declining at many state fairs, it continued in Columbia until 1926 when the State Fair dropped horse racing from its schedule during fair week. In an attempt to attract more interest in horse racing, the South Carolina Night Horse Racing Association was organized in the summer of 1914. This organization was completely separate from the State Fair and planned to hold night races (the fair's horse races were in the afternoon). The premium list for the night horse races included thirty-eight classes with prizes totaling $5,400 in cash and trophies. The $3,200 in cash prizes compared with $3,000 offered for the day races.[4] The association stated "that the object is to induce horsemen from all over the country to

The South Carolina Night Horse Show Association

GEORGE D. SHORE, PRESIDENT
SUMTER, S. C.

J. N. KIRVEN, VICE-PRESIDENT
DARLINGTON, S. C.

W. S. RAY, MANAGER
ASHEVILLE, N. C.

D. F. EFIRD, SECRETARY AND TREAS.
COLUMBIA, S. C.

EXECUTIVE COMMITTEE
J. N. KIRVEN, CHAIRMAN

GEORGE T. LITTLE, Camden, S. C.   DR. F. D. KENDALL, Columbia, S. C.
A. D. HARBY, Sumter, S. C.   S. P. HARVEY, Greenwood, S. C.
D. D. WITCOVER, Darlington, S. C.   H. T. MILLS, Greenville, S. C.
T. L. HARMON, Lexington, S. C.

SHOW HELD AT COLUMBIA, OCTOBER 27, 28, 29, 1914, 8:00 P. M.
FAIR GROUNDS

(above) **Despite the elaborate letterhead and planning, the Night Horse Show scheduled for the 1914 State Fair was canceled.** Courtesy of Rodger E. Stroup

(left) **Even though horse racing was discontinued at the State Fair in 1926, the use of the fairgrounds for horse shows continued for many years.** Courtesy of the State Agricultural and Mechanical Society of South Carolina

PRIZE LIST

With Rules and Regulations
And Entry Blank For

Columbia Horse Show

| THURSDAY NIGHT MAY 31, 1934 8 P. M. | FRIDAY NIGHT JUNE 1, 1934 8 P. M. |

AT FAIR GROUNDS

| SADDLE HORSE JUDGE | JUDGE OF JUMPS |
| H. C. Barham, Milan, Tenn. | Geo. T. Little, Camden, S, C: |

OFFICERS

J. B. Westbrook .... President   L. W. Conder ...... Secy.-Treas,

EXECUTIVE COMMITTTE

Mrs. T. J. Robertson   J. Walter Conder, Jr.
J. Lomax Bryan   Cosmo L. Walker   Bob Brooks

GROUNDS COMMITTEE

Bob Brooks   W. D. Ward
C. C. Gibson   Frank Hampton

| VETERINARIAN | OFFICIAL BLACKSMITH |
| Dr. F. P: Caughman, V: M. D. | Fred Brown |

Sponsored by
FAIRWOLD RIDING CLUB

exhibit; and also to encourage the breeding of better horses of every kind in this State."[5] Despite their optimism, by October the association was forced to cancel the night horse shows when the State Fair decided to withdraw all premium on livestock. This action by the State Fair was taken because of the "distressed situation in the South" caused by the start of World War I in Europe. When war broke out, the export market for cotton disappeared and prices dropped by 50 percent, leaving farmers with cotton in the fields and no available market. Concerned that the economic situation might cause attendance to plummet, the society board suspended all premiums except for agricultural products and poultry.[6] The South Carolina Night Horse Racing Association subsequently disappeared after its brief existence.

Beginning in 1907, the track was also used for automobile racing, and 1913 saw the first motorcycle races.[7] The advent of these new attractions drew visitors away from the horses,

Many dignitaries traveled to South Carolina during the winter to attend horse-related activities and social events. In this 1949 photograph, Elizabeth Arden poses with horses, jockeys, and trainer from her Main Chance farms at the State Fairgrounds. Standing beside the thoroughbred, Mr. Busher, are (left to right) Baron Dosten, Viscountess de Maublanc, Elizabeth Arden, and William Davis, assistant trainer. Courtesy of the Russell Maxey Photograph Collection, Richland Library

eventually leading to the demise of horse racing. In 1938 and 1939 the State Fair attempted to revive an interest in horse racing but was unsuccessful until the advent of the Palmetto Trials in 1952. While horse racing was absent at the fair from 1926 to 1938, the track facilities were used by other organizations.[8] In June 1934 the Fairwold Riding Club sponsored the Columbia Horse Show featuring eighty-nine entries, making it the second-largest show in the South. A special attraction at the show was a jumping exhibition by William Taylor of North Carolina jumping Black Spot over an automobile.[9] In 1936 the Columbia Municipal Polo Field was constructed in the center of the race track at the fairgrounds, and a polo match was held in conjunction with Columbia's sesquicentennial in March.[10]

While horse racing during fair week struggled to remain viable after 1926, the growth of the equestrian facilities for training horses during the winter grew rapidly. Even before the State Fair moved to its new location on Assembly Street in 1904, some northern trainers were wintering their horses in Columbia. As early as 1897 trainer R. L. "Bob" Davis began bringing his horses from the northern tracks to winter in Columbia at the old fairgrounds. When asked in 1903 if he planned to return to Columbia the following fall, Davis replied, "You bet I do. There is no place like Columbia to winter horses."[11] When the State Fair moved to its new fairgrounds in 1904, Davis followed and used the new track and stables. In addition to the warm climate in Columbia, trainers pointed to the soil on the fairground racetrack. Max Hirsch called it "the most perfect soil in the world for race horses."[12] The sandy, loamy soil did not get packed in the horses' hoofs and did not get muddy when it was wet, helping to prevent injuries. The sandy soil also allowed the horses to train without shoes. The track drained quickly after a rain, allowing for more training time. Another attraction for Columbia was iodine

Before the 1962 Palmetto Trials, the crowds gathered in anticipation of post time. Courtesy of the State Newspaper Photograph Archive, Richland Library

that occurred naturally in the water, which was good for the horses. Finally, Columbia was closer to the northern tracks than facilities in Florida. By 1940 the Columbia facility was considered by many trainers to be the best in the South.[13]

Between 1897 and 1909 other trainers joined Bob Davis in using the facilities at the fairgrounds to winter their horses. The horses arrived after the State Fair concluded and did not participate in the races during fair week. From November through April the horses trained on the fairgrounds track, frequently drawing small crowds of locals to watch them workout. In 1907 the society sold the old fairgrounds for $30,000 and approved using part of the funds to improve the stables and racetrack to accommodate all of the requests from trainers to winter their horses in Columbia.[14] In 1908 a Virginia-Carolina circuit began, and Columbia hosted races during fair week. In 1909 Columbia hosted a spring race as part of the new circuit. There is no mention of wintering horses at the fairgrounds between 1910 and 1926. However, horse racing was a featured event at each fair, despite its dwindling popularity.[15]

In 1926 the Buxton Brothers of New York opened their winter training facilities at the fairground. In 1929–30 they wintered 40 horses in Columbia and planned to bring 150 horses the following year. In the fall of 1930 the Buxton Brothers agreed to lease the fairground facilities for five years, with a renewal privilege of five additional years. In exchange for use of the facilities and track, the Buxton Brothers agreed to make permanent improvements, including the construction of three new stables, the renovation of three existing stables, the widening of the race track, and the erection of a permanent fence around the track. While the improvements enhanced the facilities, the real winner was Columbia because all of the construction supplies would be bought locally, and all the trainers would make Columbia their home for six

As the jockeys urge their horses toward the finish line, race fans in the grandstand cheer on their favorites.

Courtesy of the State Newspaper Photograph Archives, Richland Library

months of the year. Additionally, six other New York owners planned to winter their horses in Columbia, and many of them would journey to Columbia during the winter to see their horses.[16]

In 1933 the nationally recognized trainer Max Hirsch opened the Columbia Training Stables that operated until 1969. Other well-known trainers included Woody Stephens (Cain Hoy Stable), Frank Whiteley, Eddie Kelly (Brookfield Stable), and Tom Smith (Maine Chance Farm). In addition to five Kentucky Derby winners, Columbia's winter facilities hosted four Preakness and two Belmont winners. But it was Max Hirsh, trainer for the famous King Ranch Stable that promoted and kept returning to Columbia every winter until his death in 1969.

While horse racing ended during fair week in 1926 and an attempt to resurrect it in 1938 and 1939 failed, the advent of the Palmetto Trials in 1952 revived the sport in Columbia. In 1952 the Junior League of Columbia and Max Hirsh's Columbia Training Stables established the Palmetto Trials.

Initially only horses from Max Hirsch's stable participated, but over the years the field expanded to include entries from across the country. Held in early March each year through 1968, the races were a fund raiser for the Junior League and a major social event for Columbia. In addition to the racing crowd, the races frequently attracted such well-known figures as Bernard Baruch, Elizabeth Arden, and Jane Greer.

The Palmetto Trials consisted of five or six races for two- and three-year-old horses. Probably the most entertaining race was the mule race featuring local celebrities as the jockeys. There were no cash prizes for the winners because all the proceeds went to charity, but winners were rewarded with flowers. The Saturday races were preceded by a party on Friday evening in the ballroom of the Wade Hampton Hotel.

From 1952 until 1968 the trials raised over $170,000 for the Junior League charities. However, after the 1968 races the Junior League decided to drop its affiliation, and horse racing at the fairgrounds came to an end.[17] While the loss of the Junior League's sponsorship was a major factor in ending

Max Hirsch, the trainer for King Ranch Stables, gazes over the racetrack in 1968, the final year of the Palmetto Trials.
Courtesy of the State Newspaper Photograph Archive, Richland Library

the Palmetto Trials, there were other issues in play. In 1967 the society engaged Horwath & Horwath, a strategic planning consultant, to review the operations of the fair and make recommendations for improvements. The study pointed out that the income from the horse operations was less than 20 percent of the income per acre for the rest of the property, and the future of the horse operations was dim unless contracts could be secured from at least three stables of between three hundred to four hundred horses each. In early 1968 an article by Max Hirsch in *The Blood Horse,* a national weekly magazine on thoroughbred racing, criticized the track and stable facilities at the fairground. Both the racetrack and the stables were in poor condition, motivating many trainers to find accommodations elsewhere. For several months the society board struggled over whether to spend substantial sums to repair the facilities or to discontinue the wintering of horses at the fairgrounds.[18] By the fall of 1969 the fate of the stables was sealed after Max Hirsch's death in April and the decision by the Guggenheim stables to winter its horses elsewhere.

At the society's annual meeting in October, President Frank Hampton reported that there "was little or no chance of operating the stables."[19] In 1969 the racetrack and grandstand were demolished, and the society leased the parking lot to the University of South Carolina for football parking. The stables continued in use for the horse shows until they were demolished in 1986.

From the earliest colonial fairs through the middle of the twentieth century, horses and racing were an integral part of the State Fair. Even after automobile and motorcycle races became popular at the racetrack in the early twentieth century, the society struggled to keep horse racing at the fair. The advent of the Palmetto Trials enabled the racing to remain viable for almost two more decades until its final demise in 1969. However, without the wintering of horses at the fairgrounds from the 1890s until the 1960s, it is likely that the racetrack and races would have ended much earlier.

7

1946–1964

Integration and the Civic Center

In the years following World War II, the society continued searching for ways to both expand the fair and attract more visitors. During the war, upgrades and on-going maintenance of the facilities were put on hold. Over the next twenty-five years the society focused on upgrading existing facilities while constructing new amenities to meet the increases in attendance. Conscious of the demands put on the physical plant, the society entered in the early 1960s into an agreement with City of Columbia to develop a joint project at the fairgrounds that would not only contain facilities for the annual State Fair but also feature a convention center, a performing arts auditorium, and a basketball arena for the University of South Carolina basketball team. Following several years of planning, this concept was eventually abandoned.

The 1946 fair featured a large exhibit of military hardware that was developed and used during the war. Another attraction was a new automatic voting machine that was touted as "apparently incapable of error or mishandling." While the

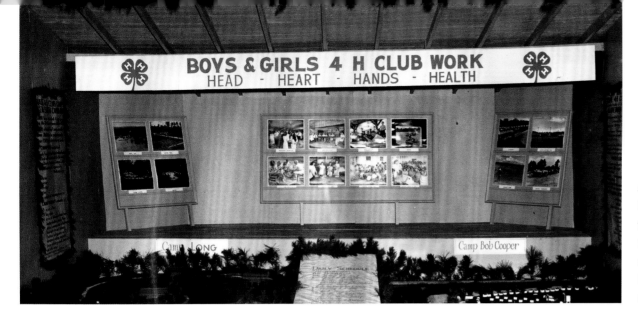

A 4-H Club exhibit at the State Fair in the late 1940s features their motto: Head–Heart–Hands–Health. Courtesy of the State Agricultural and Mechanical Society of South Carolina

midway with its three Ferris wheels and two grandstand shows each evening attracted many visitors, efforts were implemented to enhance the fair's agricultural focus. In 1946 all 4-H Club members were admitted free (but they were required to pay a ten-cent admission tax).[1] In 1947 the fairgrounds featured new swine and poultry barns, paved walkways in the steel building and a fresh coat of paint on many buildings. Finally, after many years the fair could boast of a first-class women's building with "a large lounge, with long mirrors, comfortable chairs and sofas, running cold water and adequate resting space for a number of people. There are several powder rooms with the most modern conveniences. At the windows are Venetian blinds."[2]

During the next several years, the State Fair introduced new activities to promote agriculture. Beginning in 1948, the Future Farmers of America and the Junior Homemakers Association sponsored special events attracting more than eleven thousand students.[3] In addition to the new swine and poultry buildings, in 1949 all the agricultural premiums were almost doubled, increasing from $1,800 to $3,450.[4] Editorials and newspaper articles encouraged fairgoers to "take time to look at the exhibits, a side of the fair too many do not tarry to enjoy."[5]

In 1947 people attending the Carolina–Clemson game on Big Thursday no longer had to pay admission to the fair, as they had beginning in 1896, when the football stadium was located inside the old fairgrounds on Elmwood Avenue and football fans entered through the fair's main gate. This practice continued when the fair moved to the new fairgrounds in 1904 and the stadium was also located inside the fair. In 1935, when the new stadium was built across from the fairgrounds, the University of South Carolina and the society had agreed to require football patrons to purchase fair tickets to attend the game on Big Thursday. In return the society had allowed the use of its parking lot free of charge for other Carolina football games.

But in January 1947 the General Assembly appointed a special committee to "ascertain why the fair association collected fees for entering the grounds or stadium to the annual Carolina–Clemson game." The special committee reported that "it did not question the right of the fair association to charge admission fees in cases where persons desire to see the fair but we recommend that such changes be made as will permit patrons of the Carolina–Clemson football game to enter the stadium property and witness the game without being forced to pay admission to the fair grounds." Shortly after the report was issued, the University Board of Trustees voted to terminate the 1935 agreement with the society. Paul Moore, secretary for the society, acknowledged receipt of the letter terminating the agreement and commented, "We propose to proceed just as if there wasn't a football game." He predicted that "the public will suffer" because of the inadequate parking and traffic facilities.[6] Moore's prediction was on target. When a University of South Carolina home football game occurs during the State Fair, traffic and parking are a still challenge for everyone.

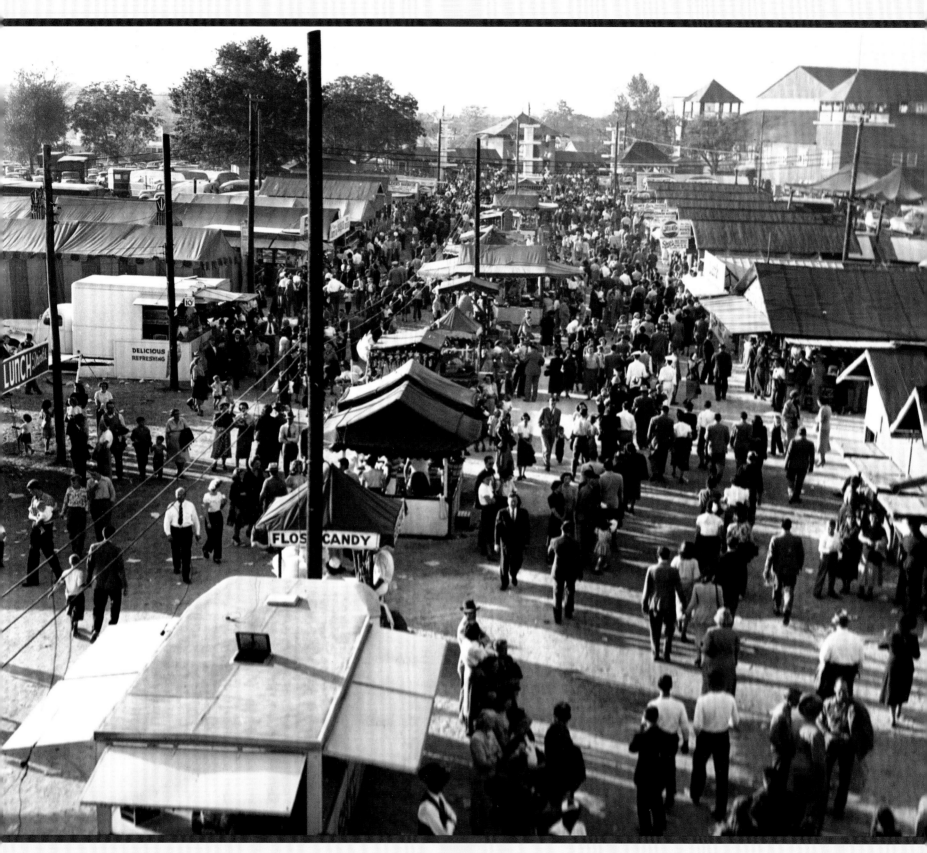

A view of the midway about 1950. The old steel building on the upper right of the image was the main exhibition building from 1913 until 1966. Courtesy of the State Agricultural and Mechanical Society of South Carolina

Several young men look over the field crop exhibit sponsored by the Future Farmers of America.
Courtesy of the State Agricultural and Mechanical Society of South Carolina

The State Highway Patrol directs traffic during the fair at the corner of Rosewood Avenue and Bluff Road in this 1950 photo.
Courtesy of the South Carolina Department of Archives & History

Rice Music House exhibit at the Anderson County Fair in 1955. Courtesy of Rice Music House

In 1952, as final preparations were under way to open the fair, a fire destroyed fifty-seven concession stands on the midway. Constructed of flimsy materials, the concession stands were quickly consumed by the fire, and only the rapid response of the Columbia Fire Department prevented the fire from spreading further. Despite the fire, all the evening's activities went on as scheduled, and by the next morning hastily erected concession stands were open.[7]

The 1952 annual meeting of the society experienced the first election of a new society president in twenty-eight years following the death of longtime president D. D. Witcover. Prior to his election as president in 1925, Witcover had served as head of the horse racing department for eight years. During his tenure, the society not only survived the Depression and World War II but also continued to add new attractions, construct badly needed facilities, and increase attendance. The newly elected president, former governor Ransome J. Williams, inherited an organization that was on a firm financial foundation due in large part to Witcover's leadership.[8]

Over the years one of the major challenges facing the State Agricultural and Mechanical Society of South Carolina was maintaining the buildings and grounds. Almost all the structures, including the Old Steel Building, were wooden

construction, which required constant painting and repair. One of the frequent structures mentioned in the board minutes was the grandstand. In 1953 President Williams reported, "The grandstand is in bad repair, and we spend money on it every year."[9] Even with the strong support of the membership, the new grandstand was not completed until four years later because of financial limitations and other commitments.[10] Constructed of concrete rather than wood, it was named in honor of D. D. Witcover, president of the society from 1923 to 1952.[11]

From the 1870s until 1915 the midway and carnival activities of the State Fair were held on Columbia's downtown streets, providing a boon for the city's merchants. Since 1915 the merchants tried several ways to attract fair visitors to the downtown stores. In 1956 the retail merchants division of the Columbia Chamber of Commerce sponsored "Fair Week Million Dollar Days." According to Joe Berry, chairman of the trade promotion committee, "Values will be offered in all lines of merchandise which would not be obtained except during an event of this type. The six days of Fair Week Million Dollar Days will be a consumer's fiesta of values this year."[12]

The election of Mayor Lester L. Bates in March 1958 saw the society work with the City of Columbia, Richland County, and the University of South Carolina to add elements to the fairgrounds that would expand year-round use of the facilities. During his twelve years as mayor, Bates proposed the development of long-range plans that would provide the city with amenities necessary for healthy growth. Among the facilities he advocated were an auditorium, a coliseum, and a convention or civic center. Only a few months after his election, Mayor Bates created a team to study how the fairgrounds could be altered to include other facilities. At an initial meeting of the group in August, informal discussions included developing a fine arts building for the university with a theater-type auditorium large enough to seat all five thousand students. There was also discussion about constructing a larger building that could be used for events ordinarily held in a field house.[13]

Over the next two months the team, led by Columbia architect William G. Lyles, developed a detailed proposal that was presented at the annual meeting of the society on October 21. The concept had evolved from the earlier meetings to include a 10,000-seat coliseum, a 2,500-seat auditorium, a large Richland County agricultural building, three new exhibit buildings to replace the steel building, and three new cattle barns. The plan would require the society to deed the fairgrounds to the city so that public funds could be used. In turn, the city would maintain the property and structures, and they would be available exclusively for the State Fair for four weeks each fall. The city would also provide a location and pay the expenses to move the racetrack to a new location and to construct fireproof stables.[14] Society members, after a lengthy discussion, voted unanimously to give the executive committee authority to work with the city on the proposed $6 million to $8 million project.[15]

Mayor Bates was anxious to get the necessary approvals and get the project moving. In May 1959 the university was recruiting a new basketball coach. When one of the candidates saw the 3,500-seat fieldhouse on the campus, he was less than impressed. Athletic Director Rex Enright immediately called Mayor Bates, who assured the candidate that the Gamecocks would be playing in the new 12,500-seat coliseum

WHAT'S IN A NICKNAME?

"State Fair" is only a nickname! The Annual Fair held in Columbia was christened: The State Agricultural and Mechnical Society of South Carolina. Each Fair is in reality a meeting of this society's members and many friends. "State Fair" is the popular nickname which you, the citizens of South Carolina, have affectionately given to this great Annual Event.

The first Fair was held in 1869 on an Elmwood Avenue site donated by the City of Columbia. As the Fair's popularity increased the need for larger grounds arose, so at the turn of the century the Fair was moved to its present location on the outskirts of your capital city.

The Fair, like Columbia, belongs to South Carolina. It is, in every sense of the word, your "State Fair." You named it and your interest has made it grow. Big Thursday, when the Carolina-Clemson Football Game is played, always brings together the largest Annual gathering of South Carolinians. The 1947 Fair will surpass all others! Why don't you plan, now, to attend your State Fair?

Columbia Merchants Association, Inc
Columbia, S. C.

Columbia belongs to South Carolina!

Each year during the run of the State Fair, Columbia merchants benefited from the patronage of fairgoers. This 1947 advertisement from the Columbia Merchants Association contains a brief history of the fair. Courtesy of the Greater Columbia Chamber of Commerce

for the 1961–62 season.[16] Despite the mayor's assurances, the State Fair society was proceeding more deliberately. In July 1959 society president James L. McIntosh indicated he would not call a special meeting of the society because many of the members were farmers and were busy with their crops at that time of year. He also did not want to bear the expense of a

1 The Coliseum will seat 14,000 for stage presentations, 12,500 for ice shows and sports events.

2 The Theater may be used with seating capacity of 1,800 or 2,600 depending on requirements of the production.

3 The Exhibition Hall, covering nearly a city block, will house conventions, science fairs, educational exhibits and new products shows (boats, cars, etc.). It will also replace the old steel building during the State Fair. The exhibit area can be converted to dining space to accommodate banquets seating up to 5,000, and in addition there will be room for meetings of from 50 to 600 people.

4 State Fair buildings in this group provide adequate area for cattle, swine, sheep and poultry.

5 State Fair Midway area will be paved to eliminate dust and mud—an improvement welcomed by Fair visitors.

INTO YOUR COMMUNITY
$$$$$ from conventions
$$$$$ from paid admissions
$$$$$ from taxes and retail sales
NEW MONEY

YOUR INVESTMENT

Market value of your home	Tax assessment value	Monthly investment	Yearly investment
$ 5,000	$ 500	21¢	$ 2.50
10,000	1,000	42¢	5.00
15,000	1,500	63¢	7.50
20,000	2,000	84¢	10.00

A brochure promoting the Richland Civic Center contains a schematic drawing showing the location of the planned facilities and describes what each would provide for the Midlands. Courtesy of Mike Safran

called meeting, planning instead to address the subject at the annual meeting in October.[17] As some began to express concern about the cost of the project, Mayor Bates began favoring a multistep approach with the auditorium coming first. In September the mayor and a special citizens' committee visited the auditorium in Greensboro, North Carolina, and came away greatly impressed.[18] Prior to the society's annual meeting in October, President McIntosh sent letters to society members outlining his reservations about deeding the fairgrounds back to the city. In response, R. Beverly Herbert Sr., chairman of the city's advisory committee, also mailed letters to society members asking for their support.[19]

At the society's annual meeting on October 20, 1959, a lengthy discussion regarding the return of the property to the city dominated the discussion. Leading the proponents of returning the property to the city were society vice-president Frank Hampton, Columbia attorney R. Beverly Herbert Sr., and Mayor Bates. Those in opposition were led by society president McIntosh; W. M. Manning, superintendent of the state penitentiary; and John Adger Manning, an attorney and local farmer. Both sides of the question had recruited new members, resulting in the election of 112 new members at the beginning of the meeting. The two primary concerns expressed by those opposed to the plan focused on segregation and the city's lack of a detailed plan. Several members argued that if the property returned to the city, the society would be forced to integrate the fair since it would be held on public property. Mayor Bates indicated that the agreement between the society and the city addressed the integration question, and there would be no change to the current status. The mayor said a detailed plan was the next step, but the federal funds needed to pay for the plan would not be available until the property was owned by the city. After a three-hour discussion, a motion was made to call for a vote. Prior to the meeting both sides collected proxy votes, and in some cases each side had votes from the same member. Discussion ensued regarding how to handle the proxy votes. After a brief recess it was decided to continue the discussion at a special called meeting

in January. Following the meeting Mayor Bates indicated that the city would go ahead with the plans on another site if the fairgrounds were not available.[20]

President McIntosh called a special meeting of the society for February 4, 1960. Again both sides solicited proxy votes from the 1,200 members of the society, and a special committee was appointed to count the proxy votes. Discussion focused on integration, but local attorney David W. Robinson pointed out that the contract with the city stipulated that the fair could remain segregated, although he emphasized that "anything on the racial situation is a calculated risk."[21] Several members who spoke against the plan in October announced their support. When the vote was taken, the contract was approved 397 to 166 including almost 400 proxy votes. The only change to the contract stipulated that if the financing was not in place within six years, the property would revert to the society. Mayor Bates commented, "This is the biggest Thursday Columbia has ever had. It meant more to more people than any Big Thursday I can conceive of. Everybody's a winner."[22] Shortly after the vote the mayor sent each member of the State Fair society a letter thanking them for their support of the planned facilities at the fairgrounds and assuring them that every effort would be made to complete the project as quickly as possible.[23]

In August 1960 the city received an interest-free federal loan of $103,000 to initiate the planning process. Local architect William G. Lyles of Lyles, Bissett, Carlisle, and Wolff would lead the planning team.[24] In early September the Coliseum Building Committee held its first meeting. Representing the State Fair society were William E. DeLoache, Frank Hampton, and Frank B. Ruff. David G. Ellison, Robert Harden, and Wallace Martin were appointed to the committee by the city.[25] On September 27, 1960, the deed to the one-hundred-acre state fairground was transferred from the State Fair society to the City of Columbia. Following the transfer of the deed, society president John L. McIntosh stated, "It is our hope that this transaction will not only provide space for anticipated buildings for the City of Columbia and the University of South

Proposed Theater Auditorium

New Midway for State Fair

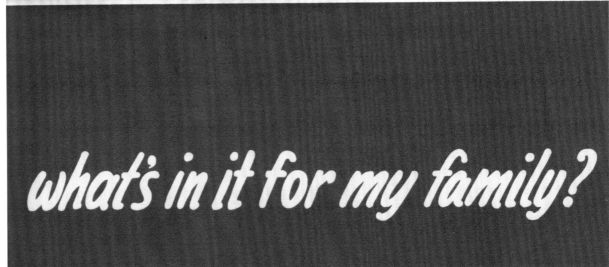

what's in it for my family?

The promotional brochure high-lights the advantages for the community, for businesses, and for families. Courtesy of Mike Safran

Carolina, but at the same time enable us to have the most modern and outstanding fair in the South."[26]

After almost a year, the planning committee completed its work and proposed developing the South Carolina Civic Center at the fairgrounds. In September 1961 the city and county appointed an eighteen-member financial advisory committee chaired by Robert S. Davis. While the initiative for the project began with the city, the need for broader support became apparent as the planning evolved. By mid-1961 Richland County had taken a leading role in the planning and, ultimately, the financing. Even before the final cost estimates were developed, Richland County representatives Crosby Lewis and Heyward Belser introduced an amendment to the state constitution that would allow the county to exclude the cost of the civic center from the limitations placed on the bonded indebtedness of the county.[27]

On August 30, 1962, the civic center committee announced that the cost of the project would be $8.9 million. This included a 14,000-seat coliseum, a theater-auditorium, and a 75,000-square-foot exhibit hall as well as special buildings and barns for the State Fair. Financing would come from the sale of Richland County general obligation bonds, payable over a thirty-year period. Both the state and Lexington County would be asked to provide funding since the facilities would be an asset to the Midlands and the whole state. Proponents of the civic center described it as a complex for the next forty years that would be unsurpassed in the Southeast.[28]

Initially there was only limited opposition to the proposed bond sale. However, five weeks before the election, letters to the editor began to appear questioning why citizens of Richland County should pay for a coliseum that would greatly benefit the university's basketball program, provide buildings for the fair, and purchase property for a racetrack and stables.[29] One letter pointed out that the city was going to spend $8.9 million for a civic center but would not commit $400,000 to save the Ainsley Hall mansion.[30] In mid-October a group called the Committee for Conservative Government began running two-column, full-length ads entitled "Tax Facts Relative to the Civic Center." Members of the group who sponsored the ads were Robert Adams Jr., Thomas C. Brown, A. Mason Gibbes, and A. Talley Moore. They pointed out that the city and county were using taxpayer money to underwrite facilities for the university, the State Fair, and the Columbia Training Stables.[31] At the annual meeting of the society on October 23, Frank Hampton, the society's vice-president, told the society members that if the proposed Richland Civic Center is approved, "we'll have the finest facilities for a fair of anyone in the Southeast."[32] As Election Day approached both sides encouraged their supporters to get out the vote.

When the votes were counted, the bond issue for the civic center was defeated in Richland County by a vote of 12,413 to 11,617. Voters in the city supported the bond issue while almost all the rural precincts were heavily opposed. In Lexington County the vote to provide county funds to the project failed by a vote of 6,224 to 3,662. However, the statewide vote to allow Richland County to exceed its bond limitations easily won approval.[33]

Following the defeat of the bond referendum, the supporters of the civic center regrouped. During the legislative session in the spring of 1963, the Richland County delegation secured a $2 million appropriation from the state. At the same time, the city amended the contract with the State Fair society, reducing their use of the fairgrounds to two weeks

IF RICHLAND COUNTY BUILDS A CIVIC CENTER AT THE EXPENSE OF THE PROPERTY TAXPAYERS AND YOU EXPECT TO OWN A NEW CAR WITHIN THE NEXT 25 YEARS THEN YOU SHOULD BE PREPARED TO PAY YOUR

CIVIC CENTER AUTO TAX!

Airplanes, boats, motors and cars are considered personal property and are taxed on a higher basis than real estate. Here is what you are paying now and what you would pay if there were now a civic center tax on automobiles.

RICHLAND COUNTY 1963
AUTOMOBILE TAX CHART—School District 1

Make of Car	County Auto Tax (75 Mills)	Proposed Civic Center Auto Tax (5 Mills)	TOTAL: County & Civic Center Auto Tax (80 Mills)	City Auto Tax (45 Mills)	TOTAL: City, County & Civic Center Auto Tax (125 Mills)
Buick	$39.00	$2.60	$41.60	$23.40	$65.00
Cadillac	69.00	4.60	73.60	41.40	115.00
Chevrolet	30.00	2.00	32.00	18.00	50.00
Chrysler	39.75	2.65	42.40	23.85	66.25
Dodge	32.25	2.15	34.40	19.35	51.60
Ford	30.00	2.00	32.00	18.00	50.00
Mercury	36.00	2.40	38.40	21.60	60.00
Oldsmobile	36.00	2.40	38.40	21.60	60.00
Plymouth	30.00	2.00	32.00	18.00	50.00
Pontiac	33.00	2.20	35.20	19.80	55.00
Rambler	30.00	2.00	32.00	18.00	50.00
Studebaker	30.00	2.00	32.00	18.00	50.00
Volkswagen	19.50	1.30	20.80	11.70	32.50

Chart Compiled from Public Records Using New Car Valuations for Popular Model of Each Make

IF YOU DO NOT LIKE THE IDEA OF PAYING HIGHER AND HIGHER TAXES ON YOUR AUTOMOBILE AND OTHER PERSONAL PROPERTY YOU HOPE TO OWN BETWEEN NOW AND 1990 THEN - - - -

VOTE "NO" CIVIC CENTER

If You Are NOT *For It* -- Be Sure to Vote *Against It!*

Committee for Conservative Government.

A. Mason Gibbes, Chairman

11-4-63

A flyer distributed by the Committee for Conservative Government encourages citizens to vote "NO" on the proposed Richland Civic Center or they would see their automobile taxes raised. Courtesy of the South Caroliniana Library, University of South Carolina, Columbia, S.C.

each fall and giving the Civic Center Commission control of the facilities the remainder of the year. In response to the opposition during the referendum, several other minor changes benefited the city. By October plans were under way for another referendum on November 11 to secure $6.9 million in Richland County bonds.[34] Even though the state appropriation reduced the bond request by $2 million, the Committee for Conservative Government again led the opposition. Their primary argument was that the county had many other needs, including overcrowded schools, a new airport facility, a new sewage treatment plant, and road repairs. They also pointed out that tax rates were already too high, and the county could not afford more bonded indebtedness. Proponents reiterated that if Columbia and South Carolina wanted to be competitive with neighboring states, these facilities were essential.[35]

When the votes were counted, the bond issue was defeated by 6,000 votes, a much larger margin than the 737 votes the previous year. Only nine of the fifty-six precincts voted yes. Following the vote R. Roy Pearce, chairman of the Citizens Committee for the Richland Civic Center, said, "We are not going to let this defeat deter us. We are coming back again and again until we get that which we feel our community needs and should have."[36] But city and county officials were ready to move on to other pressing issues. On November 27 the city council discussed returning the fairgrounds to the State Fair society. In a statement at the council meeting, Mayor Bates said, "In deference to the will of the majority of the voters and after consultation with interested groups, it has been determined that the right and just thing for the city to do now, is to tender the Fairground property back to the State Fair Association." He concluded: "Although there are honest differences of opinion regarding the various need of our growing community we are confident that the progress of the future will fulfill these needs in ways that will be generally acceptable to our citizens."[37] On December 4 the city adopted a resolution deeding the fairgrounds back to the State Fair society.[38]

Seemingly, a project like the proposed civic center, backed by most of the local politicians and businessmen, would

RICHLAND COUNTY IS ON THE MOVE

YOU, AS A REGISTERED VOTER, HAVE MADE IT POSSIBLE

THE RICHLAND COUNTY CIVIC CENTER

means FUN, RECREATION, CULTURAL ADVANCE, RELIGIOUS EXPRESSION, and EXCITEMENT for us and our children. It will provide MANY EXTRA JOB opportunities for all of us.

VOTE YES FOR THE RICHLAND COUNTY CIVIC CENTER NOVEMBER 6TH

Mailings like this one were sent in support of the Civic Center. Courtesy of the South Caroliniana Library, University of South Carolina, Columbia, S.C.

easily be approved. The defeat of the referendum on the bond issue was attributed by most observers on the reluctance of Richland County voters to pay additional taxes. But there were other factors involved. One veteran of the local political scene commented, "Both sides made mistakes and there is no such thing as a perfectly conducted campaign. But the proponents used too many names prominent in the social and civic life of the community. You set up social and economic class war that way…you alienate the lower income groups, and there are more of them." The Reverend I. DeQuincey Newman, field secretary of the South Carolina Conference of the NAACP branches, remarked that "Negroes probably voted against the Civic Center because 'poor people would have no means with which to enjoy, but would have to pay for it along with others.'" Reverend Newman said segregation was not an issue. A. P. Williams, an African American funeral director, disagreed, stating, "There never was a clear statement as far as discrimination is concerned." Williams led an African American organization opposed to the civic center. The Richland County Citizens Committee opposed the project because it felt there

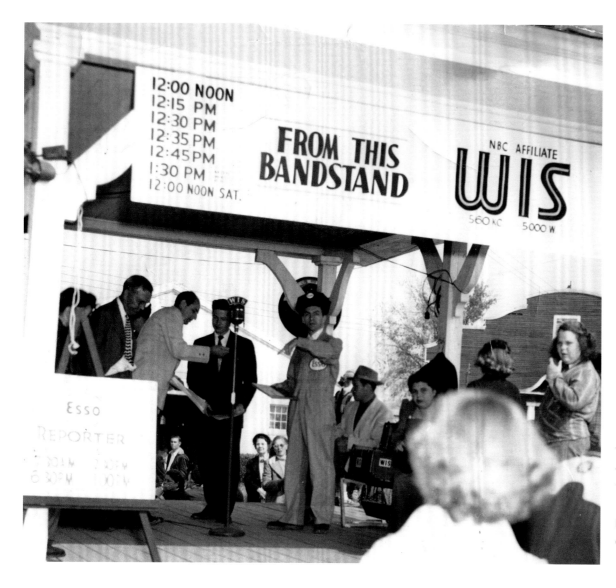

Despite the contentious struggle over the Civic Center, activities at the fair continued uninterrupted. In this early 1960 image, WIS radio personality Mackie Quave, in the Esso uniform, hosts a live broadcast from the State Fair. Courtesy of the State Agricultural and Mechanical Society of South Carolina

was an attempt "to buy our people" and because "we were not in on it at the policy-making stage." Williams pointed out that Columbia's predominantly African American ward 9 voted 274–258 against during the first referendum but voted 437–275 against it this year.[39] With the civil rights movement making headlines on a regular basis and only months away from the passage of the Civil Rights Act of 1964, race was a contributing factor in the outcome of the referendum on the civic center.

With the end of World War II, the State Fair anticipated a return to normal operations. During the first several years following the war, new facilities were constructed to accommodate increased attendance. When discussions about the possible use of the fairgrounds as the site of a Richland County civic center began in 1958, the State Fair society played an active role in the planning process but continued to focus on sustaining a quality fair each year. The need for additional facilities and the maintenance of current structures was put on hold while plans for a civic center were developed. With the return of the property in 1963, the State Fair society needed to evaluate its facilities and plan for the future. In January 1964 the society engaged Lyles, Bissett, Carlisle, and Wolff, a local architecture firm, to develop a plan for future development.

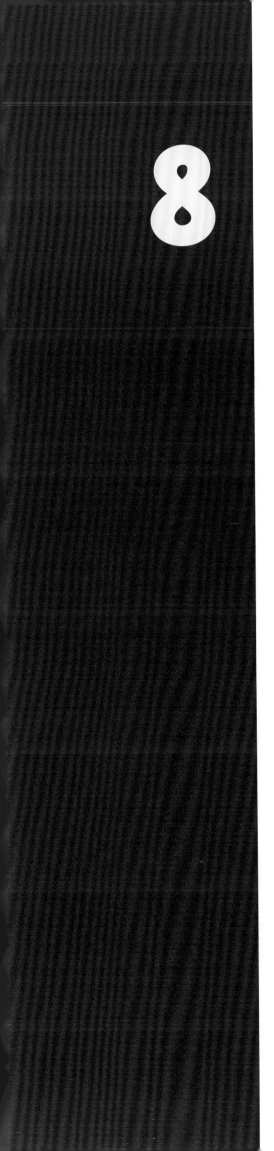

8 County and Regional Fairs

Since the early eighteenth century South Carolina planters and farmers gathered to exchange agricultural information, socialize with their neighbors, and enjoy showing off their prized livestock and crops. These informal gatherings predated the more formal gatherings sponsored by the agricultural societies that had evolved by the early nineteenth century. One of the earliest county fairs with official recognition occurred in Kershaw County in 1774. An old commission from King George III of England authorized a fair "for the benefit and advantage of the interior parts of this Province whereto the inhabitants might resort to purchase horses, cattle, pigs and other commodities which they may want or have to dispose of."[1] Prior to the Civil War the frequency of county or regional fairs varied from year to year. When the first State Fair was held in 1840, regional fairs were well established, and planters and farmers were accustomed to taking time from their fields to attend. The antebellum state fairs attracted participants from across the state, especially after 1856, when railroad travel permitted the movement of people, livestock, and crops much more easily than the inadequate dirt roads. However, even after the advent of the State Fair, district and regional fairs continued until the outbreak of the Civil War. The Newberry Agricultural Society celebrated its seventeenth fair in 1856, attended by many of its four hundred members.[2] In 1857 the *Winnsboro Register* reported, "The success of our District Fair, on Saturday was unquestionable." The article extolled the large number of entries in livestock, field crops, handiwork, foodstuffs, and the mechanical department, saying only the art department was a disappointment.[3] In 1858 even the reporter for the *Charleston Courier* remarked of the Fairfield County Fair that "the entire Fair was one highly creditable to the intelligent citizens of Fairfield." The success of the fair was only spoiled when former governor John H. Means fell through an unfinished section of the floor in the building, hitting a stove

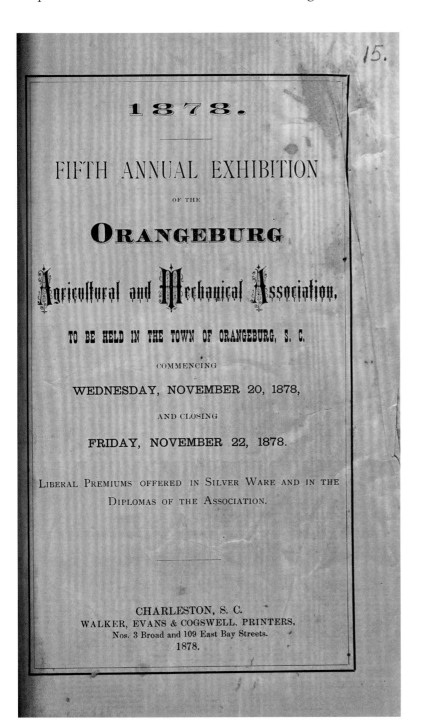

UNITED STATES RAILROAD
ADMINISTRATION
——ANNOUNCES——
VERY LOW EXCURSION RATES
——ACCOUNT——
ORANGEBURG COUNTY FAIR

From Columbia, Sumter, Charleston, S. C., and intermediate points, also all stations between Denmark and Branchville, S. C., tickets on sale November 10, 11, 13, and for trains scheduled to arrive in Orangeburg, S. C., before noon of November 14, 1919, good to reach original starting point returning prior to midnight of November 16, 1919.

Minimum round trip fare 25 cents. Ample equipment will be provided on all regular trains to handle the extra travel.

SOUTHERN RAILROAD LINES

For information and exact round trip fares apply to ticket agents or telephone Nos. 7 or 3701.

(left) Like the State Fair, many of the local fairs also published premium lists. The cover of the 1878 Orangeburg County fair premium list announces "Liberal Premiums offered in Silver Ware and in the Diplomas of the Association."
Courtesy of the South Caroliniana Library, University of South Carolina, Columbia, S.C.

(above) Following the Civil War, the State Fair and the local fairs depended on the railroads to transport fairgoers as well as exhibits. This 1919 advertisement by Southern Railways for the Orangeburg County Fair includes schedules, fares, and an assurance of "ample equipment" on all scheduled trains.
Courtesy of Rodger E. Stroup

South Carolina Fairs, 1920

NAMES AND DATES.	PLACE.	SECRETARY.
South Carolina State Fair Association, October 25-29	Columbia	D. F. Efird
Colored State Fair Association, November 2-5th	Columbia	R. W. Westberry
Orangeburg County Fair, November 9-12	Orangeburg	J. M. Hughes
Pee Dee Fair, November 2-4	Florence	A. H. Gasque
Williamsburg County Fair Association, November 9-12	Kingstree	W. H. Welch
Southeastern Fair, November 3-5	Andrews	W. W. Smoak
Sumter Fair Association, November 16-19	Sumter	E. J. Rearden
York County Fair Association, October 20-23	Rock Hill	Miss S. M. Jewel
Union Fair Association, 2nd week in November	Union	B. F. Alston
Chester Fair Association, November 2-5	Chester	H .G. Branch
Marlboro County Fair Association, November 3-4-5	Bennettsville	B. L. Stanton
Chesterfield Fair Association, November 9-12	Chesterfield	T. E. Mulloy
Piedmont Fair Association, October 20-21-22	Greenwood	W. T. King
Lexington County Fair Association, October 19-21	Lexington	S. J. Leaphart
Bamberg County Fair Association, November 17-19	Denmark	R. W. Wroten
Spartanburg County Fair Association, November 2-6	Spartanburg	P. V. Moore
Fairfield Agricultural Society, November 10-12	Winnsboro	Mary Y. Ellison

The 1920 State Fair premium list contains a list of county and regional fairs across the state. Courtesy of the State Agricultural and Mechanical Society of South Carolina

pipe and breaking two ribs.[4] The following year the *Lexington Flag* bragged of their district fair: "The number of articles on exhibition far surpassed those of last year, both in quality and number, and most especially the fine arts wrought by the hands of the 'Old Lexington's' fairest daughters."[5] In October 1860, as the secession crisis heightened, the *Abbeville Banner* proclaimed the district fair a great success, with over 432 exhibitors.[6]

The county fairs also encouraged the reestablishment of a state fair during the 1850s. At a meeting of the Newberry Agricultural Society in 1855, the society endorsed a suggestion that a "State Agricultural Society should be formed…that it should be constituted by delegates from other Societies and communities."[7] According to the editor of the *South Carolina Agriculturist,* the impetus for the establishment of a revived state agricultural society was due to a new spirit of cooperation that sprang into life during 1855. Prior to this new spirit, many planters chose to go it on their own, as highlighted in an 1844 report written by Gov. Whitemarsh B. Seabrook, Judge John Belton O'Neall, and B. F. Alston Jr.: "The habits of planters are those of separate action; they combine less

than any other class of men. Each regards his own plantation as his empire: he looks around and considers what will best promote his individual interest; and though there is no doubt that many might be induced to meet, consult and…yet some, and possibly a great many, would prefer separate action."[8]

After the start of the Civil War, except for the abbreviated State Fair in the fall of 1861, it would be the end of the decade before the fairs returned. During the war, most of the white males in the state were in the military, and many women struggled to maintain a plantation or a business. In the years immediately following the war, the uncertainties of Reconstruction and the adjustment to the new social and political climate occupied the state's citizens. However, by 1869 the realities of the war's aftermath encouraged the prewar leadership to establish organizations to resist the new order. Among these was the creation of the State Agricultural and Mechanical Society to revive the annual State Fair in Columbia. The first postwar State Fair was held November 10–12, 1869, on the rebuilt fairgrounds on Elmwood Avenue. On November 16 the Barnwell County fair opened "with a large attendance."[9] Over the next several years, county and regional fairs began

A 1913 postcard shows the household department at the Orangeburg County Fair. Courtesy of Rodger E. Stroup

to spring up across the state. By 1883 there were seven county fairs (Anderson, Greenville, Chester, Darlington, Union, Newberry, and Sumter) and another fair in Charleston sponsored by the Agricultural Society of South Carolina.[10] In 1909 the *State* newspaper reported that about half of the counties sponsored fairs. The paper continued, "These fairs are doing good; they interest the people of the communities and they encourage betterments on the farm. They are visited by many thousands who can not go to a fair in Columbia. They constantly improve. Many of them furnish the visitor from the county with carnival amusements; some of them, like that at Spartanburg this year, provide excellent horse-racing, admirably conducted, entertaining 'free' features."[11] These local fairs

were often sponsored by service organizations, including the American Legion and the Jaycees. Others fairs were not associated with an organization but were staged by interested volunteers.

By the mid-1920s there were fifteen county or regional fairs operating from the Pee Dee to the Piedmont. In 1929 the fair secretaries met in Columbia to form an organization, "with the avowed purpose of making the county fairs in South Carolina more attractive to the people, of better standard and more helpful and educative." In addition the organization agreed to cooperate with Gov. John G. Richards to "eradicate objectionable features, such as the 'wheels of chance' of all kinds, and will back him up in his law enforcement programs as regards

FIRST ANNUAL TRI-COUNTY FAIR

Georgetown, Williamsburg and Berkeley Counties

ANDREWS, SOUTH CAROLINA

Wednesday, Thursday and Friday

OCTOBER 15, 16, 17

Extensive Exhibits in

AGRICULTURE, CATTLE, SWINE, POULTRY and WOMEN'S WORK

Special U. S. Government Exhibits

Good Roads, Farm Development and Forestry

YOU OWE IT TO YOURSELF AND FAMILY TO COME

OCTOBER 15, 16, 17

It Will Be the Gala Occasion of the Pee Dee Section

AMUSEMENTS of the HIGHEST CLASS

ANDREWS, S. C.

OCTOBER 15, 16, 17

NEWBERRY COUNTY FAIR

BOARD OF DIRECTORS

J. W. Johnson	J. F. Hawkins	J. F. Clarkson
T. E. Davis	Y. T. Dickert	Claude Gilliam
H. O. Long	J. W. Abrams	J. C. Epting, Jr.

OFFICERS

J. F. Hawkins, Pres.   J. W. Johnson, Vice-Pres.
Henry Cannon, Sec.-Mgr.   James D. Brown, Treas.

American Legion Fair Committee in Charge

Frank Sutton, Mgr.

James D. Brown, Chm.; Paul Ezell, Hal Kohn, Jr., Louis Floyd, John Lindsay

ANNOUNCEMENTS

More than $2,000.00 is being offered in cash as prizes at the 1950 NEWBERRY COUNTY FAIR. The prizes are attractive and should encourage keen competition in all departments. The County Fair officials want to co-operate with the good people of the county and adjoining counties in making the exhibits at this year's fair the best in the history of Newberry County. Read the catalog and prepare your exhibits early.

Be Sure And Take In All The Midway Attractions

FREE ACTS ON MIDWAY DAILY

The COUNTY FAIR opens officially, Monday, October 23rd, at 6:00 P. M. Wednesday is School Day.

SIX BIG DAYS   -   -   SIX BIG NIGHTS

WEEK OF OCTOBER 23RD

Admission to Fair Grounds:

Adults_____50c   Children_____25c

Automobiles, 25c each

All White School Children FREE on Wednesday, October 25th, up to 6:00 P. M.

Fair Opens Officially at 6:00 P. M., Monday, October 23.

MIDWAY OPENS MONDAY NIGHT

(3)

(left) In 1919 Georgetown, Williamsburg, and Berkeley Counties established the Tri-County Fair in Andrews. This advertisement depicts the variety of activities available at the local fairs during this era. *Courtesy of Rodger E. Stroup*

(above) The local fairs' racial policies mirrored those of the State Fair. This page from the 1950 Newberry County Fair premium list notes that "All White School Children FREE on Wednesday." *Courtesy of Rodger E. Stroup*

Even during the Great Depression in the 1930s, the crowds still flocked to the Anderson County Fair.

Courtesy of the South Caroliniana Library, University of South Carolina, Columbia, S.C.

Overlooking the Orangeburg County fairgrounds during the 2005 fair. Courtesy of the State Agricultural and Mechanical Society of South Carolina

county fairs."[12] In January 1930 the group met as the South Carolina Association of Fair Secretaries and elected J. P. Moon of Newberry as president and Paul V. Moore of Columbia, secretary of the State Fair, as chairman of the executive committee. The group agreed that its purpose was to make the organization a clearinghouse for ideas and mutual support.[13] By 1942 there were twenty-nine fairs operating in the state.[14]

Following World War II, county and regional fairs continued to attract thousands of visitors each year. Beginning in the 1960s, the number of local fairs began to decline. In 1969 there were twenty-four county and regional fairs.[15] By 2017 only fourteen local fairs were still operating.[16] Several factors contributed to the decline of local fairs. The creation of the interstate highway system made travel to the State Fair easier and safer. Beginning in the 1970s the development of large amusement and theme parks like Disney World and Carowinds dwarfed the thrill rides and midway attractions at local fairs. Finally, many of the local fairs depended heavily on volunteers who drifted away over the years.

9

From Disaster to a New Vision

"We have a story of a disaster,
we have lost the Steel Building"

Following the aborted attempt by the city to develop a coliseum and convention center at the fairgrounds, the State Fair society quickly realized that it needed to address serious issues with the physical plant that had been put on hold during planning for the civic center. At a meeting in April 1964, the executive committee announced plans for a long-range construction and modernization program that was developed by the architectural firm of Lyles, Bissett, Carlisle, and Wolff. The first phase included a new main entrance on Rosewood Drive, paving the midway, and constructing three new dormitories for the stable area. A total of $35,000 was approved by the executive committee, with completion scheduled before the fair's opening in October. The second phase included construction of a new 100,000-square-foot, air-conditioned exhibit building to replace the steel building, which would be torn down. The main projects in the third phase included an agricultural building and a women's building.[1]

The morning after the fire, all that was left of the old steel building was a pile of rubble.
Courtesy of the State Newspaper Photograph Archive, Richland Library

During 1965 some minor improvements were completed at the fairgrounds while the society continued to refine plans to turn the fairgrounds into a year-round facility. The society board realized while the planning for the civic center was under way that the location of the fairgrounds had the potential to host a variety of non-fair-related activities throughout the year. These activities would not only bring people to the fairgrounds, but they would also provide a source of revenue to help maintain the physical plant.[2] While the society's board continued to refine the long-range plan and seek the necessary funds, fate intervened and forced them to move rapidly.

On April 22, 1966, the headlines in the *State* newspaper proclaimed "Fire Destroys Steel Building." Actually, despite its name, the building was constructed primarily of wood, and the fire was caused by a short circuit in an area containing poultry cases, rapidly spreading through the rafters to the entire structure. Despite the best efforts of the nine trucks and forty-two firemen from the Columbia Fire Department, within an hour the building was a smoldering ruin. Society president Frank Hampton said, "We have a story of a disaster, we have lost the Steel Building." He noted that the building was valued at $500,000 but would cost $1.5 million to replace it. President Hampton stated the building was not insured

(opposite) The smoke from the fire that destroyed the old steel building was visible from miles away.
Courtesy of the State Newspaper Photograph Archives, Richland Library

The plan developed by Dean McClure contained a remodeled football stadium in the foreground connected by a pedestrian bridge over the street to the fair exhibition facilities. Beyond is an elevated racetrack, inside of which is the parking area for the complex. This is connected by underpasses to the traffic arteries, amusement areas, and the convention center, which contains a multistory hotel, convention hall, merchandising mart, and group recreational facilities. Courtesy of the South Carolina Chapter of the American Institute of Architects

because the premium was too high. He indicated the society was working to get a new building financed, "but we haven't been too successful."[3] However, Susanne Kennedy, longtime treasurer of the society, believed that the loss of the steel building was the catalyst for the society to stop spending money repairing the old structure and develop a plan for the future development of the fairgrounds.

Only two days after the fire, President Hampton announced that two Columbia banks offered pledges of support for a building to replace the steel building. The society was moving forward with plans to construct a 65,000-square-foot building, the same size as the steel building, which could be used for conventions, trade shows, flower shows, and similar events.[4] On April 27 the society's executive committee gave

the building committee approval to solicit proposals from contractors and authorized spending $300,000. The new 160 × 400-foot building would contain a two-story section across the front with three large heated and air-conditioned meeting rooms and several modern offices. The executive committee also approved a temporary reduction in livestock premiums to help ease the financial strain caused by the fire.[5] The following day at a meeting with local bankers, business leaders, society officials, and representatives of federal agencies, several individuals suggested that more time was needed to ensure that the new building would meet the long-term needs of the fair. Architect Louis Wolff pointed out that "if hasty decisions proved wrong about the building they would have to live with it a long time." The option of using a "Big

Top" tent for the 1966 fair was suggested. The federal officials at the meeting indicated that there were no federal funds available because the society was not a government entity.[6] Following this meeting the society decided to scale back the new building and construct a 60 × 250-foot building costing $25,000, dubbed the "Little Steel Building." To provide adequate exhibit space, the poultry building was connected to the new building by a 30-foot steel extension, and the poultry exhibits would be housed in tents.[7] However, on May 9, before construction began on the new structure, a fire broke out in the debris from the Old Steel Building, which was quickly extinguished by a fire truck from the Shandon Fire Station.[8]

As the opening of the fair approached in 1966, the "Little Steel Building" was completed. However, the society needed to address the long-range need for a larger main building. The society decided to engage the School of Architecture at Clemson University to develop a long-range plan for the physical plant. Dean Harlan McClure indicated that over the previous eleven years, the School of Architecture's faculty and students had completed master plans for cities like Greenville, Hartsville, and Sumter. He said that "the State Fair survey presents the biggest and most challenging problem to date."[9]

In March 1967 Dean McClure and the fifth-year Clemson architecture students presented a comprehensive twenty-year plan to the society. With a price tag of $35 million, the plan was overly ambitious, and the executive committee did not believe the society could afford it.[10] At a meeting on April 12, 1967, the executive committee engaged the planning firm of Horwath & Horwath of Miami, Florida, to review the State Fair's physical plant and financial situation.[11] The firm developed "a plan by which the South Carolina Fairgrounds property can be revitalized with necessary new construction and refurbishing in order to better serve its purpose as a state fair. It was also our aim to find other means by which expanded use of this acreage on a year-round basis will benefit the people of South Carolina, especially Columbia, and enhance the economic utilization of the subject property." On June 7 Horwath & Horwath submitted an eighty-one-page report outlining a three-phase approach complete with physical plant plans and financial recommendations and projections.[12]

The major recommendations of the Horwath report included construction of new buildings and renovation of existing structures so they could house a variety of events throughout the year. The report suggested that all the structures needed to have adequate heat and portable exhibit equipment. It noted the poor image of the fairgrounds and called for the renovation of older restrooms and the construction of new restrooms. The concession area needed to be expanded to meet the larger crowds. A key recommendation of the report was elimination of the winter training stables. After analyzing the fair's income, the report showed that the income from the stable operations was less than 20 percent of the income per acre for the rest of the property. During the previous year the winter stables generated $62,611, while the fair and related activities generated $350,629. In 1966 only 125 horses were quartered at the fairgrounds, and the report indicated that unless 300 to 400 horses were on hand, the stable operations would continue to be far less profitable. With fifty-two of the ninety-three acres dedicated to the racetrack and stables, it would be difficult to expand other aspects of the fair. Another major recommendation of the report was the development of an amusement park that would draw people to the fairgrounds throughout the year.

It did not take long for the society to embrace much of the first phase of the Horwath report, and almost immediately the exhibition buildings and renovation of older structures were under way and completed before the 1967 fair. In August the *State* reported that the new facilities at the fairgrounds would have the state's largest seating and dining facility, capable of seating ten thousand for a meeting and six thousand for dining. In addition, a cafeteria, a new office building, new restrooms, and new cattle barns are nearing completion. The new facilities were financed with a $730,000 loan. Instead of eliminating the winter stable operations, the society approved funds to repair the stables and install an automatic sprinkler system for the racetrack. President Hampton said

A 1974 aerial photograph looking east shows the buildings that replaced the old steel building. The remnants of the racetrack are in the upper right corner of the image while the stables are at the top center. Courtesy of the Agricultural and Mechanical Society of South Carolina

Another 1974 aerial photograph looking west shows the midway, the grandstand, the former racetrack (now a parking lot), and a glimpse of the football stadium. Courtesy of the State Agricultural and Mechanical Society of South Carolina

(left) In 1967 the society hired a sales manager to market the fairground's facilities. One traditional marketing technique was posters. In this 1969 photograph a poster advertising the State Fair is on a construction fence on the corner of Gervais and Assembly Streets with the Market Restaurant in the **background.** Courtesy of the Mabel Payne Photograph Collection, Richland Library

(above) A tray from the Redwood Cafeteria that operated at the fairgrounds from 1968 to the mid-1970s. Courtesy of Burl R. Kennedy

plans were under way to increase the horse-training activities and that within five years the stables and racetrack would be completely renovated.[13]

Another major recommendation of the Horwath report encouraged the society to hire a sales manager to market the facilities at the fairgrounds on a year-round basis. They emphasized that many state fairs across the country rented their facilities, and this important source of income needed to be tapped. But the Horwath recommendation for an amusement park was never seriously considered by the society.

The recommendations in the Horwath report were a major turning point in the future operations of the State Fair. While they rejected closing the stables and in fact in 1968 spent $10,500 refurbishing the stables, they enthusiastically endorsed marketing the fairgrounds as a year-round venue for a wide variety of events. The newly constructed cafeteria was leased to the Redwood Cafeteria, which began offering lunch and dinner. For at least one season the Ruff Building was leased for roller skating to the New Palace Skate Club.[14] Over the next several years the fairgrounds were the site of trade shows, boats shows, religious revivals, traveling circuses, and an anti-Vietnam protest that "hijacked" a music festival. In March 1970 a rock 'n' roll festival at the fairgrounds featuring several local bands was taken over by a group protesting the closing of the UFO Coffeehouse on Main Street. The anti–Vietnam War coffeehouse had been closed by a court order and its owners indicted by a grand jury the previous January. Protestors showed up at the concert and displayed signs and distributed antiwar literature. The media initially reported the event as an antiwar protest, but a subsequent letter to the editor indicated that the protestors were unwanted interlopers and represented only a small percentage of the crowd.[15]

Previously the fairgrounds had been leased for other events, but following the Horwath report the facilities were aggressively promoted. Following completion of the new steel building (now the Ruff Building), an advertisement in the *Columbia Record* featured a photograph and stated, "With 15,000 sq. ft. of floor space you can use in hundreds of ways, with practically unlimited parking areas and with a location convenient to all and well known to all South Carolinians…

For its centennial in 1969, the society commissioned several special items, including a cookbook, lapel pins, and a key chain. On the top right is an invitation to the Centennial Dinner. *Courtesy of Burl R. Kennedy*

this is the ideal facility for all your sale or exhibition hall needs."[16]

As the centennial of the State Agricultural and Mechanical Society approached in 1969, a special planning committee was appointed. The planning committee selected "State Fair 100" as the theme for the celebration. In April the executive committee approved several special activities recommended by the committee. The Rocket was approved as a permanent addition to the fairgrounds. They also approved casting a special medal or coin, publishing a centennial cookbook, and purchasing hats or buttons to identify employees. Finally, a special VIP party was planned for the Friday night before the fair opened.[17] A highlight of the party at the Redwood Cafeteria was a history of the State Fair presented in song and rhyme by Ruth Ann Collins, Helen Farah, Pam Inabinet, Thom Jones, Steve Corkran (director), and Kay Holley (accompanist). Special guests of the society included Senator and Mrs. Strom Thurmond, Congressman and Mrs. James

F. Mann, Gov. Robert E. McNair and his daughter, and Major General and Mrs. James F. Hollingsworth, the commanding general at Fort Jackson.[18] The *Centennial Celebrity Cookbook* featured recipes from various South Carolina dignitaries as well as First Lady Pat Nixon and Second Lady Judy Agnew. A unique feature of the cookbook was that each of the recipes was reproduced just as they were received—some were typed but most were handwritten by the contributor.[19] Each evening of the fair featured a special fireworks display.

In 1970 South Carolina celebrated its tricentennial, and the State Fair adopted a country-western theme featuring singer Loretta Lynn. In Charleston, the Charles Towne Landing Exposition Park featured the first hundred years and colonial life in the state. The Midlands Exposition Park in Columbia featured the second hundred years covering the American Revolution through Reconstruction. In Greenville, the Piedmont Exposition Park covered the last hundred years and highlighted the growth of manufacturing in the state.

Because of design and construction problems, the Greenville park was never completed. Across the state counties organized special events and historical programs. Richland County's tricentennial activities coincided with fair week. On Friday and Saturday nights the fair featured special tricentennial fireworks.[20]

Tricentennial festivities at the fair were marred when, on October 24, 1970, a security guard was shot and killed by a visitor. Daniel Monopoli, an employee of Collins and Murray Security, challenged a twenty-three-year-old visitor who had purchased a student ticket. When confronted, the suspect pulled a revolver from his belt and shot Monopoli in the chest. The suspect fled before other officers could apprehend him.[21] With a description and sketch provided by witnesses, a suspect was arrested three weeks later.[22] However, two days later Sheriff Frank Powell released the individual, indicating he was not involved.[23] On November 17 a second suspect, James F. Moseley Jr. was arrested.[24] When the case came to trial in April 1971, Moseley pleaded guilty to manslaughter and received a two-year prison sentence. Judge Francis B. Nicholson imposed the minimum sentence because "there was a very fine point of possible self-defense in the case." Sheriff Powell said "that Moseley apparently thought Monopoli was reaching for a gun when Moseley pulled his own gun and shot the guard." Powell noted that he had received complaints that the fair guards were "giving people a bad time." The sheriff met with the guards, who were from an out-of-state company, and told them that they should be fair but firm with patrons.[25]

As attendance at the fair increased because of the new facilities, the society decided in 1972 to stop allowing free admission on Sunday, the day before the formal opening. For many years this practice had allowed free access to the fairgrounds while the final touches to rides and midway shows were being completed. Society president David G. Ellison realized that "thousands of people accustomed to bringing their children down to the fairgrounds for maybe a candied apple, cotton candy or a kiddie ride on Sunday will be disappointed." President Ellison said the decision was made for safety

Carnival operator Deggeller Attractions featured clowns on their 1977 poster promoting the State Fair. Courtesy of Burl R. Kennedy

reasons because it would allow workers setting up exhibits and midway attractions to "do their jobs more efficiently if they don't have to keep a watchful eye out for children."[26]

During the 1970s the State Fair continued to implement the improvements recommended in the 1967 Horwath report. Each year the facilities at the fairground were used by additional organizations for their meetings and trade shows. The society continued to upgrade the physical plant, including the construction in 1977 of a 44,000-square-foot building named in honor of Dr. William C. Cantey. Another major upgrade completed during the early 1970s was paving all the walkways. According to State Fair manager W. L. Abernathy, "They are really appreciated on the days it rains and the pavement allows us to do a better cleanup job."[27] Finding the right vendor to run the restaurant proved to be a challenge. After two unsuccessful ventures, the society contracted with Seawell's in 1976 to operate the restaurant, a relationship that lasted until Seawell's built its own facility across Rosewood Avenue in 1999.[28]

By the early 1980s the State Fair board once again looked for an outside consultant to review the status of the fair and its operations. T. Wilson Sparks, the executive director of the Florida State Fair Authority, spent four days visiting during the 1981 fair. In December Sparks submitted his report to the board. Most of Sparks' comments were positive, but he pointed to a couple of areas that needed attention. His primary concern was with the restrooms and food service facilities. He recommended that the signage for the restrooms should be more visible and that additional women's restrooms were needed. Sparks' biggest concern was with the food service area, especially the older permanent structures sponsored by local organizations. He recommended

that they be removed and replaced by "professionally built mobile units" because they "not only provide a more sanitary method of handling food but provide an opportunity to change the layout of the grounds from year to year so that the Fairgrounds will not look the same." In his concluding remarks Sparks highlighted the challenge facing all state fairs. He pointed out that the carnivals continue to attract younger visitors, but fairs are losing ground with the over twenty-five age group as they are "demanding more people comfort, a changing program, more entertainment than ever before and a more sophisticated type of exhibit program."[29] Over the next several years the State Fair began implementing Sparks' suggestions as the organization moved into the twenty-first century.

The society initially labeled the fire that destroyed the Old Steel Building in 1965 a disaster. However, it was a blessing in disguise because it forced the society not only to address the deteriorating physical plant but also to develop facilities that would enable year-round use of the fairgrounds and provide a much-needed new source of income and visibility for the State Fair.

10 Entertainment and the Midway

"All to win a stuffed animal I really didn't want"

From their beginnings, local and state fairs were primarily for the promotion of agricultural and industrial interests. Before radio, television, and smartphones, farmers lived an isolated existence, frequently going for extended periods of time without seeing neighbors. In addition to learning about the latest in scientific farming methods, farmers could visit with friends, show off prize livestock and crops, and enjoy the entertainment and amusements offered at the fair. During the late nineteenth century, the society began to struggle with balancing the agricultural and industrial missions of the fair midway. On several occasions during the twentieth century, the society's board recognized that the ever-growing popularity of the midway activities was a major reason for increased attendance. At the same time the board realized that many fairgoers came primarily for the entertainment, rides, and sideshows, while the agricultural exhibits and competitions were often overlooked. The board realized that its challenge was to balance the agricultural activities with the midway attractions. Several times they raised the premiums on agricultural exhibits, hoping to attract more entries, while reducing premiums in other categories. They tried different ways to showcase the agricultural activities. For example, in 1952 the grandstand show was preceded by a parade of champion and grand champion cattle winners.[1] Despite the society's efforts, the midway continued to be the main attraction for most fairgoers.

The midway at today's State Fair can trace its beginnings to the colonial fairs of the eighteenth century in South Carolina. In addition to the agricultural components, the entertainment, games, and attractions were an important element of the early fairs. As early as 1749 the Charleston newspaper reported that fairgoers enjoyed a variety of diversions including horse racing, shooting matches, raffles, and "a Schara-mouche-Dance, precisely at 3 o'Clock, by a Person from London."[2] During the early nineteenth century, fairs sponsored by local agricultural societies featured speakers on agricultural topics along with agricultural and domestic competitions for prizes. The entertainment included horse racing, shooting matches, and occasionally musical performances.

The State Fairs sponsored by the State Agricultural Society from 1840 to 1845 did not have any entertainment-related activities. Because the fairs were located on the statehouse grounds, they had limited space and lacked indoor facilities. These fairs highlighted the awarding of premiums for the best livestock and field crops and featured speakers promoting the latest in scientific farming practices.

When the State Agricultural Society was reborn in 1855 and sponsored fairs from 1856 to 1861, they were located at the new fairgrounds on Elmwood Avenue and had both outdoor and indoor facilities. It was during this time that the entertainment activities began to appear. Horse racing was always a favorite at the prewar fairs and continued to attract large crowds into the early twentieth century. Plowing demonstrations provided both a lively competition and featured the attributes of the various plow manufacturers. In 1859 the *Charleston Mercury* reported, "The plowing match drew quite a large concourse of spectators. A practical trial was made of

AMUSEMENTS

Johnny J. Jones Exposition will be the Midway attraction. We guarantee this aggregation to be clean.
The following high-class free acts have been booked:
  The Duttons.
  The Duttons Equestrians.
  Miss Nellie Jordan and Co. Dancing and Wire Walking.
  Barney Google and Spark Plug-Comedy.
  Smallest Mule in the World.
  Miss Vivian De Vere-Sensational Aerial Loop-the-Loop.
  Mechanic Comedy Riding Act.
  Gene De Kos-Famous French Clown.
  Tom Dick and Harry, Fun on the Hay Wagon.
  Old Fashioned Country Dance.
  The De Kos Bros. Comedy Acrobatic Act.
These free acts are varied and will please the most exacting.
  Band Concerts.
  Tilting Tournament—Monday Night.
  Harness Races—Tuesday, Wednesday, Thursday and Friday.
  Horse Show—Tuesday, Wednesday and Thursday Nights.
  Football Games—Tuesday and Wednesday.
  Football—Carolina-Clemson, Thursday.
  Historical Pageant—Friday and Saturday Nights.

. AMPLE PARKING SPACE FOR AUTOMOBILES!

Amusements list from 1925. Frequently the premium list contained a list of the amusements and highlights for each day. Courtesy of the State Agricultural and Mechanical Society of South Carolina

The limited space on the antebellum statehouse grounds and the lack of indoor facilities limited the exhibits and entertainment at the 1840–45 fairs. Courtesy of the South Carolina Department of Archives and History

the different variety of plows, exhibitors claiming for each respectively some important improvements over all other and of course indispensable to the planter."[3] Prior to the outbreak of the Civil War in 1861, entertainment at the fair was limited. Coverage in the newspapers focused on the agricultural aspects of the fair, but occasionally the reporters mentioned other entertainment. A major attraction at the 1857 fair was a calliope, possibly the first one seen in Columbia since it was invented only in 1855. The calliope was described as "an organ or some kind of musical instrument, made by arranging a number of whistles (similar to those used on our [rail]cars) over a steam boiler, commencing at one end with a small one, and gradually increasing in size to the other end. These whistles all have valves with cords attached to them. The cords are all brought together and attached to keys like a piano, and is played the same way as a piano."[4] In 1858 the fair featured the Carolina Minstrels and a concert by Ellen Brennan and

also hosted Bailey's Circus.[5] In 1859 the Latta Juvenile Negro Band provided the music during the exercising of horses in the amphitheater.[6]

FREAK SHOWS

From the 1850s until the 1980s, the midway usually contained exhibits featuring human and animal oddities, frequently called the "freak" shows. One of the earliest documented exhibitions of a human oddity occurred in the Carolinas in 1738 featuring an exhibit who "was taken in a wood at Guinea; tis a female about four feet high, in every part like a woman excepting her head which nearly resembles the ape."[7] The freak shows originated in the 1840s when separate traveling shows featuring a single human oddity were brought together by enterprising entrepreneurs who combined the several attractions into a traveling show that moved from community

In 1955 the freak shows were located on the midway near Billy's Carmel Crisps.

Courtesy of the State Newspaper Photograph Archive, Richland Library

to community, eventually becoming a major attraction at fairs and carnivals across the country. In 1849 a show featuring "THE LIVING SKELTON" stopped in the Charleston area and over a period of two weeks was exhibited at the Apprentice's Library Hall on Meeting Street and at several other places.[8] The 1856 State Fair featured "The Maine Giantess, the Bearded Woman, and her wooly child, and other American curiosities."[9]

These freaks of nature or, in many cases, outright fakes became an integral part of the fair midway until the 1980s. In 1898 the Fat Lady and the Skeleton Lady had a falling out when the latter "was now rolling in luxury, with some promise of getting fat, and on account of her prosperity would not speak to her former friend the fat lady." The sideshows that year also featured a Cuban *reconcentrados* family (a family displaced by the government during the revolution of 1895–98).[10] In 1916 the fair included Elizabeth, who was "said by her exhibitors to be the smallest woman living. She is known as the Living Doll and is said to be only 32 inches in height, weighs but 27 pounds and is 23 years old."[11] By contrast, in 1951 the "Heavyweights on the State Fair Midway" featured a woman weighing 585 pounds and her male counterpart, who weighed 657 pounds.[12] A 1917 midway barker enticed fairgoers to see "Nature's Mistake," the Samar Twins: "The twins

Frequently the State Fair offered exhibits that would be considered racist today. One attraction on the midway was the African Dodger. Prior to the civil rights movement, fairs and carnivals often featured a booth where fairgoers could throw baseballs at the head of an African American protruding from a hole in a banner. The African Dip found an African American sitting on a plank above a tank of water. Fairgoers would throw balls at a target, and when they hit the bullseye it would dump the sitter into the tank. The carnival show owners encouraged the targets in both games to hurl racial insults at the white patrons, thus ensuring a long line of angry customers. It is not known how frequently these concessions were at the State Fair, but an article in the *Piney Woods Kazoo* from Jayborough, South Carolina, in 1891 recorded the presence of an African Dodger concession at the State Fair that year. The reporter highlighted his day at the fair, which included "the beautiful collection of artistic tastes and the cordial invitation to see the frog boy for 10 cents; the gaily bedecked ladies and the pop-corn man's sweet lullaby; the merry children and the blissful recollection that 'every time you hit the nigger's head you get a good seegar,' the brilliant plumage of the crazy quilt and the sensuous odor of fried liver from the open air cookeries."* In 1909 the *State* reported, "The game of 'Hit the nigger; three throws for a

nickel,' continues to draw the nickels from the pockets of the rural population."† On occasion the result of the game was not good. In 1892 the *State* recounted, "There is at the fair grounds one of those perennial 'knock-the-negro-in-the-head' arrangements. Yesterday afternoon late the business for once went contrary to the rules, and the negro stuck his head through the canvas hole just in time to get a tremendous blow in the eye from a ball hurled by a brawny-armed countryman. His left eye was literally torn from its socket by the whirling ball, and the negro fell senseless. At last accounts he was still unconscious and it was feared the blow would prove fatal."‡

These concessions remained in vogue until at least the 1950s in South Carolina. In 1949 an article in the *Florence Morning News* described an African Dip concession at the local fair: "A shivering Negro, bemasked and dripping, is the piece de non-resistance for one of the more colorful concessions. At three throws for a quarter, the more sadistically inclined Fair patrons may try to win him a chilly ducking in a tank filled with water, pointedly unheated. He sits on a breakaway board, released when your accurate throw trips the connected catch."§ The presence of these games underscore the depth of the racist views held by the white population of the era.

* "Our Visit to the State Fair," *State* (Columbia), November 19, 1891.
† "State Survey," *State* (Columbia), November 5, 1909.
‡ "Record of Fairs Broken," *State* (Columbia), November 17, 1892.
§ *Florence Morning News*, November 3, 1949, cited in Arthur H. Lewis, *Carnival* (New York: Trident Press, 1970), 202.

are Filipino boys, nine years old. They are leashed together by a cartilage of flesh. They speak and understand three different languages. They have circled the globe three times."[13] The 1928 fair featured the Royal Midget Circus "composed of ten of the world's smallest and most perfectly formed Lilliputians, ranging in stature from 19 inches to 31 inches, and each is a talented and accomplished little artist."[14]

By the 1970s the freak shows were beginning to fall out of

favor. Attendance was falling, and the heightened sensitivity of Americans forced many out of business. The managers of the freak shows indicated that advances in medical science had all but eliminated unusual births in America, and they were forced to seek oddities from overseas, especially from the Caribbean, Mexico, and South America.[15] The fair managers were also less inclined to host freak shows. In 1970 the South Carolina State Fair advertised "freak animal exhibits and a circus side show of unusual people from around the world." In 1971 one freak show manager said he was "providing them an opportunity to help themselves rather than having to sit around and take money from welfare."[16] In 1974 at the South Carolina State Fair the freak show featured all animals including a chicken with fur.[17] By 1989 the State Fair dropped the freak shows. A spokesperson for the fair said that "Fairs have gotten to be more quality forms of entertainment. The fair with us is a family affair."[18]

In 1869 the first State Fair sponsored by the State Agricultural and Mechanical Society of South Carolina at the reconstructed fairgrounds on Elmwood Avenue featured a variety of entertainment. The 1869 fair also began a practice that continued well into the twentieth century, with activities and performances in downtown venues running concurrently with the fair. The activities not associated with agriculture became known as sideshows because initially they were kept outside the fairgrounds so they would not distract from the agricultural exhibits. At the South Carolina State Fair, it was more a matter of space because the fairgrounds were not large enough to accommodate the sideshows until the fair moved to the Rosewood site in 1904.

At the 1869 fair the entertainment included a band of minstrels with Mark Read and a company of dramatists from Charleston all at downtown locations.[19] The 1869 fair also featured a "monster size St. Bernard dog." Well known for their gentle behavior, this St. Bernard endured unkind treatment before finally growling at the crowd. According to a reporter, "Each lady that viewed his comely proportions must have a poke at him with their parasol; each urchin must have a pull at his tail."[20]

Except for the abbreviated fair in 1876, during the 1870s and 1880s the fair continued to sponsor attractions that would draw visitors. On November 10, 1885, the *Abbeville Messenger* reported that a cyclorama painting of the Battle of Gettysburg was featured. In 1883 Paul Philippoteaux had completed a cyclorama painting of the Battle of Gettysburg, which was shown in Chicago and Boston. By 1885 there were at least

two dozen unauthorized copies circulating at fairs across the country. According to the National Park Service, there is no record of Philippoteaux's painting appearing in Columbia. The 300-foot-long by 18-foot-tall painting at the 1885 State Fair must have been one of the unauthorized copies. The cyclorama was a huge success, and during one day of the fair school children were admitted free to see it.

The week of the State Fair was an important economic boon to Columbia. With thousands of visitors in the city, the merchants and restaurants were busy. By the early 1880s the activities of the fair had expanded down Main Street to Gervais Street. Many of the amusements and sideshows were located on Main Street between Elmwood Avenue and Gervais Street and often spilled over onto the side streets. For the 1891 fair, "expert decorators have made things look quite fair like. Yesterday they were busy all day decorating buildings and now some eight or ten are handsomely draped."[21] In 1892 the *State* reported: "As soon as darkness fell upon the city the streets quickly became crowded to their utmost, and the pavements from Elmwood avenue to the State House were packed and almost impassable. There was a perfect crush. Main street was illuminated more brilliantly and attractively than ever before. The magnificent arches, and the four thousand lanterns swung in fantastic shapes, made a scene that was beautiful beyond description."[22]

Along with activities associated with the fair, additional venues in Columbia used the influx of visitors during fair week to provide special performances. In 1891 the Opera House hosted Milton and Dolly Nobles and their drama company as they presented three plays: *A Son of Thespis*, *From Sire to Son*, and *The Phoenix*. Each play was performed on two evenings. The city also used fair week as an opportunity to steer visitors to local places of note. Included on the list were the statehouse, the state penitentiary, the lunatic asylum, the South Carolina College, Elmwood Cemetery, the South Carolina College for Women, the Richmond and Danville railroad shops, the Columbia Female Academy, and the Winthrop Training School. The United Daughters of the

During fair week, the Opera House, located in City Hall on the corner of Main and Gervais Streets, presented special shows throughout the run of the fair. Courtesy of the Russell Maxey Photograph Collection, Richland Library

Confederacy also expanded the hours of the Confederate Relic Room located in the statehouse during fair week. Of special note in 1891 was the Columbia Canal, "which has been so long building, which is to be completed next week, and on which Columbia's hopes of a brilliant future are based."[23]

While the society sponsored the fair and supervised the agricultural, industrial, and domestic competitions, by the early twentieth century one of many carnival operators provided the activities associated with the midway and were responsible for the amusements, games of chance, sideshows, rides,

and often the food vendors. It was also in the late nineteenth century that rides began to appear on the midway. The merry-go-round and carousel were the earliest rides that appeared at fairs across the country. The first modern carousel in the United States was developed in the 1860s, becoming a popular attraction by the 1890s. The 1891 South Carolina State Fair featured a merry-go-round; its popularity has endured the advent of other more thrilling rides, and it is still a staple at the fairs in the twenty-first century.[24]

Perhaps the ride most associated with fairs is the Ferris wheel. The first Ferris wheel was constructed for the World's

Chicora College for Women, Columbia, S. C.

The structures and elaborate gardens at the Chicora College for Women were popular destinations for visitors during the fair.
Courtesy of the Richland Library Historical Collections

Columbian Exposition in Chicago in 1893 by George Ferris Jr., a thirty-three-year-old engineer from Pittsburgh. The 250-foot wheel carried thirty-six cars, each capable of holding sixty people. In the expositions' nineteen-week run, more than 1.4 million people paid fifty cents each for a twenty-minute ride described as "an indescribable sensation, that of revolving through such a vast orbit in a bird cage."[25] The ride consisted of six stops for loading and unloading six cars at a time, and one nine-minute nonstop revolution. Even though this first Ferris wheel was scrapped two years later, by the late 1890s smaller versions began to appear at amusement parks and fairs. In 1900 the first Ferris wheel appeared at the South Carolina State Fair. "There are 10 buggy-carriages on the wheel and yesterday each set was kept filled throughout the day. The ride on the Ferris wheel was a novel experience to most of the people who visited the fair yesterday, this being the first time in the history of the State fairs the wheel has been exhibited." It proved to be a popular attraction as visitors were able to take a ride "around the belt and stop at the top of the buckle" and view the city.[26] In 1900 the fairgrounds were still located on Elmwood Avenue, so riders would have enjoyed a view overlooking the river and downtown.

Taken from the Ferris wheel in 1955, this photo shows the activity around the carousel.

The twin Ferris wheels at the 1955 State Fair tower over the rest of the midway in this evening photograph.
Courtesy of the State Newspaper Photograph Archive, Richland Library

In 1906 the Orangeburg Fall Carnival featured Lunette the Flying Lady and a high-dive act featured in this postcard. The following week, these acts were at the State Fair in Columbia. Courtesy of Rodger E. Stroup

Another popular attraction was the roller coaster. The first roller coaster in the United States opened in 1884 at Coney Island in Brooklyn, New York. LaMarcus Thompson's Gravity Pleasure Switchback Railway featured cars that carried ten people over the 450-foot track at six miles per hour. In 1888 America's first looping coaster appeared, also at Coney Island. While stationary roller coasters began to appear at amusement parks in the 1890s, the first ones to appear at state fairs were in the 1910s in Iowa and Indiana. It remains unknown when the roller coaster first appeared at the State Fair, but the presence of one is mentioned in 1940.[27]

By the 1890s fairs were featuring daredevils whose acts cheated death and thrilled fairgoers of all ages. Beginning in the mid-nineteenth century, daredevils ascended in balloons and parachuted back to earth. As early as 1894 the South Carolina State Fair featured balloon ascensions and

The Kochman Hell Drivers appeared at the State Fair on a regular basis from 1945 into the mid-1970s.

Courtesy of Rodger E. Stroup

parachutists.[28] In 1897 a wedding was scheduled during a balloon ascension, with "the bridal party returning from their wedding by means of parachutes." Unfortunately, the balloonist failed to show up, and the fate of the planned wedding is unknown. However, fairgoers were treated to a high diver who leaped from a sixty-foot tower into three feet of water.[29] As late as 1973 balloon ascensions were still popular at the fair, and local television personality Joe Pinner opened the fair by ascending in a balloon.[30] In 1892 a bullfight was scheduled to take place on the infield of the racetrack. However, Col. Tilman Watson, president of the Society for the Prevention of Cruelty to Animals, intervened and asked the State Fair society to stop the inhumane activity. The society agreed, canceling the fight.[31] The 1910 fair featured Frank's Diving Horse, who jumped from a seventy-foot tower with a lady on his back into twelve feet of water. Also in 1910 Zingerilla thrilled fairgoers by climbing to the top of a spiral tower and balancing herself on a huge ball that rolled up and down a

One of the challenges in doing this history of the State Fair was locating photographs and other images. The society has some images as early as the 1930s, but nothing prior to that. Searching repositories across the state and nation have turned up a few that are included. Probably the most challenging photograph to document was one of a motordrome that is in the North Carolina State Archives collection. The image was one of many acquired from an individual who sold motorcycles and is the only image in the collection from South Carolina. In the lower right-hand corner is written in ink: "Blanchard Photo/ Columbia, S.C." When the gasoline engine became readily available in the early twentieth century, automobile and motorcycle racing began to replace horse racing at fairs. In addition to racing, the automobiles and motorcycles also performed stunts and daredevil feats such as a motorcycle riding around a circular track that was almost perpendicular to the ground. Many of these tracks were called motordromes, which could be transported from town to town.

When the North Carolina Archives acquired the photo, it researched the motorcycle on the platform and dated it to about 1915. Since these activities were common at fairs and since Columbia is the site of the South Carolina State Fair, they identified the photo as possibly taken at the South Carolina State Fair. When we found the photo, it was apparent that the building on the left in the background was not a building located on the fairgrounds. A little more sleuthing by staff at the Historic Columbia Foundation found that there was an Elks' parade and carnival in Columbia in April 1913, and one of the shows was a motorcyclist named Oscar V. Babcock, who would "loop the death trap and fly the flume twice daily."[*] According to a newspaper article, the carnival activities were on Assembly Street between Lady and Washington Streets. At the same time, a sharp-eyed archivist at the North Carolina Archives noticed that just to the left of the man's head who is sitting on the steps is a sign that reads: "Fred Brown Horseshoeing." A check of the 1910 and 1915 city directories shows Brown's business at 1109 Lady Street. Exactly where the shows for the Elks' carnival were located.

It would have been nice to find an image of the motordrome that was at the State Fair. There was a motordrome at the 1915 fair, but not this one. So this image is representative of the motorcycle daredevils who visited the South Carolina State Fair.

[*] "Preparing Plans for Elks' Parade," *State* (Columbia), April 18, 1913.

1913 Motordrome at a Columbia street fair. Courtesy of the North Carolina State Archives

President William Howard Taft in front of the grandstand at the 1909 State Fair.

Courtesy of the Russell Maxey Photograph Collection, Richland Library

narrow pathway. The 1910 fair also included an exceptional Wild West Show, a feature that was frequently a part of the fair during the early twentieth century.[32] While not during fair week, the first aviation show ever held in South Carolina took place on December 7, 1910, featuring two Curtiss airplanes. The aviators used the race track enclosure at the fairgrounds as their airfield.[33]

Horse racing was a part of almost every fair before 1900. By the 1920s flat racing gave way to harness racing, but that too was dropped in the 1920s, until the advent of the Palmetto Trials in 1952, in favor of automobile races. The first automobile race at the State Fair was in 1901 on the racetrack at the old fairgrounds on Elmwood Avenue.[34] Automobile racing became a staple at the fair until World War II; rationing of gasoline during the war led the Office of Defense Transportation to prohibit all automobile and motorcycle racing after July 10, 1942.[35] Following the war, automobile racing was replaced by stunt drivers. In 1945 Jack Kochman's Hell Drivers made their debut at the State Fair. According to the *State* newspaper, they were "a collection of automobile maniacs who drove through walls of fire, over cars, drove on two wheels, etc."[36] Kochman's Hell Drivers performed at the State Fair on numerous occasions through the mid-1970s. In addition to automobile racing, the fair also hosted motorcycle racing as early as 1913 on a flat track. In 1949 the "Thrill-O-Dome" for motorcycles was introduced at the fair. "Although the 35 foot Thrill-O-Dome with its nine foot high straightwall is the largest ever to be presented on tour, the element of danger and the requirement of daring are in no way diminished."[37]

Celebrities are always an attraction at the fair. Usually they are performers at the grandstand or state politicians attending the fair, especially during election years. The only sitting United States presidents to attend the State Fair were presidents William Howard Taft and Gerald R. Ford. On November 6, 1909, President Taft addressed a crowd of thousands from a podium in the center of the athletic field at the fairgrounds. The president's speech highlighted the importance of agriculture to the nation.[38] During the final days of the 1976 presidential campaign, President Ford made a brief visit to the State Fair where a straw poll showed him favored over Jimmy Carter, 10,115 to 6,982. Local and statewide political figures frequented the fair, especially in years when elections were held only a few weeks after the fair closed.

THE PEOPLE OF THE FAIR

The midway would not be the midway without the people who operated the rides, the hawkers who enticed fairgoers to spend a little extra to see the featured attractions, the performers who appeared in a variety of sideshows, the cooks who prepared and served the ever-expanding food offerings, and myriad people who worked behind the scenes to keep everything running smoothly. At the State Fair today the midway is operated by a company that provides all the attractions, traveling from fair to fair across the country. The society contracts with the carnival operator to provide the midway activities. However, in the early years at the State Fair, the society would engage each individual sideshow and vendor, a major undertaking that kept the fair manager busy for several weeks.

Prior to the carnival operators, the activities on the midway were usually local businesses. As early as the 1870s most of these activities were not inside the fairgrounds but located on Main Street and adjacent side streets and were not sponsored by the society but sponsored and overseen by the City of Columbia. However, there were a limited number of booths and privileges inside the fairgrounds, and from the 1870s to the early 1900s these were auctioned to the highest bidder. In 1891 there were fifteen booths available, rented for $15 to $17 each. The prime privilege auctioned was the beer concession, which sold for $320.[39] In 1896, sixteen of the twenty available booths under the racecourse grandstand sold for $11 to $13 each, the lowest price in several years.[40] During the 1890s the State Fair continued to add attractions to the midway, with each one booked independently by the fair manager. In the early twentieth century booking agents began to represent many of the individual midway attractions, and the fair

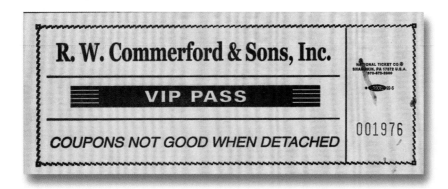

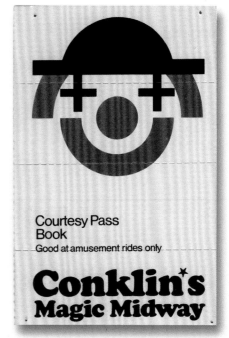

Carnival operators frequently provided dignitaries with special courtesy passes.
Courtesy of Burl R. Kennedy

manager could work with the agent to book the midway each year. By 1907 the South Atlantic Fair Association was formed to assist in scheduling the major fairs so that traveling attractions could move from one fair to another more easily.[41] By 1910 traveling carnival operators began to contract directly with fairs to provide a complete midway.

The South Carolina State Fair did not begin using a carnival operator to provide the midway shows until 1902, when the Cincinnati Carnival Company was engaged to provide the carnival component.[42] Between 1903 and 1923 the society continued to hire individual shows and activities, except when it used a carnival company in 1905 and 1906 (Barkout Carnival Show), 1911 (Johnny J. Jones Carnival Company), and 1919 (Smith Greater Shows). In 1924 the society hired

Wolfe Superior Shows as the carnival operator, and the carnival attractions have been provided by a vendor—including many of the top carnival shows in the nation—ever since.

Supplying the manpower necessary to staff the carnival at the fair was usually provided by the carnival operator. It takes a lot of people to operate the carnival at the State Fair. In 1905, when Barkout Carnival Shows provided the midway activities, the company had 170 employees who traveled with the show.[43] In the 1990s Conklin Shows estimated that they had 350 employees who traveled with the show eight months each year. In addition, they frequently hired locals at each stop. Known as a "carnie" or "carny," a term that was popularized in the early 1930s, employees constructed, operated, maintained, and tore down the rides. The carnies also operated the

In 2018, the Strates Show is the last circus or carnival operator that still moves its show by rail.
Courtesy of the Strates Show

games of chance and many of the food service facilities. They also staffed the sideshows as both performers and "barkers." The "barkers" or "talkers," as they were known, tried to entice fairgoers into their show. In 1964 Joy Purvis, owner of the "Star and Garter" revue, said about her barker, Peter Garey, "Your talker makes or breaks you. Peter is the best in the business. He works on a commission, and therefore, the more people he talks into the tent, the more he makes." Peter Garey's story is typical of many of the carnies. He started as a calliope player at the age of fourteen and on the side cleaned out the lion's cage. He then went to Hollywood and played the juvenile lead in several shows starring many top names, like Clifton Webb, Marie Wilson, and Danny Kaye. But "barking" was his first love, and after writing a musical comedy,

A RIDE TOWN

The carnival operators often focused their midway offerings depending on the most popular attraction in that community. In 1964 Hal F. Eifort, general manager of Gooding's Million Dollar Midway, said that Columbia was a "ride town." "Ride-wise this is the largest state fair in the United States this year. We have more rides—60-odd—set up here than at any state fair in the country." Other towns have reputations as "gambling" and "hanky pank" towns. Fayetteville, North Carolina, is known as the "girly show town" because of its proximity to Fort Bragg.[*]

[*] "Fair and Warmer," *State* (Columbia), October 21, 1964.

Tent Show Tonite, based on carnival life, he returned to the carnival.[44]

With the carnival shows on the road for eight or nine months a year, family life is difficult for carnies, and many bring their children with them. Moving from location to location each week prevents the children from enrolling in a local school. To ensure their children don't miss out on an education, some carnival operators and parents pool their resources and provide a school. For example, in 1994 carnival operator Conklin Magic Midway sponsored a mobile school complete with a teacher and aides. It was located behind the Dungeons and Dragons haunted house in a small trailer. Frequently the teacher had to shout to be heard above the carnival music and rowdy barkers on the midway.[45]

Moving the carnival operation from one spot to another was a major undertaking. Many of the workers traveled with the carnival from site to site, and in the early twentieth century most carnival companies moved by train. In 1943 the World of Mirth Shows transported its twenty rides, games, and midway attractions on forty railroad cars.[46] The last carnival show to arrive in Columbia by rail was the World of Mirth Shows in 1961. The following year a new operator, Allen & Allen, provided the carnival, transporting its show on fifty tractor trailer trucks.[47] With the closing of the Ringling Brothers and Barnum & Bailey Circus in 2017, the only carnival or circus troupe in the United States still using railroads as its primary carrier is the Strates Shows, a carnival operator that started in 1923.

SPECIAL EVENTS

Whenever the opportunity arose, the society took advantage of special commemorations. In 1876 many were too occupied trying to oust the Reconstruction state government to participate in the centennial of the Declaration of Independence. However, in 1925, the year before the sesquicentennial of the Declaration, the State Fair hosted a pageant celebrating the

150th anniversary of American independence. *America, the Melting Pot of Nations* was staged in the ten-thousand-seat football stadium with a cast of over one thousand mostly local actors. The production was under the direction of John T. Hall of the John B. Rogers Producing Company of Ohio. The pageant was composed of nine vignettes, six representing national events and three incidents focusing on South Carolina,

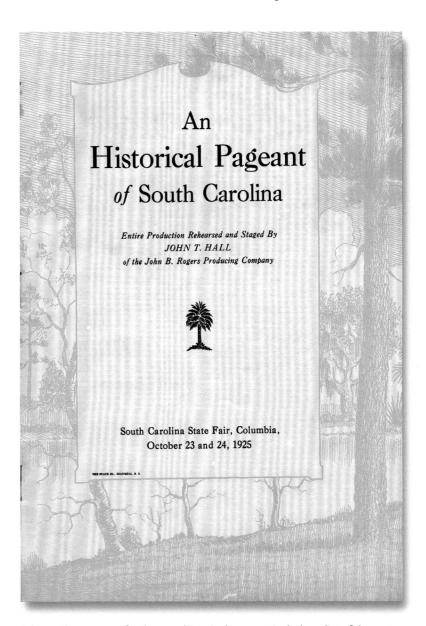

(above) The program for the 1925 historical pageant includes a list of the cast and descriptions of each act. Courtesy of Rodger E. Stroup

(opposite) Bob Hope on stage at the Bicentennial Celebration in 1976, cosponsored by the State Fair. Courtesy of the State Agricultural and Mechanical Society of South Carolina

including the ride of Emily Geiger in 1781, President George Washington's visit in 1791, and the Red Shirts campaign in 1876. Participants in the pageant represented a wide variety of organizations from the community, including groups of fifty from each area college: Columbia College, Chicora College, Benedict College, and Pacific Mills. Following opening night, the *State* reported on the pageant: "Characterized by brilliance, beauty, grace and finish, the long looked for State fair pageant was staged last night at the football stadium of the fair grounds before a host of five thousand or more people. The thousands of enthusiastic spectators followed closely the unfolding of 'The Making of America,' and the strikingly picturesque scenes of wilderness, campfire, market place and ballroom, their charm enhanced by the well executed lighting effects and the musical accompaniments of the orchestra."[48]

The 1925 pageant was so successful that the State Fair worked with the Columbia Stage Society to present an historical pageant the following year. *Hail, South Carolina* had a cast of three hundred, a chorus of three hundred, and an orchestra of forty. Performed in an area in front of the grandstand, the drama traced the state's history from its founding into the twentieth century. The first performance was staged in front of a large crowd the evening following the Carolina–Clemson football game. Following the performances at the fair, the Columbia Stage Society presented two indoor performances at the Columbia Theatre.[49] With the nation's sesquicentennial over, the presentation of pageants also ceased at the State Fair. However, in 1927 the Colored Fair presented a pageant, *The Striking of America's Hour*, featuring a cast of over one hundred that "was largely attended and was greatly enjoyed."[50]

In 1936 Columbia celebrated its sesquicentennial during the spring. The State Fair participated by sponsoring with the Elks Club the annual spring race several weeks earlier than the usual so it would coincide with the city's week-long celebration.[51] South Carolina commemorated its tricentennial in 1970, and the State Fair presented a special tricentennial fireworks performance on Friday and Saturday nights. As

A ticket for the grandstand show in 1963. The main attraction that evening was the Kochman Hell Drivers followed by a fireworks display. Courtesy of Rodger E. Stroup

the country's bicentennial approached in 1976, the State Fair presented in conjunction with the Office of the Governor and the South Carolina Bicentennial Commission *We the People: A Bicentennial Salute to America*. The program was held in Williams–Brice Stadium and featured Bob Hope, Martha Raye, Minnie Pearl, Anita Bryant, Sam Jaffe, and Betty Ackerman, with Frank Blair as the host. It was broadcast live on South Carolina ETV.[52]

FIREWORKS

In many years a fireworks display was a staple at the State Fair. As early as 1891 at both the White and Colored State Fairs, fireworks shows were held at least one night during the run of the fair.[53] In some years at the White State Fair, there was a display every night just before the fair closed. On occasion the fireworks display reproduced an historic event. For example, in 1922 the *State* newspaper headlines announced: "FAIR FIREWORKS WILL BE FEATURED." Each night would feature a different fireworks display, culminating with a reproduction of the World War I Battle of Château-Thierry.[54]

THE GRANDSTAND

When the State Fair opened in 1869 on the rebuilt fairgrounds, a grandstand was located on the racetrack a short

Special Attraction

State Fair

Gorgeous Fireworks Display

MILITARY BAND CONCERT, RIDING DUT-
TONS, AERIAL SHAWS, UP HIGH CUNNING-
HAM, TRAINED PONIES

and Several Other Free Attractions on the Race Track

On The Midway

Krause Greater Shows

The Largest Carnival Organization in the World—40 High Class Attractions for
LADIES, GENTLEMEN AND CHILDREN

FREE Gate at Night FREE

An advertisement for the 1920 fireworks display at the State Fair. Courtesy of the State Agricultural and Mechanical Society of South Carolina

distance from the main building. Originally its primary purpose was to view the horse races and stock exhibitions, but it was also used for a variety of other types of entertainment. Little mention is made of the grandstand until 1892, when a special grandstand was constructed for a major fireworks exhibition entitled "Paris, from Empire to Commune." Paris, represented by a large painting, would appear to burn each evening, followed by a spectacular pyrotechnic display. A special stage 75 × 300 feet and a grandstand seating 8,000 spectators was built for the exhibition.[55] When the fair moved to the

Rosewood Fairgrounds in 1904, a grandstand 250 feet long was constructed adjacent to the racetrack.[56] Capable of seating 2,000 spectators, the new grandstand seats "[were] carefully planned and have none of the roughness and unevenness of the old stand. The view of the track [was] exceptionally fine."[57] At the new fairgrounds a second grandstand was located at the athletic field. Moved from the old fairgrounds, this grandstand hosted the football games until the new stadium was built in 1934.

Over the years the upkeep of the grandstand was a constant drain on the society's resources. In 1926 the original grandstand burned and was replaced by a larger one capable of seating 3,000. By 1954 the grandstand was again in need of extensive repairs, forcing the society board to decide whether to repair it or replace it. For the next two years the board looked at several options and finally decided in 1956 to replace the grandstand with a new concrete structure that would seat 2,624. It was designed in sections so that two additional sections could be added later, increasing the seating capacity to 3,900.[58]

The grandstand was used not only for horse races but also automobile and motorcycle races. In addition to racing, the grandstand also became the scene of various shows and entertainment features. In 1926 the grandstand show hosted the "Parisienne Follies musical revue, featuring the Chez Paree chorus and starring 'The Lady in Bronze,' Elizabeth Graves."[59] The 1945 grandstand show celebrated the end of World War II with ten main acts displaying color, thrills, and comedy.[60]

In the past, and still true today, it is the attractions on the midway and at the grandstand that draw most people to the State Fair. The thrill of the latest ride, the opportunity to win a prize at one of the games, the challenge of eating the latest culinary concoction, and the chance to see a performance by a nationally renowned star can all be done in one visit to the State Fair. Since the society sponsored its first fair in 1869, there have been many changes to all aspects of the fair, but the excitement experienced by fairgoers over the years has not dwindled.

Gene Autry and Champion perform at the grandstand in 1960. Courtesy of the State Newspaper Photograph Archive, Richland Library

FOOD AT THE FAIR

Feeding the hordes of fairgoers has always been a challenge. At the antebellum fairs from 1840 to 1845 and again from 1856 to 1861, there was no food service provided on the fairgrounds. Nearby restaurants, taverns, and hotels served meals, and there were probably additional temporary vendors located on the streets near the fairgrounds. When the society was organized following the Civil War, the fairgrounds were rebuilt on Elmwood Avenue for the 1869 fair. Extant records don't mention a restaurant or food service on the fairgrounds. However, during the early 1870s the midway began to develop along Main Street, and food was available not only in established venues but also in temporary booths.

When the fair moved to the Rosewood Avenue location in 1904, the fairgrounds had two 150-seat restaurants that were primarily used for the noonday meal because, until 1915, the fair closed about 6 P.M., and most of the evening activities and the midway were still located on Main Street. However, by 1910 additional food vendors were located on the fairgrounds. In 1910 a fire started near the entrance, destroying the booth used by the Shandon Methodist Church "and several smaller refreshment stands near the main entrance."[61]

In addition to the restaurants on the fairgrounds and the independent food vendors, many local organizations were allowed to serve food as part of their fundraising activity.

From the early twentieth century, the organizations that sponsored food service were located to the right of the food trailers, seen in the center of this photograph. Courtesy of the State Agricultural and Mechanical Society of South Carolina

(right) The Dreher Band Booster Club operated this food concession for many years. Proceeds were used to support band activities. Courtesy of Bill and Trish Eccles

(below) Today the food concessions remain an important activity at each State Fair. Courtesy of Rodger E. Stroup

Many churches and schools, including Greene Street United Methodist Church, Dreher High School Band Booster Club, Cayce–West Columbia Lions Club, Oak Grove Civic Club, and Women in Construction, operated the "cook houses," as they were called, from the early twentieth century until 1990. Following the 1989 fair the society decided to remove the antiquated wooden structures and replace them with more sanitary and attractive food trailers. Representatives of the organizations impacted by this change were disappointed and said removal of the permanent booths was unfair. Fair manager Gary Goodman pointed out that the booths were a safety hazard to people parking on the fairgrounds and that the average lease did not cover the maintenance costs. Goodman also noted that "we're going to be putting in a new sewer system in here in about two years and the booths don't fit into the plan."[62] The society agreed to donate $5,000 to each of the groups, which they could use to help purchase a food trailer if they wanted to continue operating. However, the trailers cost between $13,000 and $15,000, and a representative of the Oak Grove Civic Club said "that would not be a practical move for any of us."[63]

Beginning with the 1990s, fair food services consisted of the independent vendors who contracted directly with the society. These were located on the independent midway—the corridor between the Rosewood Avenue entrance and the parking lot entrance. Other vendors were supplied by the carnival operator and were located on the carnival midway.

The food offerings at the State Fair have changed over the years. When the "cook houses" were run by local organizations, fairgoers could get a meal of fried chicken, mashed potatoes, vegetables, biscuit, and banana pudding. Another popular favorite was some form of barbeque. Or you could go to one of the other booths and get hot dogs and hamburgers with all the fixin's. Popular items like popcorn, cotton candy, candied apples, and elephant ears have been staples at the State Fair food booths for many years. But in recent years popular new delicacies include bacon, Oreos, or candy bars rolled in dough and deep fried. At the 2017 South Carolina State Fair, new food offerings included a "Southern Catfish Sundae" featuring hand-cut french fries, fried catfish fingerlings in a seasoned batter, a spicy remoulade sauce, and a cool white tartar sauce. If fish is not to your liking, you could try the "3B Burger" consisting of burger, bacon, and brisket with provolone served on garlic toast.

GAMES

While there is little mention of games of chance or skill at the pre–Civil War fairs, they were probably present in the city but not an official activity of the fair itself. By the 1890s, "with the State fair came a collection of about one hundred

Not all the prizes at the games were stuffed animals. In 1945 a fairgoer won this still-unopened bottle of Coca Cola at the ringtoss game. Courtesy of the South Carolina State Museum

In addition to games of skill, you could bet on the monkey races at the 1955 State Fair. Courtesy of the State Newspaper Photograph Archive, Richland Library

and fifty well trained gamblers, fakirs and sneak-thieves—all with the full intention of fleecing the visitors by a thousand and one games, alleged to be perfectly fair, and so explained to the public by them. From the very opening day of the fair they have been carrying on their business—robbery in a gentlemanly style—in various prominent places in the most open and above-board manner."[64] At the society's annual meeting in 1896, a resolution was passed directing the fair manager "to keep immoral shows and gambling games from the grounds."[65] While the newspaper accounts don't clearly describe these games, it seems that they were primarily gambling games for adult males rather than the type of games associated with the midway since the early twentieth century.

By 1910 there were games for all ages on the midway where winners received prizes rather than money: "The games are there also. To be exact, they are not games (with a capital G); for 'every number gets a prize,' so the proprietor say. Of course a prize may be a 'three-fer' cigar or a diamond tiara."[66] By 1929 gambling devices, including slot machines, were common at the State Fair. Even though gambling was illegal in South Carolina, the law frequently went unenforced. However, in 1929 Gov. John G. Richards announced, "Gambling devices will not be allowed to operate at the South Carolina State Fair. Nor will they be allowed to operate at county fairs."[67] In 1932 state constables reported to the governor that efforts were made to open gambling games on the fairgrounds, but they were shut down.[68]

The games on the midway following World War II had changed very little since the early twentieth century. Fairgoers could still try to knock over weighted milk bottles with baseballs, shoot basketballs through a standard hoop, or squeeze the trigger of a water gun to inflate a device. There was always a suspicion that the games were rigged in favor of the carnival operator. In 1967 one carnival operator

explained why the games did not need to be rigged. Benny Glass, who ran a game stand at the State Fair for over thirty years, explained the games were based on science and skill: "I mean a fellow can lose as well as win. Take my Crazy Ball. When I have a full play on all numbers—there are three lay-downs of 1-through-30—three people will always win." An inside tip suggested that you should play the busiest games because the more players there are increases your chances of winning.[69] Despite Glass's depiction of the games, two days later the Richland County Sheriff's Department arrested ten game operators and charged them with violating the laws relating to gambling devices on carnival games. The day following this crackdown other games were back operating on the midway.[70]

The midway games are an important source of income for the carnival operator. In addition to the skilled barkers enticing fairgoers to their booths, the carnival operators experimented with other incentives, such as in 1964: "Another 'modern' twist on the midway are the girls in high stockings and tights running the pitch-'til-you-win games of chance. This cheese-cake has helped business."[71] Reporting on the games at the State Fair in 1987, David L. Covington captured the essence of the midway games experienced by generations of fairgoers: "Playing the games on The State Fair Midway makes my blood rush, my palms sweat and my wallet empty—all to win a stuffed animal I don't really want."[72]

Despite the society's ongoing efforts to promote the state's agricultural and mechanical resources, the midway remained as the primary attraction for most fairgoers. While the nature of the activities has changed as technologies and cultural mores have evolved, the excitement generated along the midway continues to be the heartbeat of the State Fair.

11

The State Fair into the Twenty-first Century

"Nothing Could Be Swiner"

During the 1980s the State Fair society took to heart the recommendations in the 1981 Sparks report that outlined the need to attract an older audience with more variety in educational exhibits, grandstand shows, and amenities. The advent of theme parks in the 1960s and 1970s meant that the carnival rides on the fair's midway were now more readily available at least six months of the year and in some locales were open all year. This additional competition meant that activities and programs to attract younger fairgoers also needed to be identified and implemented.

The State Fair society also faced an identity issue. The organization that operates the fair, The State Agricultural and Mechanical Society of South Carolina, is a private nonprofit organization with no ties to state government. Most fairgoers assumed that in some way the State Fair was run by the state. To increase its visibility in the state, in the 1970s the society began to donate funds to a variety of local and statewide charitable organizations. As early as 1972 the society

When T-shirts gained popularity for advertising a variety of products and causes, the State Fair joined the bandwagon with its first staff T-shirt in the 1970s. Courtesy of Burl R. Kennedy

donated $2,000 to the Carolina–Clemson game for two $1,000 scholarships given in the names of the best offensive and defensive players in the game.[1] In 1976 the society donated $5,000 to help send the Spring Valley High School band to a national competition at the Indiana State Fair.[2] By the early 1980s the society had retired its capital debt and was able to provide donations to other organizations. In 1982 it gave $25,000 each to Clemson, the University of South Carolina, and the Riverbanks Zoo.[3]

By the 1990s the society was donating funds to a variety of organizations throughout the state. In 1998 these contributions totaled $145,000 and included $40,000 to the University of South Carolina scholarship fund, $20,000 to South Carolina Educational Television, $10,000 to Junior Achievement, $5,000 to Harvest Hope Food Bank, $3,000 to the Nurturing Center, $2,500 to Columbia Green, $2,000 to the Capitol Senior Center, $5,000 to 4-H, $5,000 to the Storm

Eye Institute at the Medical University of South Carolina, and $2,500 toward the restoration of the governor's mansion. The 1998 contributions also included $50,000 to the State Fair Scholarship Fund.[4] Initiated in 1997, the college scholarship program is for South Carolina students who attend in-state schools. Initially $40,000 was allocated for scholarships. By 2016 the society was awarding fifty scholarships of $6,000 (a total of $300,000) spread over four years as long as the student maintains a 3.0 grade point average.

Following the construction of the football stadium adjacent to the fairgrounds in 1934, the shortage of parking for football fans during the fair became an ongoing issue. From 1904, when the State Fair moved to Rosewood Avenue, until 1934, the Carolina–Clemson game was played on the fairground's field, and football fans parked free. However, when the new football stadium was built in 1934, the University of South Carolina and Clemson agreed to continue the practice of requiring football fans to purchase fair tickets for $.50 and $.25 for parking. The parking fee applied only to the Carolina–Clemson game—parking for other Carolina home games was free. In 1947 the University of South Carolina canceled the 1934 agreement. In return, the State Fair retained the $.25 parking fee for Carolina–Clemson games, but if football fans purchased a ticket to the fair, they could park free and would be given a pass enabling the holder to return to the fair after the game.[5]

In 1970, after the stables closed and the racetrack was gone, the university and the State Fair society signed a contract regarding the parking for athletic events. The university agreed to cover the expenses for the immediate development of the fairground promenade and two restrooms, developing the racetrack and infield into a suitable parking lot and fencing the property. In return for funding these improvements, the university would retain 50 percent of the net proceeds from the parking for three years, after which time they would pay the society $.50 per parking space or half of the prevailing parking fee, whichever was greater. The society agreed to a forty-year lease and allowed parking for athletic events on the midway as long as it did not conflict with other fair activities.[6]

CONGRATULATIONS 2015 SCHOLARSHIP RECIPIENTS!

These 49 recipients were chosen from over 1,200 applicants. The selection was based on academic achievement, extra-curricular activities, citizenship and need. Each recipient received a potential $6,000 scholarship to help finance their higher education. 2015 recipients will receive a total of $300,000 in scholarship awards.

SOUTH CAROLINA STATE FAIR
RIDE OF YOUR LIFE
SCHOLARSHIP PROGRAM

State Fair
Be a part of it!

For eighteen years, the South Carolina State Fair Scholarship Program has helped launch bright futures for deserving students in our state.

The list of scholarship winners following the 2015 State Fair. Courtesy of the State Agricultural and Mechanical Society of South Carolina

Between 1970 and 2010 there were several attempts to alter the parking agreement. A major point of discussion was the need to upgrade the parking lot. Negotiations revolved around the extent of the improvements and whether the society or the university would pay for them. In 1998 the society offered to take over the parking for football games, including handling all of the administrative functions. In addition, it would pay for all upkeep and improvements to the parking lot. The projected revenue for each home game was $75,000, which the society would use to maintain the facility. In return, the society would donate $50,000 each year to the university's athletic department. The university, however, decided not to change the 1970 parking agreement at that time.[7] In 2005 the society announced it would terminate the parking agreement when it expired in 2010 and would rent the spaces during the football games.[8] Over the next five years negotiations between the society and the university continued, resulting in a new agreement in 2009. Under the new agreement the university would continue to allocate parking at the newly renovated Carolina Fair Park for home football games and pay the society $900,000 per year, considerably more than the $50,000 under the 1970 agreement. Initially the society would use the new income to pay off the loans incurred for the new parking facility. Once that debt was retired, the funds would be available for other capital improvements to the fairgrounds. The new parking facility contained 4,105 spaces on forty acres, about 400 fewer spaces than before. However, the new facility featured framed grass parking spaces, paved roads, better lighting, less dust with more green space, and an extensive underground drainage system.[9]

Following the adoption of the new parking agreement, the society embarked on an ambitious master plan. Working with Populous, fairground architects and planners from Knoxville, Tennessee, it completed a master plan in late 2011. The primary objectives of the master plan were to ensure the maximum use of the grounds for the fair and football parking, to determine future building needs, and to upgrade existing building exteriors to demonstrate architectural integrity.

Because the fairgrounds are well known to South Carolinians, outside groups frequently use the fairgrounds for their activities. In the late nineteenth century, horse racing, carnivals, and football and baseball games were frequently held at the fairgrounds but were not considered a major source of income. By the late twentieth century, rental income was an important source of revenue. Through the years the fairgrounds

(opposite) **In a 2000 aerial photograph, most of the parking lot was still primarily dirt.**
Courtesy of the State Agricultural and Mechanical Society of South Carolina

Under the 2009 parking agreement with the University of South Carolina, the society upgraded the parking facility, including grass-framed parking areas, paved roads, better lighting, and expanded green spaces.

Courtesy of the State Agricultural and Mechanical Society of South Carolina

In 2015 the society constructed a new gate on Rosewood Avenue, providing a more inviting entrance and additional ticket windows.
Courtesy of the State Agricultural and Mechanical Society of South Carolina

hosted political meetings, trade shows, animal events, civic clubs, and historical pageants. The 2011 master plan strove to provide exhibit and meeting space to satisfy the increasing demand. An important factor that attracts many events is the availability of convenient, secure parking. With the completion of the new parking lot in 2009, the next step was to provide expanded meeting and exhibit facilities for both the State Fair and outside groups. The 2011 master plan provided for adding forty thousand square feet to the Cantey Building, constructing a new gate on Rosewood Avenue with additional ticket windows, improving the grandstand, and adding one portal defining the entrance into the animal area and two

shade structures on the midway. In addition, the plan called for providing architectural consistency to the varied structures by adding brick facades, trellises, brick banding, and applied graphic signage. By 2016 the Rosewood gate, the addition to the Cantey Building (named the Goodman Building after fair manager Gary Goodman) and the enhancements to the older buildings were completed. The plan also called for adding green space where possible.[10] Because the Hampton Building needed substantial work and was not air-conditioned, the society decided in 2015 to demolish it and create Hampton Plaza, a green space that provides a place for outdoor dining, tailgating, and other activities.[11]

State Fair employee identification badges. The deputy sheriff badge from the 1930s is rare because they were only issued for a short time. Courtesy of Burl R. Kennedy

Since the 1890s the society has tried to ensure that visitors can enjoy all of the activities at the fair without being concerned with their personal safety. While this issue has come to the forefront in recent years, it is not new. In 1891 Columbia's chief of police warned fairgoers that there were already many fakirs and "gentlemen of leisure" in the city "and these deft and light-fingered gentry will doubtless ply their trade to a great advantage if the proper precaution is not used."[12] In 1896 fairgoers were warned that gangs of fakirs and crooks followed the fair from Raleigh, North Carolina, to Columbia. Columbia's chief of police reported that many of these men were known to local officers, and he "instructed his men to take care of them as soon as they arrive in the city."[13] In 1911 Gov. Cole Blease, who was known for issuing pardons liberally, was criticized for pardoning several pickpockets who were caught at the State Fair.[14] During the twentieth century, newspaper accounts relate numerous instances of cash stolen from concession stands, the theft of a motor scooter, and even the pilfering of a stuffed animal from a game on the midway.[15] In 1974 the Richland County sheriff used mounted officers supplemented by mounted volunteers to patrol the parking lot at the fairgrounds to combat thefts from cars.[16]

Occasionally a fairgoer was involved in an altercation resulting in an injury. In 1957 two men got into an argument and one was stabbed by the other, resulting in serious injury. Fortunately, the victim survived.[17] However, in 2004 a fourteen-year-old student was killed following an argument and shooting just outside the gates. While the authorities did not have any evidence that the shooting was gang-related, a spokesman for the sheriff's office reported that there were other gang-related incidents inside the fairgrounds that evening.[18] Two days following the shooting, the society altered its admission rules requiring that, after 6:00 P.M., anyone younger than eighteen must be accompanied by a parent. In addition, twenty additional police officers were added to the security detail at the fair. Sheriff Leon Lott commented that the change in admission rules was "something that's needed" and predicted it would help reduce problems. Fair manager Gary Goodman said the fair would rather err on the side of caution because "we take the security of our patrons very seriously."[19] The shooting victim died five days after the incident, resulting in the arrest of a seventeen year old.[20] In 2007 the society installed metal detectors at each gate, but the resulting long lines did not cause a drop in attendance. In addition, gang colors were prohibited in the fairgrounds, and anyone refusing to adhere to the policy was not permitted to enter.[21]

While it is important to update and improve the State Fair facilities, it is also necessary to keep abreast of the latest marketing techniques. In 1986 several staff members attended a professional meeting and learned that the Minnesota State Fair began using slogans such as "Red, White and Moo" to promote the fair. The fair staff put their heads together and for the 1987 fair came up with "Nothing Could Be Swiner." After buying a hot-turquoise Hawaiian shirt from a local department store and borrowing a sixty-pound pig from a local farmer, they finally managed to get the pig dressed so that a photographer could get a picture for the logo. Fairgoers in 1987 were able to buy "fine swine" posters and T-shirts during the fair.[*] The following year fairgoers were treated to an "Udderly Fantastic" fair.[†] In addition to marketing, the fair slogans are also chosen to help with public education. In 2014, in conjunction with National Breast Cancer Awareness Month, the fair went pink to increase awareness of the need to find a cure for breast cancer. Special educational events were held, the annual Breast Cancer Run was scheduled during the fair, and a Wall of Hope was built in the Ellison Building where visitors could post a note in honor or remembrance of someone affected by breast cancer.[‡]

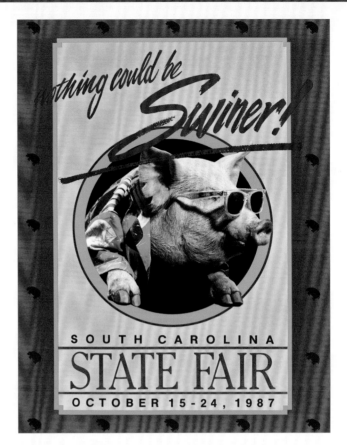

The theme for the 1987 State Fair was "Nothing Could Be Swiner."
Courtesy of Burl R. Kennedy

In 1988 State Fair general manager, Gary Goodman, poses with the model for the "Udderly Fantastic" theme.
Courtesy of the State Agricultural and Mechanical Society of South Carolina

[*] "Pig-ture This!" *State* (Columbia), September 11, 1987.
[†] "Annual Fair Celebration," *State* (Columbia), October 13, 1988.
[‡] "State Fair Going Pink to Support Breast Cancer Fight-'Celebrate the Survivors among Us,'" *State* (Columbia), October 8, 2014.

With all the activities inherent in an event like the State Fair, it is not surprising that accidents are a frequent occurrence, although the extant records of the society mention only a few accidents. Reporting of accidents in the newspapers is inconsistent, perhaps because accidents were more frequent than in today's increasingly regulated environment. The earliest documented accident occurred at the 1869 fair when William Guignard was thrown from his horse during a race and was killed.[22] In 1908 a jockey and rider were injured while on a training run when the horse got away and ran through a gap in the fence, cutting himself and severely bruising the jockey.[23] With the advent of motorized racing, accidents became more frequent. During an automobile race at the fairgrounds in 1914, local photographer W. L. Blanchard was filming the race when an accident occurred. He was able to take movie film of workers extracting the drivers from the cars as well as some still images.[24] Motorcycle racing was popular at the fairgrounds during the early twentieth century. In a 1915 article, the unbanked dirt track was blamed for a dozen automobile and motorcycle accidents, including the deaths of two motorcyclists and one rider who became permanently disabled.[25]

Between 1920 and 1980 the newspapers contain few accounts of accidents occurring at the fairgrounds. There were certainly accidents, but they apparently were not newsworthy enough to make the paper. Prior to the early 1970s there were no requirements for government inspection of rides at amusement parks. In 1972 Congress passed an act creating the Consumer Product Safety Commission and empowered it with the authority to oversee the safety of rides at both permanent and mobile amusement parks. State inspections of rides vary, but in South Carolina they are inspected by a certified inspector from the State Department of Labor, Licensing and Review. Perhaps because of more stringent government oversight, reports of accidents at the fair again appear in the media by the mid-1980s. In 1985 a suit was filed against the carnival operator Deggeller Attractions for injuries a child received while coming down a slide.[26] In 1987 three Columbia boys

were injured after they were thrown from the Music Express Ride when they tried to change seats while the ride was operating.[27] A carnival worker was killed in 2008 when he was in a secured area of the Inverter and was hit by a part of the ride.[28] In 2010 a carnival worker was electrocuted and died when he was working on the electronics on the Rainbow.[29]

Perhaps the most unusual accident at the fair occurred in 1897 when a bull apparently "committed suicide." According to the newspaper account,

> On Thursday night the bull was put in the stall on the fair grounds for the night. At some time during the night another bull managed to break loose and get out of his stall. He came near the stall in which Mr. Sanders' bull was fastened, and the latter became greatly enraged. He was tied to the building by a heavy rope which was fastened about his neck. It is supposed that he endeavored to pull loose in order to fight his enemy. At any rate when daylight came and the attendant went to see about the big fellow he found him dead in the stall. The rope around the neck had slipped and tightened until at last the animal was choked to death, having effectively hung himself.[30]

As the twenty-first century approached, the State Fair enhanced its visibility across the state by sponsoring college scholarships and using the rapidly expanding technologies available through the Internet. After years of discussions with the University of South Carolina, the perennial parking situation prevalent during football games was resolved, providing the society with a revenue stream to improve and maintain the parking lot and ultimately to assist with other capital needs. At the same time, societal changes required the society to alter its admission policy for children and youth and to increase security measures at the fair. Despite these challenges, the State Fair remains a major attraction, providing South Carolinians of every age with both educational and entertainment opportunities.

(opposite) **In 2014 even the Rocket helped promote the annual theme by wearing a pink ribbon in conjunction with National Breast Cancer Awareness Month.**
Courtesy of the State Agricultural and Mechanical Society of South Carolina

12 Exhibits and Premiums

Exhibits are an important component of any fair. The State Fair provides an opportunity for exposure to thousands of people, whether in an exhibit for a piece of artwork created by an individual, the latest tractor built by a manufacturer, or a panel exhibit touting an organization's mission. Individuals enter their creations in the competitive exhibits category, trying to win the first premium in their category and bragging rights until the next fair. Businesses and manufacturers demonstrate their merchandise and services in the commercial exhibits category, knowing that winning the first premium adds creditability to their product. Organizations seek to create an awareness of their activities.

Over the years the categories for competitive exhibitors have included agriculture, flowers, home and craft, fine art, student art, beef cattle, dairy cattle, dairy goats, sheep, small stock, swine, and youth horse. In 2014 there were 3,658 competitive exhibitors, with a total of 18,466 entries. The exhibits in the commercial category vary widely. For example, in 1952 the exhibits in the Old Steel

Building ranged from the famous Borden cow, "Elsie," to a display by a New York stock brokerage firm. Other exhibitors featured steel buildings, electric appliances, butane gas displays, mattresses, metal awnings, religious exhibits, sewing machines, hearing aids, and jewelry. Organizational exhibitors included the Cancer Society, Clemson College, the University of South Carolina, Winthrop College, the State Highway Department, the State Forestry Commission, and the State Department of Labor.[1]

Premiums or prizes for the best entry in a category have always been an important part of agricultural fairs. Whether the premium is a valuable engraved sterling silver trophy or a simple paper diploma, winners know that they have prevailed over their competitors. Winning a premium at the State Fair also added value when advertising an item for sale. In 1856 Thomas G. Bacon of Edgefield advertised a horse for sale, bragging that "he is the Stallion that took first premium at our State Fair in Columbia in November past."[2] The following year the Saluda Cotton Factory announced it had changed its name to Columbia Mills and in the same announcement

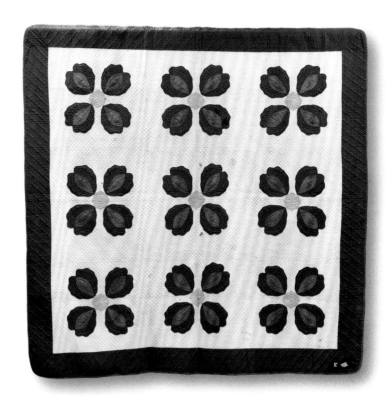

(above) **Entered in the 1897 State Fair, this quilt still has a remnant of an entry tag cherished over the years by the quilt's owners.** Courtesy of the South Carolina State Museum

(below) **The State Highway Department was a frequent exhibitor at the State Fair. This 1930 exhibit encourages safe driving.** Courtesy of the State Agricultural and Mechanical Society of South Carolina

In the early twentieth century, the State Fair began to award ribbons as premiums. Ribbons are still used today to recognize the top entries in many categories.

Courtesy of Rodger E. Stroup

boasted that their osnaburg cloth took first premium at the State Fair.[3]

Beginning with the first antebellum fairs, thousands of cash awards, trophies, medals, ribbons, diplomas, and other special premiums have been awarded. During hard economic times, it was not uncommon for the society to cancel premiums in some categories. Each year from 1869 until 2001 the society published its premium list detailing the rules for entering and listing all of the categories and premiums. In addition, the premium lists carried advertisements for local merchants as well as promoting national brands. Since 2002 the premium list is distributed electronically.

From the earliest South Carolina regional fairs in the early eighteenth century, winners received a premium in addition to the satisfaction of having the best entry. In 1751 the *South Carolina Gazette* reported that "a Role of Tobacco and 3 Gross of Pipes *to be grinn'd for by old Women*."[4] At most colonial fairs the premiums were small, and the winners were satisfied with the bragging rights. In 1795 the Agricultural Society of South Carolina was established to encourage the use of scientific farming practices. While it did not hold a statewide fair, it did award premiums for a variety of field crops and livestock. In addition, many of the local agricultural societies also offered premiums at annual membership gatherings.

Following the creation of the State Agricultural Society in 1839, the first statewide fair was held in Columbia in 1840. Premiums were awarded for entries in both livestock and field crops, but the proceedings of the society failed to indicate the nature of the premiums. However, following the 1841 fair, the premium list for horses and cattle indicated that the winners in each category received both a silver cup and a cash prize of twenty dollars.[5] Unfortunately, while the winners in all the other categories were listed, the premiums were not described. In 1842 the society's minutes indicated cash awards for field crops, with the winner receiving twenty dollars. Generally, the society prepared the premium list and

(above) **Silver items by Charleston silversmiths were frequently awarded as premiums at the antebellum State Fairs. This unusual sterling ear trumpet is an excellent example of John Ewan's work.** Courtesy of the South Carolina State Museum

(left) **The premiums awarded at both the State Fair and local fairs before the Civil War were often not ribbons or silver trophies. Catherine Parr Summer received a pair of mercury vases for a winning entry at either the State Fair or the Newberry County Fair.** Courtesy of Tom and Beth Evers

published it during the summer prior to the fair. But on occasion a special premium was awarded. For example, in 1842 Dr. Robert W. Gibbes moved that a silver cup be presented to Mary Dantzler of Spartanburg District for the splendid silk handkerchiefs she made and presented at the fair. Dr. Gibbes's motion passed unanimously. Following the 1845 fair, the society struggled to remain active. In 1846 and 1847 the society sponsored meetings featuring orations on agricultural topics, but no competitions were held.[6]

When the revived society sponsored the 1856 fair, it was at the new fairgrounds on Elmwood Avenue instead of on the statehouse grounds. The revitalized State Fair featured permanent structures, a racetrack, and more premiums. In addition to silver trophies in many categories, the cash premiums were increased. The presentation of premiums was the culmination of fair week. "Yesterday the premiums were read out, and as the name of each successful competitor was called out, he was called up and received his prize in *propria persona,* from the hands of Col. A. G. Summer, the untiring and indefatigable Secretary."[7]

Perhaps the most unusual special premium was awarded at the 1859 State Fair. A. M. Hunt of the United States Hotel commissioned a handsome silver pitcher valued at $60 ($1,625 in 2017) "as a premium for the best specimen of a native African imported in 1858 or 1859." The richly decorated pitcher featured "two Africans...represented hoeing in a field—a farm house in the distance." The reporter for the *Charleston Mercury* described the entries in this category: "two 'natives' were exhibited in front of the Amphitheatre standing erect in a buggy neatly dressed looking well and decidedly pleased. Our curiosity prompted us to examine them. The eldest, *Napoleon,* about 18 or 14 years of age, has his two upper front teeth sharpened to a point. He is a likely boy, of good countenance and feature. The other, *Isaac,* is about 11 or 12 years old. He is tattooed, but not so much as to disfigure him. Upon him the choice of the committee fell. The little fellow evidently felt gratified at the result, and held the pitcher aloft triumphantly." Unfortunately the reporter failed to identify Isaac's owner, and the whereabouts of the pitcher is unknown. The other interesting aspect of this premium is that the legal importation of slaves had ceased in 1808. However, the illegal importation of slaves continued until the eve of the Civil War, and this event reflects how poorly the law was enforced.[8]

The premium list for 1859 offered over 700 premiums allocated to the various departments: field crops, 54; domestic

The 1841 premium list indicates that the premium for the best ewe was a silver cup valued at twenty dollars. The same premium was also awarded in 1842. Courtesy of the *Charleston Courier*

1842 SILVER TROPHY

The earliest known premium from the South Carolina State Fair is a silver cup for the best Ewe won in 1842. The name of the winner was never inscribed on the cup, but it descended in the Gibbes family of Columbia. The cup is marked "Wm. Glaze." Glaze was a Columbia silversmith and jeweler who also founded and operated the Palmetto Armory on Arsenal Hill during the 1850s.

According to family tradition, this silver cup for the best ewe was won by Wade Hampton at the 1842 State Fair. It is the earliest known premium from the antebellum fair and has the maker's mark of Columbia silversmith William Glaze. Courtesy of Barry Gibbes

(left) William Summer of Pomaria won this bronze equestrian sculpture "Mare and Colt" by Christopher Fratin at either the State Fair or the Newberry County Fair in the late 1850s.
Courtesy of Tom and Beth Evers

(below) A fruit knife made in New York City by Albert Cole was a premium won by William Summer at the State Fair before 1860.
Courtesy of Tom and Beth Evers

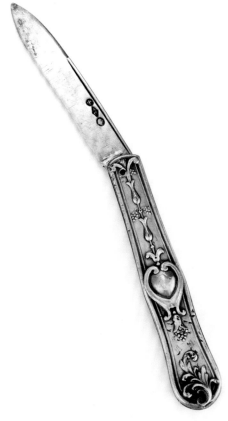

animals, 215; household department, 260; Southern manufacturing, 27; mechanical department, 108; plowing match, 6; sculpture and paintings, 23; and essays, 4. The premiums ranged from five dollars to the sixty-dollar silver trophy mentioned above. The most valuable regular premium offered by the society was thirty dollars for the best sculpture or painting. Among the intriguing premiums was ten dollars for the best South Carolina mill rock for grinding Indian corn and a silver cup valued at ten dollars for the "best case or chest of genuine medicine suitable for family use and the Southern practitioner."[9]

In 1860 in addition to the usual premium list, the Agricultural Society of South Carolina published an amendment to the premium list specifically for long staple cotton grown only on the Sea Islands. A premium of thirty dollars was offered for "the greatest production upon five acres of restored land by the aid of DOMESTIC MANURES with the mode of cultivation, the amount and kind of manure used, the preparation of the soil, period of planting, the number of times plowed and hoed, the variety of cotton, the land to be measured, and the cotton weighed and vouched for by affidavit."[10] Several additional premiums for long staple cotton were also included in the amendment. While not mentioned in the advertisement, this addition to the premium list was probably an attempt to attract lowcountry planters to participate in the State Fair in addition to their participation in the South Carolina Institute Fair based in Charleston.

When the State Agricultural and Mechanical Society of South Carolina was organized in 1869 to sponsor a statewide fair, it offered an extensive premium list. The 1869 premium list, published in the *Charleston Courier,* included $2,965 in cash prizes, 12 gold medals, and 214 pieces of silverware purchased from W. G. Whilden & Company of Charleston for over $4,000. The silverware premiums included flatware, goblets, ladles, porte-monnaies, and card cases.[11] Unlike the prewar fairs, which focused on agriculture and domestic activities, the 1869 fair's categories were expanded to feature the state's industrial products including machinery, manufactures in wood and iron, and manufactures in stone and marble. However, the premiums for agricultural entries received the largest cash awards. For example, in 1883 the society awarded $2691 in cash premiums: field crops, $300; cattle, $740; horses, $715; mules, $80; sheep, $84; goats, $43; swine, $330; poultry, $279; household, $40; and fruits and gardens, $80.[12]

While there were slight variations in categories and premiums each year, cash and medals were the primary awards. Occasionally the society would offer different awards. For example, in 1878 the winners in several categories received diplomas rather than cash or medals. The use of less expensive awards coincides with those years when the society was struggling financially. But even in lean years, stock and field crop winners received cash awards and medals.

Almost every year the premium list contains special prizes offered by organizations, businesses, and individuals. While the prewar fairs featured silver trophies in several categories,

MEDALS

For several years in the late nineteenth and early twentieth centuries the society awarded gold, silver, and bronze medals. These 1¾" medals depicted the society's logo of a palmetto tree with crops and industrial equipment at its base on the front. The reverse contained a blank space where the name of the winner and the category was inscribed. The medals were made by Peter L. Krider and Company of Philadelphia, one of the country's largest manufactures of medals.

In 1899 and 1900 Cornelia Earle won these medals at the State Fair. The 1899 bronze medal on the right was for "Water Color Painting Flowers from Copy." The 1900 silver medal on the left was for "Best Collection of China." Courtesy of Rodger E. Stroup

the postwar fairs only occasionally mention a silver trophy, and these were special prizes. For example, in 1913 the Carolina Life Insurance Company "provided three handsome silver trophy cups, for the best ten ears of corn in the boys' and men's corn clubs and the best score on points on variety of canned products in the girls' tomato clubs."[13] The trophy for the best ten ears of corn in the boys' club "stands 13 inches high, and is mounted on an ebony base 5⅓ inches high."[14] In 1915 the American Berkshire Association offered a solid silver trophy valued at fifty dollars for the best herd of Berkshires consisting of a boar and three sows.[15] By 1920 most premiums were cash or ribbons, with only a few medals awarded in special areas. For example, in 1963 the State Record Company provided a silver pitcher for the best collection of old roses at the State Fair.[16]

THE DAHLIA TROPHY

In 1929 the premium for the best dahlia was a sterling silver trophy. Each year the winner's name was engraved on the trophy, and they would get to keep it until the next fair. The hope of each entrant was to win the trophy three times, in which case they would be able to keep it permanently. The trophy was won in 1929 and 1930 by R.W. Crosland. In 1931 and 1932 it was won by Robert G. McCreight. As the State Fair approached, both men carefully tended their dahlias, hoping to win the trophy for a third time. When the judging concluded, McCreight's thirteen-inch diameter "Jane Cowl" won the day, and he became the permanent recipient of the trophy.*

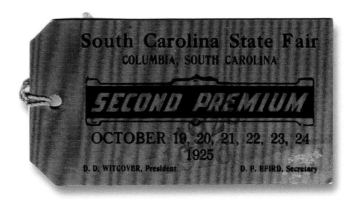

This premium tag was placed on a second place entry at the 1925 State Fair.

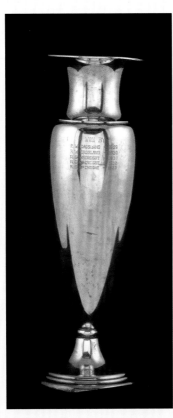

In the early 1930s the trophy for the best dahlia was sponsored by the *State* newspaper. After winning the trophy three years in a row, Robert G. McCreight was allowed to keep it permanently. Each year the name of the winner was inscribed on the trophy. Courtesy of Patricia McCreight Lunn

* George Bowman Hartness, *Gardens, Friends & Prevarications of a South Carolinian* (Canada: Integria, 2004), 25–27.

County Fairs also awarded premiums sponsored by affiliated organizations. The Farmers Cooperative Exchange sponsored this trophy for the champion Angus Cow at the 1953 Sumter County Fair. Unfortunately, the name of the winner was not inscribed on the trophy. Courtesy of Rodger E. Stroup

By 1897 the premium list published in the newspapers contained over sixty special prizes offered by businesses and organizations. Most of these special prizes were merchandise or services provided by the sponsor. In addition to paying for an advertisement in the premium list, the special prize provided the merchant more exposure to fairgoers interested in his merchandise or services. For example, in 1915 the American Agricultural & Chemical Company awarded one ton of blood and bone 8-3-3 fertilizer for the best display of grain, while Lorick & Lowrance of Columbia gave the second-best display of grain a one-horse Oliver plow.[17] In 1920 W. A. Guignard provided the winner of the largest number of premiums in the field crop department with a registered Berkshire or Poland China pig, while the second-place winner received two thousand bricks.[18] In 1927 S. B. McMaster, Inc. provided a forty-five-dollar L. C. Smith shotgun to the girl or boy making and showing the heaviest ear of corn when dried.[19] At the depth of the Depression, the 1933 premium list was shorter and featured only cash awards and ribbons with no special prizes listed.

Silver trophies have always been prized as premiums at the State Fair. Four Oaks Farm in Lexington won these trophies in 1951 and 1955 for their grand champion Berkshire hogs. Courtesy of Four Oaks Farm

OLD LADIES' WORK

Following World War I, the State Fair began to offer additional premiums in many departments. Among these was a category in the woman's department for "Old Ladies' Work." The qualifier stated that "competitors in this work must be over seventy years of age at the time of making article for exhibit."* Presumably men were not permitted to enter this category. Extant premium lists carry this category from 1922 to 1942. By the 1980s the category was changed to "Work of Adults—Seventy and Over." This modification portrays once again how the State Fair adapts to changes in our society.

Premium List South Carolina State Fair Day and Night 1927 (Columbia, South Carolina: State Agricultural and Mechanical Society of South Carolina, 1927), 71.

STATE FAIR 69

BOOK 50—OLD LADIES' WORK

Competitors in this work must be over seventy years of age at the time of making article for exhibit

Class No.		1st	2nd
710.	Knit Bedspread	$ 2.00	$1.00
711.	Crocheted Bedspread	2.00	1.00
712.	Afghan	2.00	1.00
713.	Quilt Patchwork	2.00	1.00
714.	Silk Quilt	2.00	1.00
715.	Sweater	2.00	1.00
716.	Socks	1.00	.50
717.	Cotton or Linen Embroidery	1.00	.50
718.	Silk Embroidery	1.00	.50
719.	Tatting	1.00	.50

The 1926 premium list contains a category for "Old Ladies' Work."
Courtesy of the State Agricultural and Mechanical Society of South Carolina

Each year the State Fair has thousands of entries, each striving to win a trophy, ribbon, or other premium symbolizing the best entry in that category. While the early fairs featured the agricultural and mechanical categories, as the number of competitive categories increased over the years, more and more people were drawn to the fair as a way to display their talents. Certainly, winning is important, as seen by competitors trying to win the same premium, usually a silver trophy, for several consecutive years, which allowed them to keep it permanently. The monetary value of the premium was inconsequential to many competitors, but its symbolism was the important thing. Nobody entered the competitive exhibits expecting to gain financially but rather to gain recognition as—at least for that year—the best in that category.

13 Icons of the State Fair

"_____, meet your mother at the rocket"

Each generation of fairgoers remembers an aspect of the State Fair that symbolizes their visit. In the antebellum years, all the activity was on the grounds of the old statehouse. After the Civil War, the annual horse races were a mainstay of each year's fair. From the 1870s until 1914, the midway and many of the rides were on Main Street between Elmwood Avenue and Gervais Street in the evening after the fair closed. Shortly after the fairgrounds moved to Assembly Street, the erection of the steel building dominated the fairgrounds until it was destroyed by a fire in 1966. The racetrack featured racing by horses, automobiles, and motorcycles from 1904 to 1969. Each winter from 1890 to 1969, the stables housed some of the nation's top thoroughbred horses. The grandstand performances, frequently featuring nationally prominent stars, were one reason many people came to the fair. Undoubtedly the most popular memory of fairgoers during the first half of the twentieth century was the annual Carolina–Clemson game played on Big Thursday from 1896 to 1959.

BIG THURSDAY

For over a half-century Big Thursday, featuring the annual football game between South Carolina and Clemson, was synonymous with the State Fair. Even before football became the focus on Thursday of fair week, headlines in the *State* newspaper in 1893 announced "This Is Big Thursday," and there was not even a Carolina–Clemson game that year.[1] Big Thursday was designated a state holiday by the General Assembly in 1906 not because of the football contest but rather because Thursday was always the busiest day of fair week and included the state ball on Thursday night.[2] From 1896 to 1959 the Carolina–Clemson game was played on Thursday of fair week except for 1903 to 1909, when the schools agreed not to play following a riot after the 1902 game. The riot was instigated following Carolina's 12–6 victory when students "borrowed" from a merchant on Main Street "a big transparency in his store window depicting a gamecock crowing over a poor, bedraggled tiger." The Carolina students began parading the transparency up and down the street despite comments from the Clemson cadets that it would be poor judgment to do so; the local police agreed, but the students did it anyway. After the Clemson military parade, the cadets were dismissed at the statehouse and they headed to the Horseshoe on the Carolina campus with sabers and bayonets. About thirty Carolina students armed with rifles and pistols crouched behind hastily built barricades. Officials from both schools arrived before anyone was hurt, but the series was suspended until 1909.[3] The only other year the game was not played in conjunction with the fair was 1918, when the State Fair was canceled because of the influenza epidemic. However, the game took place at Davis Field, Carolina's stadium, on Thursday of "fair" week.

Following the resumption of the Carolina–Clemson game in 1909, Big Thursday became a highlight of the fair, drawing large crowds each year. Even before the advent of today's modern highways, fans from across the state could attend without having to spend a night in Columbia. In 1914 the *State* reported that it was possible to ride a train to Columbia, attend the football game, and catch a train home that evening to almost anywhere in the state.[4] Even the U.S. Post Office recognized the importance of Big Thursday. In 1916 they notified Columbians that there would be no mail delivery after 4:00 P.M., "in view of the fact that this is the 'big' day of the fair, and it was decided to allow the carriers to have the afternoon off."[5]

The 1896 contest between Carolina and Clemson was not the first football game at the State Fair. In 1891 Trinity College (now Duke University) beat Furman 96–0.[6] Until the State Fair moved to the current fairgrounds on Rosewood Avenue, the games were played on the infield of the racetrack at the old fairgrounds on Elmwood Avenue. When the fair moved to Rosewood Avenue, the games were played in the stadium located at the corner of Rosewood Avenue and Bluff Road until the forerunner of Williams–Brice Stadium was constructed in 1934. While the Carolina–Clemson game was always the premier football game during fair week, on many occasions there were other games during the week. In 1915 there were three football games during the fair.[7]

During the 1950s legendary Clemson football coach Frank Howard wanted to end the Big Thursday game because he felt South Carolina had a home field advantage every year. As early as 1948 rumors circulated that the two schools were considering ending the Big Thursday contest and going to a home and home series. In 1948 former and later again Speaker of the State House of Representative Solomon Blatt wrote a letter to University of South Carolina president Norman Smith and Clemson president R. F. Poole: "I have heard it rumored that an effort is being made to change the Carolina–Clemson football game from Fair Week to the end of November, the game to be one year at Clemson and the other year at Columbia." Blatt went on "I hope this rumor is not correct." Blatt pointed out that Clemson did not have the restaurants or hotels to accommodate all those wanting to see the game. He also pointed out that the stadium in Columbia was being expanded to hold two or three thousand more people. Blatt concluded,

By 1928 the State Fair and the annual Carolina–Clemson game on Big Thursday, as the program states, was a "South Carolina Football Classic."
Courtesy of the University of South Carolina Archives

The program and a ticket for the final Big Thursday game in 1959.
Courtesy of Burl R. Kennedy

"Any effort to transfer this game from Columbia will cause a howl in this State. I am calling this to your attention with the hope that those of us interested in the two institutions can in the future go to Columbia and see the game played there."[8] Speaker Blatt's letter may have slowed down the demise of Big Thursday game. However, Frank Howard worked with South Carolina coach Rex Enright during the 1950s, and the two schools agreed that 1959 would be the last game at the State Fair and every other year the game would be at Clemson. After fifty-eight games on Big Thursday, the final tally was 34–21–3 in favor of Clemson.[9] However, Big Thursday continued as a state holiday until 1966, when the General Assembly passed legislation ending its designation as a state holiday.

Even though the annual Carolina–Clemson game during fair week created traffic nightmares before and after the game, the State Fair was reluctant to give up football during the fair. In 1960 the University of South Carolina freshmen team and Clemson freshmen team met on Thursday in what was called "Little Big Thursday." Two days later, on Saturday, the University of South Carolina played the University of North Carolina in their regularly scheduled game.[10] In 1961 the Gamecock and Tiger freshmen teams met on Thursday during fair week, but with little fanfare. There was no mention of Little Big Thursday for the 1961 game between the freshmen teams.[11] Since the demise of Big Thursday, the Gamecocks frequently have football games on a Saturday during the fair, and the media frequently reminds fans to leave early and be patient in traffic. Reflecting on the importance of Big Thursday the *State* noted in 1958, "Perhaps Big Thursday, more than anything else, makes the South Carolina

Clemson fans—presumably, because nobody is wearing any distinctive clothing—tear down the goalposts following the Tigers 27–0 win in the last Big Thursday game. Courtesy of the State Newspaper Photograph Archive, Richland Library

Fair unique. Other states have more elaborate exhibits, but few surpass our own affair in drawing power. For Columbia, Big Thursday means the biggest crowds of the year, the most excitement, and the most drama."[12]

The tradition of a football game on Thursday during fair week also became a signature part of the Colored State Fair. By the early 1920s a football game was played featuring teams from local African American colleges including Allen, the State Agricultural and Mechanical College (South Carolina State), Benedict, and Claflin.

THE ROCKET

On October 17, 1963, the U.S. Air Force presented to the City of Columbia a medium-range Jupiter ballistic missile in a

For over sixty years the Carolina–Clemson game on Big Thursday and the State Fair were synonymous. Until 1947 football fans had to purchase a ticket to the fair and enter the stadium through the fairgrounds. Reporters for the local papers furthered this image. In 1947 a Spartanburg man lost a diamond ring worth $3,000 ($32,300 in 2016 dollars) while attending the football game. He told reporters he had the 3¾ carat ring in an envelope in his inside coat pocket. During the game he took his coat off and when he got back to Spartanburg he realized the ring was gone. Even though this happened in the stadium during the football game, the paper headlines read: "$3,000 Ring Lost at the State Fair."*

*"$3,000 Ring Lost at the State Fair," *State* (Columbia), October 25, 1947.

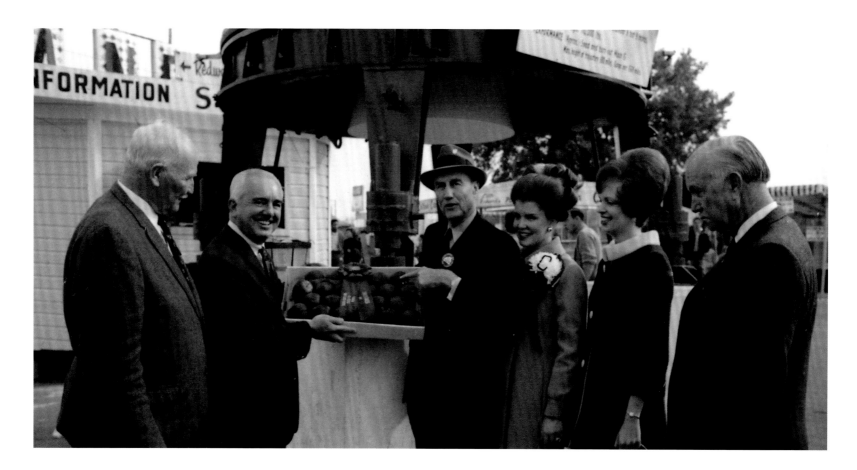

ceremony at the fairgrounds. The Jupiter was the first inter-mediate-range ballistic missile launched by the United States in 1958 and, according to Maj. Gen. Emmett B. Cassidy, commander of the Mobile, Alabama, Material Area, "stood a lonely vigil for the North Atlantic Treaty Organization in Italy and Turkey from July 1960 to the early spring of 1963." After the missile was retired from service in mid-1963, General Cassidy said it was donated to the city to "stand as a monument to deterrence, adding prestige to the glorious military traditions of South Carolina that were born with men like Gadsden, Pickens, and Sumter, and have been multiplied thousands of times by your men whenever this nation has fought for its freedom." The missile was accepted for the city by Mayor Pro-Tem Hyman Rubin and Councilman William C. Ouzts. The Jupiter arrived on a dolly-type trailer after being flown on a C-124 from Huntsville, Alabama, where it had been manufactured, to Shaw Air Force Base in Sumter. According to an article in the *State,* the missile would be erected in an upright position, and "a technician is being sent to Columbia to supervise the job."[13]

(top) The Rocket has served as a background for thousands of photographs. In 1969 Sen. Strom Thurmond was presented prize-winning apples to take as a gift to President Richard Nixon by Dr. William Cantey, then president of the society. On the far left is society past president Frank Hampton. To Senator Thurmond's right is Mrs. Thurmond. Courtesy of the State Newspaper Photograph Archive, Richland Library

(bottom) When this commemorative envelope was released in 1988, the Rocket was already a major symbol of the State Fair. Courtesy of Rodger E. Stroup

(opposite) In 2015 the Rocket was raised twelve feet and placed on a new base so it would be more visible around the fairgrounds. Courtesy of the State Agricultural and Mechanical Society of South Carolina

However, it would be exactly six years to the day before "the Rocket," as it became known in Columbia, would finally be installed at the fairgrounds. For six years the missile sat on the trailer at the fairgrounds near the corner of Rosewood Drive and Assembly Street. The impetus to have the missile finally erected came from the society's retiring president, Frank Hampton. In early September a detail from Fort Jackson painted the missile, and the plan was to display it on its trailer or erect it upright if a plan could be developed that would ensure its safe installation.[14] Hampton contacted several local contractors, but they all declined to undertake the project on such short notice. The Thursday before the fair opened, Hampton contacted Bill Law of W. P. Law, Inc., who agreed to help. Law later recalled:

> That Friday I went out through the weeds, looked and measured, figured the wind load (the weight was negligible), sketched the required concrete, and even went to see Lewis Ashford. Lewis agreed to take Saturday off from Palmetto Quarries and pour the footings. He got his material together Friday for forms, etc., while my shop was making the anchor bolts and base plates, and the State Fair labor was rolling the Juno [he meant Jupiter] out of the weeds and cleaning it up for painting, and Mr. Hampton was arranging for an Army Engineer Company at Ft. Jackson to erect it and paint it as a field exercise. And Monday I picked up steel and had our shop make the hold-down plate and the long tie-down rods. Tuesday, the thing was up, standing 7 stories tall, and painting was begun. The painting was finished Wednesday and the fair opened on Thursday with wet paint shining.

Since the original painting was done in early September, the painting that Law recalls was probably for the underside and where the missile was sitting on the trailer. Law recalled that the bill for material from Columbia Supply was about $350, and Ashford's bill for the concrete, labor, and plywood was about the same.[15]

Initially the missile did not receive a lot of attention. The *State* newspaper only had a photo and a short cutline the day following its completion.[16] Since its installation inside the Rosewood Drive gate in 1969, the Rocket has been an iconic symbol of the fair. Not long after it was installed, the public address system announcer began using it as the site for reuniting lost fairgoers. For over forty-five years, parents have been summoned to the Rocket to claim lost children, while older children have been asked to "meet your mother at the Rocket."

In 2015 the Rocket received a lift—that is, it was raised twelve feet and installed on a new foundation. Gary Goodman, the manager of the fair since 1984, remarked, "Trees have grown up all around the Rocket and it became very hard to meet your mother at the Rocket when you couldn't see it or find it. People of my generation, we all remember the Rocket as a meeting place. We're doing this so the next generation can remember it the way we did." Just as with the initial installation in 1969, the raising of the Rocket was a cooperative effort with the help of the University of South Carolina School of Engineering and several Columbia businesses.[17]

LITTLE RED SCHOOLHOUSE

In 1962 the State Fair Association purchased and moved to the fairgrounds the "Little Red Schoolhouse." Built in 1867 and owned and operated by Ellen Janney as a private school in her backyard at 1410 Blanding Street, the structure was used as the headquarters for the first annual Senior Citizens Day at the fair.[18] For several years the Little Red Schoolhouse welcomed seniors to the fair. On September 23, 1983, it was moved to Riverfront Park.[19]

GIRLIE SHOWS

From the late nineteenth century until 1975, the "girlie shows" were a mainstay of the midway at the South Carolina State Fair. When Frank Hampton, a former president of the society, was asked in 1974 what his favorite midway attraction was when he was growing up, he replied with a twinkle in his eye, "Girl shows."[20] The term "girlie show" or "hootchy-kootchy

By the middle of the twentieth century, the girlie show was located in the northwest corner of the fairgrounds.
The white building to the right of the Spook Rides housed the girlie show in this 1955 photograph.
Courtesy of the State Newspaper Photograph Archive, Richland Library

show" referred to the exotic dancers and burlesque shows that became part of the traveling midway.

Nobody knows when the first girlie show appeared at a regional or state fair. A report from the Michigan Department of Agriculture in 1882 refers to a "'Circassian Beauty' that captivating syren, who has infested agricultural fairs" since the early 1800s.[21] However, it was not until the late nineteenth century that female dancers began to appear at fairs on a regular basis. At the 1893 World's Columbian Exposition

in Chicago, the Algerian and Egyptian dancing girls performing the *dance du ventre* (belly dance) were a major attraction. Although the dancers "wore baggy trousers, or multiple petticoats, bloomers and stockings, and loose, midriff-length tops," their appeal centered on the dance that "involved an energetic series of spins, shoulder and hip shimmies, hip locks, and pirouettes." This type of dance became known as the "hootchy-kootchy" and within a few years began to appear at state and county fairs across the country. The star

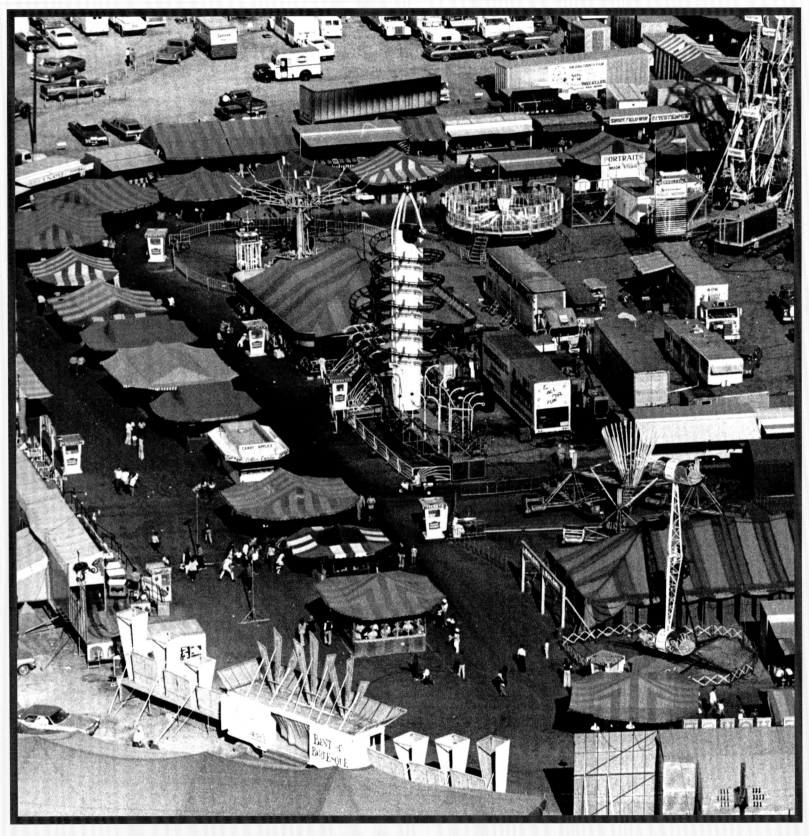

In 1974, the year before the end of the girlie shows at the State Fair, they were still located in the northwest corner. In this photograph the "Best of Burlesque" sign is on the trailer.

of the show was "Little Egypt."[22] Following the 1893 World's Fair, state and regional fairs began featuring "Little Egypt," who had emerged from nowhere and became the "putative grandmother of modern striptease."[23] In 1901 the Anderson County Fair featured one of the many "Little Egypt" dancers crisscrossing the country, capitalizing on the success of the 1893 World's Fair.[24]

The earliest girlie shows at the South Carolina State Fair appeared before the midway and carnival activities permanently moved to the fairgrounds in 1915. Prior to 1915, Main Street housed rides, musical reviews, and family-oriented activities, while the side streets featured the seamier side of the carnival, including the girlie shows. In 1909 Richard Carroll, who ran the Colored State Fair, "protested against the indecent exhibitions by white women, in tent shows open to both races."[25] In 1910 a local reporter noted, "All the old familiar shows are on the midway this year. The Oriental dancers,... are probably Bowery belles."[26]

While there were occasional negative references to the presence of the girlie shows, they became an accepted part of the fair from the 1910s until 1975. In 1914 the society management "has taken care to see that there will be nothing offensive or objectionable to anyone on the midway at the fair grounds next week and they feel confident that everyone who visits the State Fair, October 26–30, will enjoy the gay midway."[27] In 1920 the manager of Krause Greater Shows guaranteed "each and every show to be high class, moral and refined, with the absence of the lewd and immoral. Dancing girl slums and '49 camps' [a girlie show with a western theme] are noticeable by their absence."[28] The society board only addressed this issue at one meeting during this time. At an executive committee meeting in January 1939, the committee received "Petitions and protests...from several sources complaining of indecent girl shows and the sale of intoxicating liquors on the Grounds. A full and free discussion was entered into. The Secretary was instructed to handle this matter as diplomatically as possible, state that the Executive Committee stood for higher things of this life and that our Fairs would be pitched upon the highest

possible plane. It was suggested that the Secretary refrain from any unnecessary detail."[29] Neither the society minutes nor the local media contain any additional details, and the shows continued.

Following World War II, the local newspapers began to publish features about the girlie shows. On November 22, 1948, a reporter for the State recounted his interview with several of the performers. The featured dancer was Doree, who explained that she was a ballet dancer, but several of the other dancers described the style as a fan dance. In 1951 a reporter interviewed fairgoers asking them about their plans for their visit. One couple from Batesburg replied that they came "to see the Hereford show and the girlie show."[30] During the late 1960s the nature of the shows began changing from exotic dancers to burlesque. In 1966 the Star and Garter show featured an exotic dancer. Joy Midnight's performance included a dance where she "moves as if she had no bones, bouncing, writhing and keeping perfect time with the music" while she seductively removed her costume, ending with a small bikini before she left the stage "leaving her audience apparently feeling they've gotten their dollar's worth and more from her performance."[31] The headliner in 1973 was Sandy O'Hara, a former Miss Armed Forces Pinup Girl of the Year, a title previously held by Marilyn Monroe and Betty Grable. O'Hara was back in 1975 in a show entitled "The Best of Burlesque," which had the format "of a variety show, with comedy skits, Broadway-style dances, musical selections and the production strip as the finale." According to the performers in the show, their audiences were composed equally of men and women. "The Best of Burlesque" was the finale of the girlie shows at the State Fair.[32]

But the State Fair was not the only venue in South Carolina for the girlie shows. Many of the county and regional fairs across the state also featured a midway with girlie shows. While state law clearly defined illegal nudity, it was generally up to the local law enforcement agency to enforce the law, and that varied from place to place. Perhaps the county fair with the reputation for the "best" girlie shows was in Newberry. Bill McDonald, a well-known columnist for the State, recounted

At the 1955 State Fair a barker entices the crowds to buy a ticket to the "Club 18 Burlesque" show.
Courtesy of the State Newspaper Photograph Archive, Richland Library

a visit to the Newberry County Fair in 1972 hoping to see Delilah, Queen of the Temptresses. On arriving at the fair, he found nothing of the sort, and when he questioned a midway employee he was told, "You got the wrong fair buddy. We don't have that kind of thing around here. This here's a family fair."[33] A week later Bill got a message from a Newberry City councilman, who told him, "You hit the Newberry County Fair on 'Kiddies Day.' Bring a photographer over Saturday night and we'll show you a hootchie-kootchie show."[34] A few days later Bill got a call from a University of South Carolina student who said, "You got the wrong information about the Newberry County Fair. Me and two of my buddies went last night, and we saw about the most provocative girlie shows imaginable."[35] Perhaps kiddie day was when the local sheriff visited.

But not all the local fairs had the same "provocative" shows as Newberry. Writing years later, a sixteen-year-old girl recounted her visit in the 1950s to the Eastern Carolina Agricultural Fair in Florence. "I was about 16 years old and my date 17, but the bored ticket-taker acted like he thought we were grownups and let us in. We huddled like criminals in the dimly-lit tent but when the show started there wasn't much to see. A plump lady wearing lots of greasepaint, pink feathers, silver sequins and high-heel slippers did a modified burlesque number, flung her feather boa into the 'crowd' (all five of us), then ducked behind a curtain and tossed out what was supposedly the rest of her costume."[36]

Another venue for the girlie shows in the state was the Colored State Fair. Following redemption of the state from Reconstruction, the Jim Crow laws imposed on African Americans saw them all but shut out of the fair. The first Colored State Fair was held in 1889. It is not certain when the girlie shows first appeared at the Colored State Fair, but a 1931 advertisement lists a Hawaiian Revue on the midway.[37] Another advertisement in 1961 promotes "The New Orleans Revue," and one in 1963 highlights "A Glamourous Girl Revue."[38] It is interesting that at the colored fair, the girlie shows were advertised as revues.

What led to the disappearance of the girlie shows at the State Fair? The United States had just come through the "free love" 1960s. Pornography came out of the back room and was readily available. In 1954 the State Theatre in Columbia was presenting adult movies, as noted by an ad in the local newspaper for the "Striporama" featuring the movie "Cinderella's Love Lesson."[39] Lamenting the changes at the State Fair, a reporter noted in 1966 that "the Girlie Show remains about the same. I think it has been said that the fashions worn by girls' today are a lot more suggestive than the costumes worn in the girlie shows."[40] In 1975 the general manager of the Southeastern Fair in Atlanta said that "the topless nightclubs have caused the 'hootchie kootchie' dancers in the Star and Garter Review to lose some of their glamor."[41] By the mid-1970s X-rated movies were available on home video recorders. Popular magazines like *Playboy* and *Penthouse* were available through subscriptions, at newsstands, and from magazine retailers across the country. The continually skimpier bikinis at the beach and at local pools also made the midway shows seem tame. All these changes caused attendance at the girlie shows to decline. One carnival operator reported that between 1969 and 1974, he lost $50,000 on the girlie shows. Carnival operators quickly learned they could make more money on a high-capacity ride than on a sideshow.[42]

4-H CLUBS

Since the mid-1910s a major component of each State Fair has been the participation and competition of 4-H Clubs and students from across the state. Until the early twentieth century there were no premiums offered at the South Carolina State Fair specifically for children or youth. However, they were not prohibited from entering in the regular categories. For example, the 1878 premium list does not contain any awards for children or youth. By 1915 there were special categories and premiums for boys, girls, and children.

At the end of the nineteenth century many young people were moving from rural areas to the cities. Rather than taking

At the 1930 State Fair, the 4-H Club exhibit featured the "The 4-H Club Beauty Shoppe."

Courtesy of the State Agricultural and Mechanical Society of South Carolina

over the family farms, they were seeking other career paths. In response to this migration, several separate movements across the country began to focus on educating rural youth to help keep them in the agricultural arena. In 1904 Corn Clubs were founded in Indiana, Iowa, and Georgia. These clubs sponsored contests with prizes. Within a few years the Corn Clubs began to hold their contests at state fairs. In 1905 Nebraska founded the Nebraska Boys Agricultural Association and the Nebraska Girls Domestic Science Association. The boy's association exhibited corn, garden products, and livestock, while the girl's association exhibited sewing, handwork, and cooking. From 1905 to 1914 similar clubs were started in nearly all the states, including South Carolina.[43]

The passage of the Smith–Lever Act in 1914 laid the groundwork that enabled the youth agricultural clubs to thrive. Prior to the passage of the Smith–Lever Act, Clemson already had an extension program known as the "Clemson Model." It was adopted by other states, and many of the provisions in the act were based on Clemson's program. The act established the cooperative extension services at land grant colleges and provided the land grant institutions, including Clemson University, the funding to establish innovative research and vital educational programs for youth and adults. Following the passage of the Smith–Lever Act, many of the youth agricultural programs formed the national 4-H organization, and by 1924 it adopted the familiar green, four-leaf clover emblem with a white H on each leaf standing for head, heart, hands, and health.

In South Carolina the first Boys' Corn Club was organized in Marlboro County in 1908 by A. L. Easterling, the

The 4-H Club exhibit in 1930 showcased the work of the students. Courtesy of the State Agricultural and Mechanical Society of South Carolina.

superintendent of the county schools. In 1910 Marie Cromer, an Aiken County school teacher, following guidelines provided by the U.S. Department of Agriculture, organized the first Girls' Tomato Canning Club in the country. In 1911 Dora D. Walker of Barnwell County was appointed the "County Tomato Club Agent," the first county home demonstration agent in the world. Beginning in 1910 the State Fair began awarding premiums for entries by children. The 1920 premium list includes cash premiums for boys in corn, peanuts, and pigs; for girls in household, needle, and fancy work; and for children under age fourteen in the fine art department. By 1927 separate premiums were offered for youth entries in many categories. By the mid-1930s there were thirty thousand 4-H Club members across South Carolina, approximately one-third of whom were African American.[44]

Extension services were available to African American farmers prior to the opening of Clemson College and the development of the Clemson Extension Service. In 1890 Congress passed the second Morrill Act, extending the status of land grant institution to primarily African American colleges in the former Southern states whose white land grant colleges refused admission to African Americans. South Carolina State College was designated as the African American Land Grant institution in the state and began offering services to African American farmers. With the passage of the Smith–Lever Act in 1914, Clemson entered into an agreement with South Carolina State College to provide the funds for six cooperative extension service agents to assist African American farmers. In addition to assisting farmers, other cooperative extension service employees at South Carolina

In this late 1960s photograph, Ralph Riley from Saluda, South Carolina, poses with his trophy, the Model Holstein-Friesian Cow. Presenting the trophy is Gordon Newton, president of the South Carolina Holstein Association. Courtesy of Ralph Nichols Riley

State organized and supported various community groups, including 4-H Clubs. By the early 1920s African American 4-H students were competing for premiums at the Colored State Fair. During segregation, the funding available for African American farmers was well below the amount provided for white farmers. Likewise, the funds for the African American 4-H program were also inadequate to provide the resources necessary for them to match the white 4-H Clubs. Until 1965, following the passage of the Civil Rights Act of 1964, the extension services were separate, and the activities of the 4-H Clubs remained segregated.[45]

The passage of the Civil Rights Act of 1964 brought change to both the Clemson Extension Service and the 4-H Clubs. In June 1965 Clemson president Robert C. Edwards announced that by the end of the year all programs and committees would be integrated, including the 4-H programs. He pointed out that over sixty-eight thousand students participated in 4-H Clubs across the state, 52 percent of whom were white; under the new legislation, all activities would be integrated. The separate two white and one African American camps would not operate in 1965, and their future would be determined at a later date. All local 4-H Clubs would be integrated, and since most of them were based in public schools, they would follow school attendance patterns.[46] However, in practice it appears that the African American 4-H students continued to compete at the Colored State Fair until its demise in 1969. Contemporary accounts report that the first fully integrated State Fair was in 1971.

None of the State Fair icons remain from the society's first fair in 1869, and the only one still extant today, the Rocket, is the most recent icon. Other icons of different eras were discussed elsewhere, such as the state ball, horse racing, the Colored State Fair, and the freak shows. Each in their own way are representative of the era in which they thrived, and each reinforces how the State Fair reflects the cultural and social norms of the day.

Conclusion

Most of the current sources on the history of fairs in the United States cite a 1765 agricultural fair in Windsor, Nova Scotia, as the earliest fair in North America. Other sources mention a fair in Pittsfield, Massachusetts, in 1807 as the first fair in the United States. However, primary sources that I discovered while researching this book report agricultural fairs in lowcountry South Carolina as early as the 1720s. These rural fairs, held in both the spring and fall, were organized by local merchants who operated stores in Dorchester, Ashley Ferry, and Childsbury. While selling and trading enslaved persons, cattle, horses, provisions, and other merchandise was the initial purpose for fairs, these gatherings took on the character of later fairs as people came from great distances and stayed for all four days, competed in a variety of activities for prizes, and visited with neighbors.

Today's South Carolina State Fair traces its origin to early-nineteenth-century county and regional fairs held across the state. During the late 1830s there was widespread interest in establishing a statewide fair. The State Agricultural

Society was founded in 1839 expressly to host a State Fair in Columbia, the capital city located in the center of the state. While the fairs held between 1840 and 1845 were deemed successful, they failed to attract many participants from beyond fifty miles primarily due to the difficulty in transporting people and livestock on the state's dirt roads. When the State Agricultural Society reincarnated the fair in 1856, railroads were completed between Columbia and Charleston, Charlotte, and Greenville, and within the next few years to Spartanburg and Florence. The state fairs from 1856 to 1861 attracted participants from across the state and began to offer entertainment and the first vestiges of later midway activities.

Following the Civil War, the state's prewar leadership wanted to throw off the Reconstruction regimes imposed by the federal government. Rather than revive the State Agricultural Society in 1869, they chose to expand the scope of the fair and established the State Agricultural and Mechanical Society of South Carolina. The expanded scope reflected in the name of the new organization recognized the need to develop more industry in the state. Held on the reconstructed fairgrounds on Elmwood Avenue, the 1869 fair hosted the founding of several organizations destined to emerge as leaders in ending Reconstruction in the state.

Throughout its history, the State Fair has not only promoted agriculture and industry but also reflected the culture and mores of the state. Evidence indicates that the early fairs were integrated, but by the late 1880s the African American community was being pushed aside, leading to the founding of the Colored State Fair in 1890. Even after the colored fair began staging an annual event in 1908, Richard Carroll, the president of the Colored State Fair, commented in 1909 on the presence of men of both races at the girlie show at the White State Fair. The presence at the White State Fair of racially tainted activities, like the African Dodger prior to World War II, mirror the racial attitudes present in the state. Following World War II, the Colored State Fair changed its name to the Palmetto State Fair, abandoning the increasingly unpopular colored designation. The separate fairs continued to operate until 1969. However, following the Civil Rights Act of 1964, the white fair saw the 4-H program integrated at the 1965 State Fair.

While even the earliest colonial fairs had entertainment activities, the focus was on agriculture. The fairs before the Civil War contained entertainment and began to offer premiums in categories like fine arts that were not associated with agriculture. In the early twentieth century the development of the midway, with its rides, games, and sideshows, saw the focus begin to shift away from agriculture to the midway activities. On numerous occasions the society board addressed this change of focus at their meetings but were not able to find ways to refocus on agriculture without the potential loss of visitors. An editorial in the *State* on October 18, 1965, summarized the dilemma: "For many, entertainment is the primary lure of the fair and this is not to be underrated. It is that variety of entertainment which children and adults find nowhere else. For thousands at the State Fair each year it provides moments of merriment and excitement." In addition, over the years the ever-expanding categories of entries brought more people to the fair as both participants and visitors.

With over a half-million visitors each year, the State Fair still has an avid following. Perhaps the best characterization of the fair's attraction appeared in an editorial in the *State* on October 18, 1960: "The South Carolina State Fair may mean different things to different people, but it is still what it is, and the need is for the individual to rise to it. It is not in any real sense the games of chance, the girlie shows, the cages and caterpillar rides of the Midway. In a very real sense it is the opportunity to take stock within our state as to where we stand in agriculture and industry, in science and art and history. It is foremost the reflection of our educational values and where we put our faith."

APPENDIX

The State Agricultural and Mechanical Society of South Carolina

PRESIDENTS

Gen. Johnson Hagood 1869–72

Maj. Thomas W. Woodward 1873–74

Col. Thomas Taylor 1875–76

B. F. Crayton, Esq. 1877–81

D. P. Duncan 1882–86

Capt. J. B. Humbert 1887–88

Col. E. R. McIver 1889–90

R. A. Love, Esq. 1891–92

Thomas J. Moore, Esq. 1893–94

Lysander D. Childs, Esq. 1895–96

T. J. Cunningham 1897–98

W. D. Evans, Esq. 1899–1900

A. H. White, Esq. 1901–1902

R. P. Hamer Jr., Esq. 1903

G. A. Guignard, Esq. 1904–6

J. G. Mobley, Esq. 1907–9

J. A. Banks, Esq.. 1910–12

J. N. Kirvin, Esq. 1913–21

R. M. Cooper 1922–24

David Witcover 1925–52

Ransome J. Williams 1952–58

James L. McIntosh 1959–64

Frank Hampton 1965–69

Dr. William C. Cantey 1970–80

David G. Ellison 1980–89

John Cantey Heath 1990–2005

William C. Cantey Jr. 2005–2018

J. Cantey Heath, Jr. 2018–

SECRETARIES/GENERAL MANAGERS

D. Wyatt Aiken 1869–75

Thomas W. Holloway 1875–1903

A. W. Love 1903–10

D. F. Efird 1910

J. M. Cantey 1911–13

D. F. Efird 1913–22

J. W. Fleming 1922–24

D. F. Efird 1924–27

Paul V. Moore 1927–60

Frank B. Ruff 1960–69

W. L. Abernathy Jr. 1969–85

Gary L. Goodman 1986–2017

Nancy L. Smith 2018–

NOTES

1: Colonial and Antebellum Fairs, 1720–1865

1. George C. Rogers, Jr., *Charleston in the Age of the Pinckneys* (Columbia: University of South Carolina Press, 1984), 12–13. The term "grinn'd" probably came from John Milton's *Paradise Lost*, book 2, line 846: "Death grinn'd horrible a ghastly smile, to hear his famine should be fill'd." Apparently they were looking for the worst smile.

2. Walter B. Edgar, *South Carolina: A History* (Columbia: University of South Carolina Press, 1998), 277; and David Duncan Wallace, *The History of South Carolina*, vol. 2 (New York: American Historical Society, 1934), 376.

3. Yates Snowden, *History of South Carolina*, vol. 2 (Chicago: Lewis Publishing, 1920), 606–7.

4. *History of the State Agricultural Society of South Carolina from 1839–1845, Inclusive of the State Agricultural Society....* (Columbia, S.C.: R. L. Bryan, 1916), 1–13; hereafter, *Society History*.

5. *Proceedings of the Agricultural Convention and of the State Agricultural Society of South Carolina from 1839 to 1845 Inclusive* (Columbia, S.C.: Summer and Carroll, 1846), 30–40.

6. *Society History*, 33.

7. *Society History*, 15–16.

8. Cited in "The State Fair," *Charleston Courier*, October 24, 1856.

9. "State Fair of the Agricultural Society," *Charleston Courier*, November 6, 1856.

10. "South Carolina State Fair," *Charleston Courier*, November 6, 1857.

11. "Correspondence of the Courier, Columbia, S.C. Nov. 13," *Charleston Courier*, November 17. 1856.

12. Marion Brunson Lucas, *Sherman and the Burning of Columbia* (College Station: Texas A&M Press), 24, 26, 123.

2: Fair on Elmwood Avenue, 1869–1903

1. Thomas J. Brown, *Civil War Canon: Sites of Confederate Memory in South Carolina* (Chapel Hill: University of North Carolina Press, 2015), 93–94.

2. *History of the State Agricultural Society of South Carolina from 1839 to 1861*, 24–38, 85.

3. Mayor John McKenzie to John R. Tomlinson, State Auditor, September 7, 1869. South Carolina Department of Archives and History, S165249, Box 16, General Assembly, Green File, Legislative System, City of Columbia, State Fair Folder.

4. *Society History*, 26–28.

5. *Society History*, 28–29.

6. *Society History*, 29–31.

7. "Through Dixie Summary of Southern News," *Fairfield News & Herald*, November 13, 1889.

8. "The Columbia Fair Association," *State* (Columbia), September 9, 1891.

9. "Last Fair...Century Has Closed," *State* (Columbia), November 14, 1900.

10. "To Make a Success of the Fair City Fair Association Has Discontinued Its Existence...," *State* (Columbia), June 23, 1903.

11. "Putting on Gala Dress," *State* (Columbia), November 5, 1891.

12. John Hammond Moore, *Columbia and Richland County: A South Carolina Community, 1740–1990* (Columbia: University of South Carolina Press, 1993), 41.

13. Annie Perry Jester to Dr. John R. Jester, November 2, 1896. Annie Perry Jester Papers, South Caroliniana Library.

14. "State Ball's Great Success," *State* (Columbia), November 18, 1898.

15. "Champions at Football," *State* (Columbia), November 15, 1891.

16. "The Fair Grounds Secured," *State* (Columbia), August 15, 1893.

17. "An Interesting Game," *State* (Columbia), December 2, 1897.

18. J. W. Floyd, *Historical Roster and Itinerary of South Carolina Volunteer Troops Who Served in the Late War between the United States and Spain, 1898* (Columbia: R. L. Bryan Company, 1901).

19. "A Great Feature of the State Fair," *State* (Columbia), October 31, 1903.

20. *Society History*, 39–50.

3: The Greater State Fair, 1904–1920

1. "Planning and Working for 'Greater State Fair,'" *State* (Columbia), June 12, 1904.

2. "The Greater State Fair as Seen by the Editors," *State* (Columbia), November 5, 1904.

3. "Fair Week at Hand and All Is Ready," *State* (Columbia), October 23, 1905.

4. *Society History*, 50.

5. "South Carolinians and Taft," *State* (Columbia), November 7, 1909.

6. "Board of Health Met Yesterday," *State* (Columbia), October 13, 1911.

7. "State Fair Society against Street Shows," *State* (Columbia), February 2, 1905.

8. "Jno. G. Mobley Doubtful about Columbia People," *State* (Columbia), November 3, 1910.

9. "A Greater Fair for Columbia," *State* (Columbia), November 4, 1910.

10. "Position of City as to State Fair," *State* (Columbia), November 8, 1910.

11. "Moving Pictures to Exploit City," *State* (Columbia), October 2, 1911.

12. "Columbian Recalls Gonzales' Drive to Bring Steel Building Here," *State* (Columbia), April 29, 1956.

13. "Will Use Tent at State Fair," *State* (Columbia), October 20, 1911.

14. "Insurance Rates Limit Capacity," *State* (Columbia), November 11, 1914.

15. "Railroads Unable to Run Extras for State Fair—Rates Not Reduced," *State* (Columbia), November 11, 1917.

16. "Women Welcomed by Fair Society," *State* (Columbia), February 22, 1917.

17. Minutes of the Annual Meeting, State Agricultural and Mechanical Society of South Carolina, October 25, 1922. The Society's minutes and other records are kept in a safe. State Agricultural and Mechanical Society Archives, 1400 Rosewood Drive, Columbia, S.C., 29201.

18. "Influenza Fight Postpones Fair," *State* (Columbia), November 9, 1918.
19. Ibid.
20. "The Great Exhibition," *State* (Columbia), November 1, 1919.
21. "South Carolina State Fair," *Charleston News & Courier*, 1919, clipped advertisement.

4: The Colored State Fair, 1890–1969

1. *Premium List of the State Agricultural Society for the Fourth Annual Fair to be Held at Columbia, South Carolina on the 8th, 9th, 10th and 11th of November 1859*, 7. (Cover missing with publication information. Copy at South Caroliniana Library.)
2. *Premium List of the State Agricultural and Mechanical Society for the Tenth Annual Fair to Be Held in Columbia, S.C. Beginning on Tuesday Morning, the 12th of November, 1878, and Ending on Friday Evening, November 15th, 1878* (Columbia: The Daily Register, 1878), 32.
3. "The State Survey," *State* (Columbia), November 11, 1909.
4. Minutes of the Board, State Agricultural and Mechanical Society of South Carolina, December 21, 1926.
5. "Man Resembles Magazine Photo," *State* (Columbia), October 22, 1932.
6. "A Colored State Fair," *Newberry Herald and News*, October 31, 1889.
7. "The Colored State Fair," *Newberry Herald and News*, January 9, 1890.
8. "The Coming Colored State Ball," *State* (Columbia), December 9, 1892.
9. "The Colored State Fair," *Watchman and Southron* (Sumter), October 8, 1890.
10. "A Trades Display: Progress of the Colored State Fair, Military Feature," *State* (Columbia), November 25, 1891.
11. "Not a Howling Success," *State* (Columbia), November 28, 1891.
12. "A Fight for Fair Fame; The Rival Colored Fair Associations," *State* (Columbia), August 6, 1892; and "Two Colored Fairs Now," *State* (Columbia), September 30, 1892.
13. "A 'Busted' Fair: The Hampton Colored State Fair a Dead Failure," *State* (Columbia), December 1, 1892.
14. "The Colored Fair's Success," *State* (Columbia), December 29, 1892.
15. "The Colored State Fair," *State* (Columbia), December 18, 1893.
16. "The Proper Thing: The Colored State Fair Called Off on Account of Hard Times," *State* (Columbia), November 21, 1894.
17. "The State's Survey," *State* (Columbia), November 27, 1896; and "No More Fake Fairs," *State* (Columbia), November 27, 1896.
18. "Sponsored Industrial Fair," *Watchman and Southron* (Sumter), September 18, 1895.
19. "Making Plans for State Fair," *State* (Columbia), February 2, 1907.
20. "Colored People to Have a Fair," *State* (Columbia), July 21, 1908.
21. "Richard Carroll Makes Statement," *State* (Columbia), November 22, 1908.
22. "As to the Negro State Fair," *State* (Columbia), June 3, 1909.
23. "Negro Fair Closes after Great Success," *State* (Columbia), November 13, 1909.
24. "The Colored State Fair," *State* (Columbia), November 5, 1910; and "Negro State Fair Opens Next Week," *State* (Columbia), November 3, 1910.
25. "Negroes Are Urged to Exhibit at State Fair," *State* (Columbia), August 5, 1911.
26. "Outlook Bright for Negro Fair," *State* (Columbia), October 29, 1915.
27. "Negro State Fair Week from Today," *State* (Columbia), October 23, 1922.
28. "Not Long before the Colored State Fair," *Palmetto Leader*, September 10, 1927.
29. "South Carolina State Fair," *State* (Columbia), October 14, 1933.
30. "Bihari's Restaurant," *State* (Columbia), October 27, 1936.
31. "Dance at the Annual State Ball with Joe Williams…," *State* (Columbia), October 22, 1939.
32. "Plans Complete for Negro Fair," *State* (Columbia), October 17, 1943.
33. "Negroes Open Big Fair Here on Monday," *State* (Columbia), October 28, 1945.
34. "Annual SC Colored State Fair Moves into High Gear; 2,500 Autos Jam the Parking Space," *State* (Columbia), October 28, 1952.
35. "Thousands Pass through Free Gates to See Opening of 49th Colored State Fair Here," *State* (Columbia), October 17, 1953; and "Grand Stand Attraction Set at State Fair," *State* (Columbia), October 17, 1953.
36. "Mammoth Crowd Launches State's 56th Colored Fair," *State* (Columbia), October 25, 1960.
37. "An Ape Made a Monkey Out of Me," *State* (Columbia), November 3, 1963.
38. "Certificate of Incorporation," Secretary of State, State of South Carolina, February 9, 1897, South Carolina Department of Archives and History, Columbia.
39. "Certificate of Incorporation," Secretary of State, State of South Carolina, March 26, 1941, South Carolina Department of Archives and History, Columbia.
40. "Events, Month by Month, In South Carolina," *State* (Columbia), March 15, 1955.
41. "Palmetto State Fair Schedule Opening Oct. 25," *State* (Columbia), October 18, 1965.
42. "Collins to Retire; Palmetto Fair No More," *State* (Columbia), December 2, 1971.

5: The Depression and World War II, 1921–1945

1. Minutes of the Board, State Agricultural and Mechanical Society of South Carolina, February 16, 1921.
2. Minutes of the Executive Committee, State Agricultural and Mechanical Society of South Carolina, April 19–20, 1922.
3. "Committee Plans for Bigger Fair," *State* (Columbia), April 21, 1922.
4. "Columbia Backs State Fair Plan," *State* (Columbia), June 19, 1922.
5. "Teams Canvass for State Fair," *State* (Columbia), June 24, 1922.
6. "Support Given State Fair Plan," *State* (Columbia), June 20, 1922.
7. "Money to Keep Fair Raised Last Night," *State* (Columbia), August 9, 1922.
8. "Committee Plans for Bigger Fair," *State* (Columbia), April 21, 1922.
9. "State Fair Plans Handsome Stadium," *State* (Columbia), June 3, 1922.
10. "Many Changes at Fair Grounds," *State* (Columbia), October 15, 1922.
11. "Baldwin to Do Landscape Work," *State* (Columbia), July 10, 1922.
12. "Bright Prospects for Greater Fair," *State* (Columbia), September 17, 1922.
13. "May Check Babes at State Fair," *State* (Columbia), October 14, 1922.
14. "Greatest Circus in the City's History," *State* (Columbia), October 28, 1922.
15. "Display of Birds Best in History," *State* (Columbia), October 15, 1925.

16. "Fair Grounds Road Built Very Soon," *State* (Columbia), June 21, 1926.

17. Minutes of the Board, State Agricultural and Mechanical Society of South Carolina, February 20, 1924.

18. "Fire Destroys Stand at Fair," *State* (Columbia), June 12, 1926.

19. "New Grandstand Rises Very Soon," *State* (Columbia), June 15, 1926.

20. "Witcover again Heads State Fair," *State* (Columbia), October 23, 1930.

21. Minutes of the Executive Committee, State Agricultural and Mechanical Society of South Carolina, December 16, 1930.

22. "Will Broadcast News of Fair," *State* (Columbia), October 19, 1930.

23. "Witcover Wins Fair Presidency after Contest," *State* (Columbia), October 22, 1931.

24. "State Fair List Limited to State," *State* (Columbia), July 9, 1933; and "State Fair Premiums for Home People Only," *State* (Columbia), September 9, 1933.

25. "Stadium Site on Taylor Land," *State* (Columbia), July 14, 1933.

26. "Long Felt Want About Realized," *State* (Columbia), June 26, 1933.

27. "City Fathers Talk of Stadium," *State* (Columbia), September 26, 1934.

28. "Columbia's Municipal Stadium Unexcelled in Orientation," *State* (Columbia), August 20, 1934.

29. "Toe of Fellers Leads Tiger Way," *State* (Columbia), October 26, 1934.

30. "Columbia's Offer on City Stadium," *State* (Columbia), August 20, 1935.

31. Minutes of the Annual Meeting, State Agricultural and Mechanical Society of South Carolina, October 19, 1938; and "Witcover again Elected President of State Fair," *State* (Columbia), October 20, 1938.

32. Minutes of the Annual Meeting, State Agricultural and Mechanical Society of South Carolina, October 22, 1940; and "Witcover Will again Head Fair Group," *State* (Columbia), October 23, 1940.

33. Minutes of the Executive Committee, State Agricultural and Mechanical Society of South Carolina, January 21, 1941.

34. Minutes of the Executive Committee, State Agricultural and Mechanical Society of South Carolina, January 21, 1941, June 5, 1941.

35. Minutes of the Board, State Agricultural and Mechanical Society of South Carolina, April 28, 1942.

36. "Around the State House," *State* (Columbia), June 22, 1942.

37. "Crowds Find No Shortage of Good Entertainment at State Fair Midway," *State* (Columbia), October 20, 1942.

38. "State Fair to Be Held October 18–23," *State* (Columbia), June 4, 1943.

39. "Army to Have Huge Exhibit at State Fair," *State* (Columbia), August 21, 1943.

40. "Takes 40 Flatcars to Haul Show," *State* (Columbia), October 17, 1943.

41. "Adequate Bus Service to State Fair Grounds to Be Given, Moore Assured," *State* (Columbia), October 12, 1943.

42. "Saturday," *State* (Columbia), October 25, 1943.

43. "Richland Fair Planned as SC Fair Canceled," *State* (Columbia), July 26, 1945.

44. Minutes of the Audit Committee, State Agricultural and Mechanical Society of South Carolina, January 10, 1946.

6: "The Grooming Ground of Champions," 1890–1969

1. Jami Cassidy Boone, "'The Grooming Ground of Champions': The Local History and National Legacy of Columbia's Forgotten Racetrack" (master's thesis, University of South Carolina, 2006), 4–10.

2. Walter Edgar, ed., *The South Carolina Encyclopedia* (Columbia: University of South Carolina Press, 2006), 461–62.

3. "The State Fair," *Charleston Mercury,* November 12, 1859.

4. "Plan Horse Show during Fair," *State* (Columbia), June 27, 1914.

5. "Premium List for State Fair," *State* (Columbia), August 19, 1914.

6. "No Horse Show at State Fair," *State* (Columbia), October 3, 1914.

7. Boone, "The Grooming Ground of Champions," 21–22.

8. "Pacers, Trotters to Show Wares," *State* (Columbia), October 17, 1938.

9. "Columbia Horse Show Gets Off to Brilliant Start: Closes Tonight," *State* (Columbia), June 1, 1934.

10. "Polo Field Is Laid Out," *State* (Columbia), March 6, 1936.

11. "'Bob' Davis Departs," *State* (Columbia), May 19, 1903.

12. James Roach, "Horses Gallop Barefoot in South Carolina Winter Training," *New York Times,* January 15, 1955, cited in Boone, "The Grooming Ground of Champions," 27.

13. Boone, "The Grooming Ground of Champions," 27–28.

14. "Proposition to Sell Old Fairgrounds," *State* (Columbia), February 14, 1907.

15. "The Romance of the Race Course," *State* (Columbia), November 2, 1909.

16. "Buxton Brothers to Lease Track," *State* (Columbia), October 9, 1930.

17. Boone, "The Grooming Ground of Champions," 32–36.

18. Minutes of the State Agricultural and Mechanical Society of South Carolina, (executive committee) April 12, 1967, (finance committee) April 25, 1968, and (finance committee) July 3, 1968.

19. "Minutes of the Society" (annual meeting), October 21, 1969.

7: Integration and the Civic Center, 1946–1964

1. "SC Farm Youths Take Over Fair," *State* (Columbia), October 23, 1946.

2. "State Fair Women's Lounge Spacious and Lovely; Many Other Improvements Noted," *State* (Columbia), October 18, 1947; see also "You'll Be Surprised When You See the State Fair Grounds," *State* (Columbia), October 11, 1947.

3. "State Fair Attendance Passes 80,000 Mark," *State* (Columbia), October 19, 1949.

4. "1949 State Fair to Put Stress on Agriculture," *State* (Columbia), September 9, 1949.

5. "State Fair," *State* (Columbia), May 8, 1952.

6. "State Fair Admission Charge at Carolina, Clemson Game Abolished," *State* (Columbia), July 7, 1947.

7. "New Booths Set Up after Disastrous $75,000 Fire," *State* (Columbia), October 22, 1952.

8. "Witcover of the Fair," *State* (Columbia), November 18, 1951; and "New Fair Officers," *State* (Columbia), October 23, 1952.

9. "State Fair May Build Grandstand," *State* (Columbia), October 21, 1953.

10. Minutes of the Annual Meeting, State Agricultural and Mechanical Society of South Carolina, October 27, 1957.

11. "Grandstand at Fair Honors D. D. Witcover," *State* (Columbia), July 25, 1957.

12. "Fair Week Trade Promotion Called Biggest of Its Kind," *State* (Columbia), October 21, 1956.

13. "Fair Grounds to Be Surveyed for Possible Year Round Use," *State* (Columbia), August 20, 1958.

14. "Study Plan Is Given Green Light," *State* (Columbia), October 22, 1958.

15. Minutes of the Annual Meeting, State Agricultural and Mechanical Society of South Carolina, October 21, 1958.

16. "In the Press Box with Jake Penland," *State* (Columbia), June 24, 1959.

17. "Action Delayed on Return of Fair Grounds to City," *State* (Columbia), July 2, 1959.

18. "Bates Greatly Impressed by Greensboro Auditorium," *State* (Columbia), October 10, 1959.

19. "State Fair Members Asked to Consider Use of Grounds," *State* (Columbia), October 15, 1959.

20. Minutes of the Annual Meeting, State Agricultural and Mechanical Society of South Carolina, October 20, 1959; and "Decision Delayed on Use of Land for Civic Center," *State* (Columbia), October 21, 1959.

21. "Columbia Gets Use of Fairgrounds for Giant Coliseum," *State* (Columbia), February 5, 1960.

22. " 'City's Biggest Thursday,' Bates Says," *State* (Columbia), February 5, 1960.

23. "A Neat Gesture," *State* (Columbia), February 24, 1960.

24. "Acceptance Seen of Loan for Auditorium Building," *State* (Columbia), August 17, 1960.

25. "Coliseum Building Committee to Meet," *State* (Columbia), September 2, 1960.

26. "100-Acre State Fairground Deeded to City of Columbia," *State* (Columbia), September 28, 1960; see also Minutes of the Executive Committee, State Agricultural and Mechanical Society of South Carolina, April 27, 1960.

27. "Initial Steps Taken Toward Civic Center," *State* (Columbia), March 28, 1960.

28. "Richland Civic Center Will Cost $8,900,000," *State* (Columbia), August 31, 1962.

29. "Center's Foes See It as a Mistake," *State* (Columbia), October 13, 1962.

30. "Ainsley Hall Home and Proposed Coliseum," *State* (Columbia), September 6, 1962.

31. "Tax Facts Relative to the Civic Center," *State* (Columbia), October 23, 1962.

32. "Richland Civic Center Win Boost from Fair Association," *State* (Columbia), October 24, 1962.

33. "Richland Civic Center Voted Down," *State* (Columbia), November 7, 1962; and "Lexington Turns Down Role in Center Finance," *State* (Columbia), November 15, 1962.

34. "Civic Center Vote Due in 2 Months," *State* (Columbia), October 3, 1963.

35. "Vote Comes Tuesday on Civic Center," *State* (Columbia), November 11, 1963.

36. "Margin of Defeat Is 6,000," *State* (Columbia), November 13, 1963.

37. Minutes of the Columbia City Council, Special Meeting, November 27, 1963.

38. "City Council Handles Heavy Business Agenda," *State* (Columbia), December 5, 1963.

39. "Why Did the Voters Turn Down the Proposed Civic Center," *State* (Columbia), November 14, 1963.

8: County and Regional Fairs

1. "First Fair," *State* (Columbia)," October 2, 1975.

2. "Newberry Agricultural Society," *Charleston Courier,* July 21, 1856.

3. "Fairfield District Fair," *Winnsboro Register,* cited in *Charleston Courier,* November 11, 1857.

4. "Winnsboro' Fair—Accident to Ex-Governor Means, &c.," *Charleston Courier,* November 1, 1858.

5. "The Fair," *Lexington Flag,* cited in *Charleston Mercury,* October 30, 1858.

6. "The Abbeville District Fair," *Charleston Mercury,* October 20, 1860.

7. "Newberry Agricultural Society," *Charleston Courier,* June 23, 1855.

8. *Society History,* 14–17.

9. "City Affairs," *Charleston Courier,* November 17, 1869.

10. *Premium List of the South Carolina Agricultural and Mechanical Society for the Fifteenth Annual Fair....* (Greenville, South Carolina: Hoyt & Keys, Book and Job Printers, 1883). 77.

11. "The State Fair—Need of Radical Changes in Scope," *State* (Columbia), November 2, 1909.

12. "Fair Secretaries Form Association," *State* (Columbia), October 2, 1929.

13. "Fair Managers Form Association," *State* (Columbia), January 24, 1930.

14. *Premium Seventy-third Annual [South Carolina] State Fair* (Columbia, S.C.: State Agricultural and Mechanical Society, 1942), 75.

15. "1969 S. C. Fall Fair Schedule," *State* (Columbia), August 31, 1969.

16. Interview with Nancy Smith, assistant general manager, South Carolina State Fair, April 5, 2017.

9: From Disaster to a New Vision, 1965–1983

1. Minutes of the Executive Committee, State Agricultural and Mechanical Society of South Carolina, April 22, 1964; and "Fairgrounds to Go to Year-Round Operations," *State* (Columbia), April 24, 1964.

2. Minutes of the Executive Committee, State Agricultural and Mechanical Society of South Carolina, January 19, 1966.

3. "Fire Destroys Steel Building," *State* (Columbia), April 22, 1966.

4. "Pledges of Support Spark Move to Replace Building," *State* (Columbia), April 23, 1966.

5. Minutes of the Executive Committee, State Agricultural and Mechanical Society of South Carolina, April 27, 1966; and "New State Fair Exhibition Building Approved by Board," *State* (Columbia), April 28, 1966.

6. "Big Top Proposal Is Voiced for Fair," *State* (Columbia), April 29, 1966.

7. "New 'Little Steel' Building Readied for State Fair," *State* (Columbia), August 2, 1966.

8. "Fair Steel Building Fire Ignites Again," *State* (Columbia), May 10, 1966.

9. "All-Year Facilities Planned for Fairgrounds," *State* (Columbia), October 2, 1966.

10. "Fair Group Gets Preview of Improvements," *State* (Columbia), March 31, 1967.

11. Minutes of the Executive Committee, State Agricultural and Mechanical Society of South Carolina, April 12, 1967.

12. "The South Carolina Fairgrounds Columbia, South Carolina Special Study May 1967," Horwath & Horwath, Miami, Florida, 1967. Typescript in Society Archives safe.

13. "Fairgrounds Being Geared for Year 'Round Activities," *Columbia Record,* August 20, 1967.

14. "The New Palace Skate Club of Columbia," *State* (Columbia), December 4, 1968 (advertisement).

15. "UFO Closing in Protested," *State* (Columbia), March 9, 1970; and "Youths 'Used' at Festival," *State* (Columbia), March 22, 1970.

16. "Planning a Big…," *Columbia Record*, April 30, 1967 (advertisement).

17. Minutes of Executive Committee, State Agricultural and Mechanical Society of South Carolina, April 16, 1969.

18. "Song, Rhyme Tell Story of S. C. Fair," *State* (Columbia), October 18, 1969.

19. *Centennial Celebrity Cookbook* (Columbia: State Agricultural and Mechanical Society of South Carolina, 1969).

20. "101st State Fair Opens Monday," *State* (Columbia), October 18, 1970.

21. "Slaying Suspect Search Continues," *State* (Columbia), November 5, 1970.

22. "Man Charged in Fair Killing," *State* (Columbia), November 14, 1970.

23. "Charges in Slaying Dropped after Probe," *State* (Columbia), November 16, 1970.

24. "Fair Shooting Suspect Charged," *State* (Columbia), November 18, 1970.

25. "Man Gets 2 Years in Killing," *State* (Columbia), April 22, 1971.

26. "S.C. Fair Gated Closed to Public before Opening," *State* (Columbia), October 6, 1972.

27. "Part of the Fair Changes, Part Stays the Same," *State* (Columbia), October 13, 1982.

28. Minutes of the Executive Committee, State Agricultural and Mechanical Society of South Carolina, *State* (Columbia), April 29, 1976.

29. T. Wilson Sparks to David G. Ellison, December 14, 1981, Minutes book, located in Society Archives safe.

10: Entertainment and the Midway

1. "State Fair Exhibits Range from 'Elsie' to Securities," *State* (Columbia), September 12, 1952.

2. Rogers, *Charleston in the Age of the Pinckneys*, 13.

3. "The State Fair," *Charleston Mercury*, November 11, 1859.

4. "Correspondence of the Keowee Courier," *Keowee Courier*, October 17, 1857.

5. "Opening of the State Fair," *Courier Charleston*," November 9, 1858.

6. "The State Fair," *Charleston Mercury*, November 12, 1859.

7. Robert Bogdan, *Freak Show: Presenting Human Oddities for Amusement and Profit* (Chicago: University of Chicago Press, 1988), 25.

8. "The Living Skelton &c.," *Charleston Courier*, August 28, 1849.

9. "Correspondence of the Courier," *Charleston Courier*, November 11, 1856.

10. "Plenty of the People," *State* (Columbia), November 11, 1898.

11. "Tiniest of Women Found on Midway," *State* (Columbia), October 24, 1916.

12. "Heavyweights on State Fair Midway," *State* (Columbia), October 24, 1951.

13. "Visitors to Fair to See Samar Twins," *State* (Columbia), October 21, 1917.

14. "Many Side Shows on Gay Midway," *State* (Columbia), October 20, 1928.

15. "'Freak Show' Owner Says Science Hurts Business," *State* (Columbia), October 19, 1967.

16. "'Freak Show' Manager Says He's Giving 'Opportunity,'" *State* (Columbia), October 22, 1971.

17. "Ever See a Chicken with Fur?" *State* (Columbia), October 20, 1974.

18. "Following Trend, Fair Drops Freak Shows," *State* (Columbia), October 21, 1989.

19. "From the State Capital," *Charleston Courier*, November 11, 1869.

20. "The State Agricultural Fair," *Charleston Courier*, November 13, 1869.

21. "Putting on Gala Dress," *State* (Columbia), November 5, 1891.

22. "Record of Fairs Broken," *State* (Columbia), November 17, 1892.

23. "Fair Week Program," *State* (Columbia), November 9, 1891.

24. "Biggest and Best of Fairs," *State* (Columbia), November 10, 1891.

25. Jamie Malanowski, "The Brief History of the Ferris Wheel," *Smithsonian Magazine*, June 2015, http://www.smithsonianmag.com/history/history-ferris-wheel-180955300/.

26. "Opening Day of State Fair," *State* (Columbia), October 30, 1900; and "Records Have Been Broken," *State* (Columbia), October 31, 1900.

27. "Initial Game of the Series Saw Showers," *State* (Columbia), October 22, 1940.

28. "The Last Working Day…," *State* (Columbia), November 10, 1894.

29. "Big Day of the State Fair," *State* (Columbia), November 11, 1897; and "Fair Week Races," *State* (Columbia), October 17, 1897.

30. Minutes of the Board, State Agricultural and Mechanical Society of South Carolina, January 17, 1974.

31. "Big Thursday Bigger," *State* (Columbia), 18, 1892.

32. "Fair's First Day Showed Up Well," *State* (Columbia), November 1, 1910.

33. "Aviators Invade Columbia's Air," *State* (Columbia), December 7, 1910.

34. "All the Space Has Been Applied For," *State* (Columbia), October 27, 1901.

35. "Auto Racing Is Eliminated for Duration," *State* (Columbia), July 4, 1942.

36. "School Kids Take State Fair Today," *State* (Columbia), October 25, 1946.

37. "Motorcycle Thrill Show Is Feature of Midway at Fair," *State* (Columbia), October 15, 1949.

38. "Mr. Taft at the State Fair," *State* (Columbia), October 12, 1909.

39. "Putting on Gala Dress," *State* (Columbia), November 5, 1891.

40. "'All the Boys and Girls,'" *State* (Columbia), October 31, 1896.

41. "High Class Shows at State Fair," *State* (Columbia), October 7, 1907.

42. "South Carolina News and Gossip," *State* (Columbia), October 29, 1902.

43. "Carnival Shows Here in Abundance," *State* (Columbia), October 22, 1905.

44. "Fair and Warmer," *State* (Columbia), October 21, 1964.

45. "Mobile Class Keeps Fair Families Together," *State* (Columbia), October 13, 1994.

46. "Midway, Top Grandstand Show," *State* (Columbia), October 17, 1943.

47. "Fairgrounds Hum with Activity," *State* (Columbia), October 18, 1963.

48. "Thousands View Staging of Historical Pageant," *State* (Columbia), October 24, 1925.

49. "Crowd Witnesses Pageant at Fair," *State* (Columbia), October 22, 1926; and "Repeats Pageant Indoors," *State* (Columbia), October 31, 1926.

50. "Football Feature at Negro Fair," *State* (Columbia), October 27, 1927.

51. "Elks to Sponsor Events on Turf," *State* (Columbia), March 17, 1936.

52. "Bob Hope in We the People," *State* (Columbia), October 28, 1976.

53. "Rain Spoiled the Fair," *State* (Columbia), November 27, 1891.

54. "Fair Fireworks Will Be Feature," *State* (Columbia), October 13, 1922.

55. "Only Seven Days More," *State* (Columbia), November 6, 1892; and "Paris Aglow on Monday," *State* (Columbia), November 12, 1892.

56. "Planning and Working for 'Greater State Fair,'" *State* (Columbia), June 12, 1904.

57. "The Greater State Fair and Its Many Attractions," *State* (Columbia), October 3, 1904.

58. "State Fair May Build Grandstand," *State* (Columbia), October 21, 1953; Minutes of the Executive Committee, State Agricultural and Mechanical Society of South Carolina, August 5, 1953, April 1, 1954, and February 23, 1955; and Minutes of the Annual Meeting, State Agricultural and Mechanical Society of South Carolina, October 27, 1957.

59. "Grandstand Show Has Big Program," *State* (Columbia), October 11, 1935.

60. "State Fair Grandstand Show Delights Audience of 3,000," *State* (Columbia), October 24, 1945.

61. "Blaze Destroys One Building," *State* (Columbia), November 5, 1910.

62. "Fair's New Power Plan," *State* (Columbia), May 18, 1989.

63. "Non-Profit Groups Say Ban Unfair," *State* (Columbia), May 12, 1989.

64. "The Game Suddenly Called," *State* (Columbia), November 19, 1892.

65. "Dances and Races," *State* (Columbia), February 6, 1896.

66. "A Very Lively Midway," *State* (Columbia), November 2, 1910.

67. "No More Wheels on Fair Midways," *State* (Columbia), May 2, 1929.

68. "State Constables Remain at Fair," *State* (Columbia), October 26, 1932.

69. "Taking a Chance," *State* (Columbia), October 19, 1967.

70. "Stands Normal Again after Charge Flurry," *State* (Columbia), October 21, 1967.

71. "Along the Midway," *State* (Columbia), October 23, 1964.

72. "Fair Game," *State* (Columbia), October 17, 1987.

11: The State Fair into the Twenty-First Century, 1984–2019

1. Minutes of the Executive Committee, State Agricultural and Mechanical Society of South Carolina, January 19, 1972.

2. Minutes of the Executive Committee, State Agricultural and Mechanical Society of South Carolina, April 29, 1976.

3. Minutes of the Executive Committee, State Agricultural and Mechanical Society of South Carolina, February 25, 1982.

4. Minutes of the Executive Committee, State Agricultural and Mechanical Society of South Carolina, January 18, 1998.

5. "SC Fair Group Cites Contract on Grid Charges," *State* (Columbia), March 12, 1947; and "State Fair Admission Charge at Carolina, Clemson Game Abolished," *State* (Columbia), August 7, 1947.

6. "USC Signs Pact for Fairgrounds," *State* (Columbia), August 21, 1970.

7. Minutes of the Board, State Agricultural and Mechanical Society of South Carolina, January 28, 1998.

8. "USC Club to Lose Fairground Parking," *State* (Columbia), October 5, 2005.

9. Gary Goodman (general manager, South Carolina State Fair), discussion with the author August 3, 2016; and "Fair Touts Spiffed-up Parking," *State* (Columbia), September 5, 2009.

10. "South Carolina State Fair Master Plan" (Populous, Fairground Architects and Planners, Knoxville, Tennessee, 2011), typescript in Society Archives safe.

11. "State Fair Plowing Ahead with Facility Upgrades," *State* (Columbia), February 16, 2015.

12. "Good Morning, Fair Friends," *State* (Columbia), November 8, 1892.

13. "Fixing Fair Fakirs," *State* (Columbia), November 6, 1896.

14. "Robbers Paroled," *State* (Columbia), October 28, 1911.

15. "Yesterday at the Courthouse," *State* (Columbia), January 6, 1942; "Motor Scooter Stolen," *State* (Columbia), October 26, 1948; and "'Hey Rube' Is a Cry of the Past," *State* (Columbia), October 24, 1963.

16. "Sheriff's Posse Helps at Fair," *State* (Columbia), October 21, 1974.

17. "Fair Stabbing Victim Is Still on Danger List," *State* (Columbia), October 30, 1957.

18. "Teen Critical after Fair Shooting," *State* (Columbia), October 11, 2004.

19. "State Fair Alters Admission Rules," *State* (Columbia), October 13, 2004.

20. "Teen Shot at Fair Dies—Youth Arrested," *State* (Columbia), October 16, 2004.

21. "New System Isn't Fail-Safe-Not all Attendees Have to Go through Safety Measures, Including Metal Detectors," *State* (Columbia), October 16, 2007.

22. "The State Agricultural Fair," *Charleston Courier*, November 15, 1869.

23. "Race Horse Baldy Hurt," *State* (Columbia), October 18, 1908.

24. "Johnny Was There and Got the Pictures," *State* (Columbia), September 8, 1914.

25. "Another Accident at Fair Grounds," *State* (Columbia), September 4, 1915.

26. "Guardians Sue Deggeller for Children's Injuries," *State* (Columbia), November 20, 1985.

27. "Three Columbia Boys Injured after Being Thrown from Fair Ride," *State* (Columbia), October 20, 1987.

28. "Fairworker Killed When Ride Strikes Him," *State* (Columbia), October 20, 2008.

29. "Carnival Worker Electrocuted during State Fair Setup," *State* (Columbia), October 12, 2010.

30. "A Bull's Suicide," *State* (Columbia), November 13, 1897.

12: Exhibits and Premiums

1. "State Fair Exhibits Range from 'Elsie' to Securities," *State* (Columbia), September 12, 1952.

2. "A Fine Horse for Sale," *Edgefield Advertiser*, December 24, 1856.

3. "Glances at Our Exchanges," *Edgefield Advertiser*, April 22, 1857.

4. Rogers, *Charleston in the Age of the Pinckneys*, 12–13.

5. "The State Agricultural Society of South Carolina Premium List for 1841," *Charleston Courier*, August 12, 1841.

6. *Proceedings of the Agricultural Convention and of the State Agricultural Society of South Carolina from 1839 to 1845 Inclusive* (Columbia, S.C.: Summer and Carroll, 1846), 35–40.

7. "Correspondence of the Courier," *Charleston Courier*, November 17, 1856.

8. "The State Fair," *Charleston Mercury*, November 14, 1859.

9. *Premium List . . . for the Fourth Annual Fair . . . 1859*.

10. "Amendment of the Premium List of the State Agricultural Society, Field Crops—Long Staple Cotton," *Charleston Mercury*, April 10, 1860.

11. "Premium List of the Agricultural and Mechanical Society for the Sixth Annual Fair," *Charleston Courier,* October 23, 1869.

12. *Premium List...for the Fifteenth Annual Fair.* Handwritten note listing total amounts found in publication.

13. "To Award Prizes for Best Corn," *State* (Columbia), October 30, 1913.

14. Ibid.

15. *Premium List 1915 South Carolina State Fair* (Columbia: State Agricultural and Mechanical Society of South Carolina, 1915), 50.

16. "Fripp Win State-Record Old Rose Pitcher Again," *State* (Columbia), October 24, 1963.

17. *Premium List 1915 South Carolina State Fair,* 1915, 26.

18. *Premium List of the State Agricultural and Mechanical Society of South Carolina Columbia, S.C. 1920* (Columbia, South Carolina: State Agricultural and Mechanical Society of South Carolina, 1920), 27.

19. *Premium List South Carolina State Fair Day and Night 1927* (Columbia, South Carolina: State Agricultural and Mechanical Society of South Carolina, 1927), 71.

13: Icons of the State Fair

1. "This Is Big Thursday," *State* (Columbia), November 9, 1893.

2. "Live Wire," *Columbia Record,* February 17, 1982.

3. Daniel W. Hollis, *University of South Carolina: College to University,* vol. 2 (Columbia: University of South Carolina Press, 1956), 227–28; and John Chandler Griffin, *Carolina vs. Clemson: A Century of Unparalleled Rivalry in College Football* (Columbia, S.C.: Summerhouse Press, 1998), 23–24.

4. "Tickets on Sale for Big Battle," *State* (Columbia), October 24, 1914.

5. "Restricted Mail Delivery," *Columbia Record,* October 26, 1916.

6. "Champions at Football," *State* (Columbia), November 15, 1891.

7. "Football of Class for Greatest Fair," *State* (Columbia), October 19, 1915.

8. Solomon Blatt to R. F. Poole and Admiral Norman Smith, September 6, 1948, Solomon Blatt Papers, Public Papers, South Carolina Political Collections, University of South Carolina.

9. Henry H. Lesesne, *A History of the University of South Carolina, 1940–2000* (Columbia: University of South Carolina Press, 2001), 116.

10. "New State Fair Premium List to Be Larger than Last Year," *State* (Columbia), September 4, 1960.

11. "Carolina Frosh Clobber Clemson," *State* (Columbia), October 21, 1961.

12. "The State Fair," *State* (Columbia), October 9, 1958.

13. "Columbia Gets Missile as Permanent Memorial," *State* (Columbia), October 18, 1963.

14. "Fixing Up for the State Fair," *State* (Columbia), September 10, 1969.

15. Bill Law to The Young Folks at W. P. Law, Inc., June 10, 1996, typescript in Society Archives safe.

16. "Finally Standing Tall," *State* (Columbia), October 17, 1969.

17. "State Fair Icon Is Rising—Literally," *State* (Columbia), August 13, 2015.

18. "Full Day Planned for Senior Citizens," *State* (Columbia), October 15, 1967.

19. "A New Place to Call Home," *State* (Columbia), September 26, 1983.

20. "Elders Recall Fairs of Past," *State* (Columbia), October 13, 1974.

21. Derek Nelson, *The American State Fair* (Osceola, Wisc.: MBI Publishing, 1999), 110.

22. Ibid. 109.

23. Rachel Shteir, *Striptease: The Untold History of the Girlie Show* (New York: Oxford University Press, 2004), 43.

24. Nelson, *The American State Fair,* 109.

25. "The State Survey," *State* (Columbia), November 11, 1909.

26. "A Very Lively Midway," *State* (Columbia), November 2, 1910.

27. "Midway Promised Jolly and Clean," *State* (Columbia), October 25, 1914.

28. "Krause Furnishes State Fair Shows," *State* (Columbia), October 16, 1920.

29. Minutes of the Executive Committee, State Agricultural and Mechanical Society of South Carolina, January 27, 1939.

30. "Seen Here and There," *State* (Columbia), October 27, 1951.

31. "They Dance, Rain or Shine," *State* (Columbia), October 21, 1966.

32. "Burlesque—In Fine Form at the Fair," *State* (Columbia), October 17, 1975.

33. "Even Cows Are Tame," *State* (Columbia), October 6, 1972.

34. "Bargain Basement Briefs," *State* (Columbia), October 13, 1972.

35. "Bugs Bring Instant Fame," *State* (Columbia), October 9, 1972.

36. Elizabeth Cox, "Girlie Show at the Fair," in *SC Family Memories* (blog), November 8, 2011, https://scfamilymemories.wordpress.com/2011/11/08/girlie-show-at-the-fair/. In a subsequent email, Cox identified the fair as the Eastern Carolina Agricultural Fair.

37. "A National Institution," *State* (Columbia), October 18, 1931.

38. Advertisement, *State* (Columbia), October 25, 1961; and "Come to the South Carolina State Colored Fair," *State* (Columbia), November 11, 1963.

39. "Striporama," *State* (Columbia), April 2, 1954.

40. "Fair Not Result of Magic," *State* (Columbia), October 16, 1966.

41. "Fair May Soon Be a Memory," *State* (Columbia), December 18, 1975.

42. Advertisement illustrated in A. W. Stemce, *Girl Show: Into the Canvas World of Bump and Grind* (Toronto: ECW Press, 1999), 231.

43. "Opinions Differ as to Size of Crop," *State* (Columbia), October 6, 1910.

44. *Favorite Recipes of South Carolina 4-H Families* (Nashville: Favorite Recipes Press, 1984), 6–21.

45. "The Integration of South Carolina's Cooperative Extension Program," Clemson Libraries, http://library.clemson.edu/depts/specialcollections/2014/02/25/the-integration-of-south-carolinas-cooperative-extension-program/.

46. "Rights Act Touches Extension Service Activities," *State* (Columbia), June 9, 1965; and "Farm Services Seen Progressing on Compliance," *State* (Columbia), August 5, 1965.

INDEX

Page numbers in *italic type* refer to illustrations.

Abernathy, W. L., 98
Ackerman, Betty, 118
Adam Forepaugh & Sells Bros. circus, 29
Adams, Ben, 58–59
Adams, Robert, Jr., 79
African Dip, 103
African Dodger, 103, 163
Agnew, Judy, 96
agricultural building, 27, 30, 51, 89
agricultural societies, 1–3
Agricultural Society of South Carolina, 2, 85, 138–42
agriculture, 11–12; exhibits of, 28, 30; and fairs, 1–2, 162; focus of at fair, 4, 9, 11, 18, 49, 59–61, 71, 162, 163; premiums for exhibits of, 71, 100; promotion of in South, 32
Aiken, David Wyatt, 11, 13, 18
Aiken, William D., 17
Alexander Foundry, 8
Allen & Allen, 116
Allen College, 44, 55, 149
Alston, B. F., Jr., 84
Alston, F. W., 17
American Agricultural & Chemical Company, 145
American Berkshire Association, 142
American Legion, 85
amusement park, 50–51
Anderson County Fair, *87*, 155
Arden, Elizabeth, *66*, 68
art exhibits, 27
Ashford, Lewis, 152
Assault (horse), 62
Assembly (social club), 22
athletic field, 27, 50–51, 113
Atlantic Coast Line Railroad, 30, *38*
auditorium, 74, 78
automobile daredevils, 46–47
automobile races, 33, 113, 119, 135, 146; replacing horse races, 59, 65–66, 111
Autry, Gene, *120*
aviation show, 113

Babcock, J. W., 31
Babcock, Oscar V., 111

Bacon, Thomas G., 137
Bailey's Circus, 101
Baldwin, George, 51
Banks, J. Arthur, 31
barkers, 115
Barkout Carnival Show, 114
barns, 52, 61, 78; addition of, 71, 75, 79, 93
Barnum & Bailey Circus, 24, 116
Barron, Charles H., 50
Baruch, Bernard, 68
baseball games, 22, 53, 128
Bates, Lester L., 74–75, 77
Battle of Gettysburg painting, 104
Beatie, W. J., *63*
Bellinger, Edmund C., 14
Belser, Heyward, 78
Benedict College, 44, 46, 55, 118, 149
Benet, Christie, 50
Berry, Joe, 74
Big Thursday: and Colored State Fair, 44; and football games, *56*, 61, 71, 146–49; and Harvest Jubilee parade, 36; popularity of, 30
Blair, Frank, 118
Blanchard, W. L., 135
Blatt, Solomon, 147–48
Blease, Cole, 132
Boinest, T. S., 12
Bold Venture, 62
Brady, P., *63*
Breast Cancer Run, 133
Brennan, Ellen, 101
Brookfield Stable, 62, 68
Brookmeade Stable, 62
Brooks, Preston, 8
Brown, Thomas C., 79
Bryant, Anita, 118
Butler, Andrew, 8
Buxton Brothers, 62, 67

Cain Hoy Stable, 62, 68
calliope, 101
Camp Prospect, 23–24
Campsen Mills, 15–16

Cancer Society, 137

Cantey, William, 98, *150*

Cantey Building, 97–98, 131

Capitol Senior Center, 127

carnies, 114–16

carnival operators, 26, 59, 97, 105, 113–15; and food services, 123; and games, 125

carnivals, 98, 111, 114–16, 128; at Colored State Fair, 44; in downtown, 19–20, 24, 28, 33–34, 55, 74; at fairgrounds, 22–24, 128; and freak shows, 102; games at, 103, 125; and girlie shows, 155

Carolina-Clemson football game, 36, 61, 146–49; on fairgrounds, 25, 127; and fair ticket purchase, 69, 71, 127; at municipal football stadium, 54–56; and parking, 71, 127–28; popularity of, 33; reduced prices of, 37; scholarships for, 127

Carolina Life Insurance Company, 142

Carolina Minstrels, 101

Carolina Stadium, 56

carousel, 105, *107*

Carroll, Richard, *41*, *42*, 43, 44, 155, 163

Carter, Jimmy, 113

Cassidy, Emmett B., 150

Catawba pottery, 22

Caughman Feed and Seed, *54*

Cavalcade, 62

Cayce-West Columbia Lions Club, 123

Centennial Celebrity Cookbook, 96

Champion, *120*

Charleston Chamber of Commerce, 14

Charles Towne Landing Exposition Park, 96

Charlotte Railroad Company, 8

Chez Paree chorus, 119

Chicora College for Women, *106*, 118

Cincinnati Carnival Company, 19, 26, 114

civic center, 74

Civil Rights Act, 160, 163

Civil War, 9, 10, 16

Claflin College, 149

Claussen' Steam Bakery, 16

Clemson, Thomas Green, 11

Clemson University, 93, 137; extension services of, 60, 158–60

Coca-Cola, 28

Coker, James Lide, 11

Cole, Albert, *141*

coliseum, 74, 78

Collins, A. J., 48

Collins, Ruth Ann, 96

Colored Agricultural and Mechanical Exposition, 41

Colored State Fair, 40, 60; 4-H exhibits at, 160; activities at, 41–42, 44–48, 118; in Batesburg, 44; football games during, 44–46, 149; founding of, 163; girlie shows at, 157; renting fairgrounds, 43; and state ball, 41, 45

Colored State Fair Association, 43

Columbia (S.C.): appropriating funds for fair, 55; and fairgrounds, 6, 14–15, 55, 75, 77–78, 80; and football stadium, 54–56; hosing National Corn Show, 31–33; hosting downtown fair events, 19–20, 24–26, 31, 33–34, 113, 114; joint project of with State Agricultural and Mechanical Society, 70, 74–75, 77–81

Columbia Ad Club, 32

Columbia Canal, 105

Columbia Carnival, 24

Columbia Chamber of Commerce: ending downtown fair events, 34–35; and Fair Week Million Dollar Days, 74; hosting downtown fair events, 19, 28, 31

Columbia City Council: ending downtown fair events, 31, 34; and fairgrounds, 14–15, 80; on municipal football stadium, 55

Columbia College, 118

Columbia Fair Association, 19, 28

Columbia Female Academy, 104

Columbia Green, 127

Columbia Horse Show, 66

Columbia Mills, 137–38

Columbia Municipal Polo Field, 66

Columbiana, 62

Columbia Orchestra, 21

Columbia Stage Society, 118

Columbia Street Railway, 30

Columbia Training Stables, 68, 79

commerce building, 28

commercial building, 31

Committee for Conservative Government, 79, 80

concession stands, 120, *121–22*, 123; auctions for, 19, 41, 113; destroyed by fire, 74

Coney Island, 109

Confederate Relic Room, 105

Confederate States of America, 9, 16

Confederate Survivors' Association, 11

Conklin Magic Midway, 116

Conklin Shows, 114

Consumer Product Safety Commission, 135

Cooper, R. M., 49–52

Corkran, Steve, 96

Corn Clubs, 158

cotton, 36–37, 39, 43, 49, 65

Covington, David L., 125

Cromer, Marie, 159

Crosland, R. W., 143

dance exhibitions, 2
Dantzler, Mary, 139
daredevils, 109–10, 113
Davie, William R., 3
Davis, R. L. "Bob," 66, 67
Davis, Robert S., 78
Davis Field, 147
Deggeller Attractions, 97, 135
DeLoache, William E., 77
Democratic Party, 11
Depression, 53, 54, 56, 58
domestic exhibits, 8, 9, 16, 25; premiums for, 18; in women's building, 27, 28
dormitories, 89
Dovilliers, Eugene, 7
Drayton, N., 64
Dreher High School Band Booster Club, *122*, 123

Earle, Cornelia, 142
Easterling, A. L., 158–59
Eastern Carolina Agricultural Fair, 157
Eastman, Joseph B., 60
Edwards, Robert C., 160
Efird, D. F., 34
Eifort, Hal F., 115
Elks Club, 19, 111, 118
Ellison, David G., 54, 77, 97
Ellison Building, 133
Elmwood Cemetery, 104
Enright, Rex, 75, 148
entryway, 89, *131*
Ewan, John, 139
exhibit buildings, 78, 89, 131
extension services, 159–60

4-H Clubs, 71, 157–60, 163
Fairfield County Fair, 83–84
fairs, 1–2, 6, 82–86, 88
Fair Week Million Dollar Days, 74
Fairwold Riding Club, 66
fancy work exhibits, 18, 28
Farah, Helen, 96
Farmers' Association, 18–19
Farmers Cooperative Exchange, *143*
Ferris, George, Jr., 106
Ferris wheel, 105–6, *108*
field crop premiums, 18, 28, 100, 138, 141–42, 144, 145
fine arts exhibits, 18, 163

fireworks display, 118, 119
football games, 128; at Colored State Fair, 44–46, 149; at fairgrounds, 22, 23, 33, 147; grandstand for viewing of, 119
football stadium, 54–56, *57*, 61, 71, 94
Ford, Gerald R., 113
Fort Jackson, 152
Four Oaks Farm, *144*
Frank's Diving Horse, 110
Fratin, Christopher, *141*
freak shows, 8, 33–2, 101–4
Furman College, 22, 147
Future Farmers of America, 71, 73

Gage, Robert J., 13–14
gambling devices, 125
games, 123, *124*, 125
Garey, Peter, 115–16
Garner, William, 36
Gary, Martin W., 11
Gary, William T., 17
Geiger, Emily, 118
Gibbes, A. Mason, 79
Gibbes, Robert W., 139
Gibbes, Thomas H., 31
girlie shows, 152–53, *154*, *156*, 157
Girls' Tomato Canning Club, 159
Glass, Benny, 125
Glaze, William, 140
Gonzales, Ambrose E., 32
Gonzales, N. G., 24
Gooding's Million Dollar Midway, 115
Goodman, Gary, 123, 131, 132, *133*, 152
Goodman Building, 131
Goodwin, John H., 44
Governor's Guard of Columbia, *20*
grandstand, 27, *28*, 51, *68*, 94; demolished, 69; improvements to, 58, 74, 131; performances at, 118–19, 146; rebuilt after fire, 53; value of, 52
Graveley, C., 15
Greater State Fair, 27, 30
Greene Street United Methodist Church, 123
green spaces, 131
Greenville State Fair, 4
Greer, Jane, 68
Grogan, T., *63*
Guggenheim, 62
Guggenheim stables, 69
Guignard, W. A., 145
Guignard, William, 17, 135

Hagood, Johnson, 11
Hall, John T., 116
Hamby, A. McP., 31
Hampton, A. E., 42–43
Hampton, David, 17
Hampton, Frank, 77, 79, 91–92, *150, 152*; on horse facilities, 69, 93, 95
Hampton, Wade, 11, 17, 18
Hampton Building, 131
Hampton Plaza, 131
Harden, Robert, 77
Harvest Hope Food Bank, 127
Harvest Jubilee, 35–36
Haskell, Alexander, 11
Haskell, Paul, 17
Herbert, R. Beverly, 54
Herbert, R. Beverly, Sr., 77
Heyward, J. S., 17
High Gun, 62
Hirsch, Max, 62, 66, 68, 69
Holley, Kay, 96
Hollingsworth, James F., 96
Hope, Bob, *117*, 118
horse races, 2, 22, 33, 63–64, 100, 128; accident at, 17, 135; automobile races replacing, 59, 65–66, 111, 113; canceled at State Fair, 65–66, 68; grandstand for viewing of, 119; popularity of, 17, 30, 33, 67, 146; premiums for, 64–65
horse stables, *94*, 127; improvements to, 67, 93, 95; winter facilities for, 58, 61, 62–63, 66–68, 146
Horwath & Horwath, 69, 93, 95, 97
housing accommodations, 8–9, 15, 19, *29*, 30
Howard, Frank, 147, 148
Hunt, A. M., 139

Immigration Society of Newberry, 12
Inabinet, Pam, 96
industrial developments, 11, 12; exhibits of, 8, 27, 28, 30
influenza, 37

Jack Kochman's Hell Drivers, 113
Jackson, Andrew, 17
Jackson Vase, 17
Jacques, D. H., 12
Jaff, Sam, 118
Janney, Ellen, 152
Jaycees, 85
Jester, Annie Perry, 20
Jet Pilot, 62
Jewel, Mille, 36

Johnny J. Jones Carnival Company, 114
Johnny J. Jones Exposition Shows & Trained Wild Animal Exhibition, 33–34
Johnson, Monroe, 61
Joint Greater State Fair Committee, 24, 27
Jones, Thom, 96
Junior Achievement, 127
Junior Homemakers Association, 71
Junior League of Columbia, 68–69
Jupiter ballistic missile, 149–50

Kaye, Danny, 116
Kelly, Eddie, 68
Kennedy, Susanne, 92
Kilgo, J. P., 58–59
King Ranch Stable, 62, 68
Kochman Hell Drivers, *110*
Krause Greater Shows, 155

Labor Day celebration, 22–23
Langley, A. B., 54
Latta Juvenile Negro Band, 101
Laurens Manufacturing Company, 28
Law, Bill, 152
Lawton, W. M., 14
Lebby, William, 8
LeConte, Joseph, 9
Lee County Extension Service, 37
Leon W. Washburn's Mighty Midway Shows, 36
Lewis, Crosby, 78
Lillard, John W., 34–35
Little Egypt, 155
Little Red Schoolhouse, 152
Little Steel Building, 93
livestock, 2; exhibits of, 16, 27–28, 119; premiums for, 18, 100, 138, 144; transport of by railroads, 8
Logan, Charles, 24
Lorick & Lowrance, 145
Lott, Leon, 132
Love, A. W., 31
Lyles, Bissett, Carlisle, and Wolff, 77, 81, 89
Lyles, William G., 75, 77
Lynn, Loretta, 96

Maine Chance Farms, 62, 68
Malone, Blondelle, 22, 25
Malone, Miles Alexander, 22
Mann, James F., 96
Manning, John Adger, 77

Manning, W. M., 77
manufacturing exhibits, 15, 17, 18
Martin, Wallace, 77
McClure, Harlan, *92, 93*
McCreight, Robert G., 143
McDonald, Bill, 155, 157
McIntosh, James L., 75, 77
McIntosh, John L., 77
McKenzie, John, 15
McLaurin, John L., 37
McMahan, John J., 54
McNair, Robert E., 96
Means, John H., 83–84
mechanical advancements, 15, 18
Melton, W. D., 50
merry-go-round, 105
Middleground, 62
Midlands Exposition Park, 96
Midnight, Joy, 155
midway, 31, 60–61, 72, *94*, 113–14; in downtown, 24, 28, 33, 55, 74, 113;
    games at, *47*, 103; and girlie shows, 155; improvements to, 89, 131;
    popularity of, 30, 99–100, 125, 146, 163
Military Hall, *4*
Minnesota State Fair, 133
Mobley, John G., 31, 33
Monopoli, Daniel, 97
Moon, J. P., 88
Moore, A. Talley, 79
Moore, Paul V., 53, 61, 71, 88
Morrill Act, 159
Moseley, James F., Jr., 97
Moses, Franklin J., Jr., *12*
motorcycle races, 65–66, 111, 113, 119, 135, 146
motordrome, 111

National Breast Cancer Awareness Month, 133, *134*
National Corn Show, 31–33
National Red show, 52
Nebraska Boys Agricultural Association, 158
Nebraska Girls Domestic Science Association, 158
needlework exhibits, 18
Nettles, Joseph L., 59
Newberry Agricultural Society, 6, 8, 83, 84
Newberry County Fair, 8, *86*, 155, 157
Newman, I. DeQuincey, 80
New Palace Skate Club, 95
Newton, Gordon, *160*
Nicholson, Francis B., 97
Night Horse Racing Association, 64–65

Nixon, Pat, 96
Nobles, Dolly, 104
Nobles, Milton, 104
Nurturing Center, 127

Oak Grove Civic Club, 123
O'Hara, Sandy, 155
"Old Ladies' Work," 144
old steel building, *32–34, 57*, 89, 146; exhibits at, *52*, 136–37; fire at, *90*,
    98; improvements to, 51, 71; replacement of, 92–93
O'Neall, John Belton, 84
O'Neill, Dan, 46–47
Opera House, 104, *105*
Orangeburg County Fair, *83, 85, 88*
Orangeburg Fall Carnival, *109*
Ouzts, William C., 150

Pacific Mills., 118
pageants, 116, 118
Palmer, John B., 12, 14
Palmetto Regiment Association, 17
Palmetto State Fair, 40, 48, 163
Palmetto Trials, 62, 68–69
parking, 30, 51, 71, 127–28, *129–30*, 131, 135
Passmore & Wilhelm, 16
Patrons of Husbandry, 18
Pearce, R. Roy, 80
Pearl, Minnie, 118
Pendleton Farmers' Society Hall, *2*
Peter L. Krider and Company, 142
petrified man, 22, 23
Philippoteaux, Paul, 21, 104
Piedmont Exposition Park, 96
Pinner, Joe, 110
plow demonstrations, 17, 100–101
polo ground, 27
Poole, R. F., 147
Populous, 128
poultry shows, *51, 52*
Powell, Frank, 97
premiums, 2, *4–6, 84*; adding credibility, 136–38; for agricultural
    exhibits, 71, 100; by Agricultural Society of South Carolina,
    138–42; for Catawba pottery, 22; for children's exhibits, 159; during
    Depression, 54; for domestic exhibits, 18; for field crops, 18, 28,
    100, 138, 141–42, 144, 145; for horse races, 64–65; by legislature, 6,
    8, 18, 30, 55; for livestock, 18, 100, 138, 144; by State Agricultural
    and Mechanical Society, 138–45; during World War I, 65
press room, 20–21
product exhibits, 15–16

Propst, L. L., 53
Purvis, Joy, 115

Quave, Mackie, *81*

racetrack, 27, *28, 57, 94*, 127; grandstand at, 118–19; for horse racing, 64–65, 69; improvements to, 58, 67, 93, 95; uses for, 65–66, 146, 147; value of, 52
radio broadcast, 53
railroads: access to, 4–6, 8, 147; moving carnival operations, *115*, 116; support of fair by, 8, *29, 38, 39, 83*; during World War II, 37
Raye, Martha, 118
Reconstruction, 10–11
Red Shirts, 118
Redwood Cafeteria, 95, 96
Reed, Bessie Eugenia, 46
restaurants, 27, 120
Revere, Vincent, 36
Rice Music House, 74
Richards, John G., 85, 125
Richland Civic Center, *76*
Richland County Citizens Committee, 80–81
Richmond and Danville Railroad, 104
Riley, Ralph, *160*
Ringling Brothers Circus, 51, 116
Riverbanks Zoo, 127
Robinson, David W., 77
Rocket, 96, *134, 150–51*, 152
Rock Hill Buggy Company, 28
roller coaster, 109
Rotary Club, 50
Rubin, Hyman, 150
Ruff, Frank B., 77
Ruff Building, 95
Rural Carolinian, The, 13

Saluda Cotton Factory, 137–38
Sapp, Claud N., 50
Sawyer, E. J., 44
S. B. McMaster, Inc., 145
S.C. Legislature, 6, 8, 18, 30, 55
Seabiscuit, 62
Seaboard Airline Railroad, 45
Seabrook, Whitemarsh B., 3, 84
Seawell's, 98
Seneca Chief, 64
Senior Citizens Day, 152
Shand & LaFaye, 24, 27

Shandon Methodist Church, 120
Shaw Air Force Base, 150
Sherman, William T., 16
Shiver, H. H., 21
Shiver, Robert C., 16
sideshows, 104, 115
Smith, Norman, 147
Smith, Tom, 68
Smith Greater Shows, 114
Smith–Lever Act, 158, 159
Society for Promoting and Improving Agriculture and Other Rural Concerns, 2
South Atlantic Fair Association, 114
South Carolina Agricultural Society, 1
South Carolina Association of Fair Secretaries, 85, 88
South Carolina Civic Center, 78–79
South Carolina Club, 11, 17, *18*, 21–22
South Carolina College, 3, 9, 104
South Carolina College for Women, 104
South Carolina Educational Television, 127
South Carolina Institute, *4*, 5–6
South Carolina Monument Association, 11
South Carolina Society, 3
South Carolina State University, 149, 159
Southeastern Fair, 157
Southern Farmers' Alliance, 19
Southern Railway, 28
Southern Scale and Fixture Company, 28
Sparks, T. Wilson, 98, 126
Springs, Leroy, 8
Spring Valley High School, 127
Star and Garter show, 155
State Agricultural and Mechanical Society: agricultural and industrial mission of, 11–13, 50, 99–100; and agricultural building, 30; agricultural focus of, 49, 59–61, 163; and agricultural societies, 18–19; and centennial commemoration, 96; and Colored State Fair, 43; creation of, 11, 84, 163; donations by, 126–27; and downtown fair activities, 31, 34–35; elections held by, 53–54, 58–59, 74; and fairgrounds, 24, 75, 77–78, 80; and food services, 123; and football stadium, 54–56, 69, 71, 127, 149; on girlie shows, 155; on horse facilities, 69; improvements by, 89, 93, 95, 97–98; joint project of with Columbia, 70, 74–75, 77–81; member drive of, 14, 50; officers of, 165; and parking agreement with USC, 71, 127–28, 135; premiums offered by, 65, 138–45; publications of, *6*, 12–13; replacement of Old Steel Building by, 92–93; women added to, 38; and year-round events, 91, 95–96, 128, 131
State Agricultural Society, 11–12, 162–63; fairs held by, 3–6, 8–9
State Auxiliary and Joint Stock Company, 16

state ball, 21–22, 25
State Department of Labor, 137
State Department of Labor, Licensing and Review, 135
State Fair, 82–83; advertising for, 95; amusements list for, *100*; cancellation of, 37, 39; employee badges of, *132*; expansion of, 24–25; financial success of, 55, 58; improvements to grounds of, 51–53, 58, 71, 89, 93, 95, 97–98; integration of, 40, 48, 160; origins of, 1, 3, 162–63; as private organization, 55; relocation of, 19, 24, 26–27; revival of, 6, 11, 14–15, 84; rides at, 105; and segregation, 43, 77, 163; on statehouse grounds, 3–4, 100, *101*, 146; themes of, 133; tricentennial celebration at, 96–97, 118; during World War II, 60–61
State Fair Scholarship Fund, 127, *128*
State Forestry Commission, 137
State Highway Department, 137
State Record Company, 142
State Theatre, 157
Stephens, Woody, 62, 68
Storm Eye Institute, 127
Strates Shows, *115*, 116
stunt drivers, 113
Stymie, 62
Summer, A. G., 139
Summer, Catherine Parr, *139*
Summer, William, *141*
Sumner, Charles, 8
Sumwalt, Mrs. Robert L., *63*
Sun Beau, 62
Swamp Robin, 64
Sylvan Jewelers, 36

Taft, William Howard, 30, 111, 113
Tarantella, 22
Taylor, William, 66
Tent Show Tonite, 116
textile mills, 12
Thomas, John P., 14
Thomas, J. W., 15
Thompson, LaMarcus, 109
Thurmond, Nancy, *150*
Thurmond, Strom, 96, *150*
Tillman, Benjamin F., 18–19, 24
Tozer engine, 15, *16*
Trades Parade, *35*
Tri-County Fair, *86*
Trinity College (Duke University), 22, 147

UFO Coffeehouse, 95
United Agricultural Society of South Carolina, 3
United Ancona Club, 52
University of South Carolina: agreement with State Agricultural and Mechanical Society on stadium, 69, 71; coliseum of, 75, 78, 79; exhibits by, 137; and municipal football stadium, 55, 56; and parking, 71, 127–28, 135; and scholarship fund, 127; School of Engineering of, 152
U.S. Air Force, 149–50

Vanderbilt, Mrs. George, 51
Victory Fair, 60

Walker, Dora D., 159
Wallace, William, 14
Wall of Hope, 133
war exhibits, 39, 61, 70
Washington, George, 118
Watson, Tilman, 110
Watts, J. Washington, 18
Webb, Clifton, 116
Weston, Mrs. Thomas I., 35
W. G. Whilden & Company, 142
Whiteley, Frank, 68
Wild West Show, 113
Williams, A. P., 80–81
Williams, J. H., *41*, 42–43
Williams, Joe, 45
Williams, Ransome J., 74
Willis Jno A., 31
Wilson, Marie, 116
Winter Stables Incorporated, 58
Winthrop College, 137
Winthrop Training School, 104
Witcover, D. D., 54, 58–59, 61, 74
Wolff, Louis, 92
Women in Construction, 123
women's building, 27, 28, 51, 71, 89
World of Mirth Shows, *59*, 60–61, 116
World's Columbian Exposition, 105–6, 153
World War I, 36–37
World War II, 59–60

Young Men's Christian Association, 11
Young's Mill, 7